Chinese Whispers

Chinese Whispers

*The True Story Behind Britain's
Hidden Army of Labour*

HSIAO-HUNG PAI

PENGUIN BOOKS

PENGUIN BOOKS

Published by the Penguin Group
Penguin Books Ltd, 80 Strand, London WC2R 0RL, England
Penguin Group (USA), Inc., 375 Hudson Street, New York, New York 10014, USA
Penguin Group (Canada), 90 Eglinton Avenue East, Suite 700, Toronto, Ontario, Canada M4P 2Y3
(a division of Pearson Penguin Canada Inc.)
Penguin Ireland, 25 St Stephen's Green, Dublin 2, Ireland (a division of Penguin Books Ltd)
Penguin Group (Australia), 250 Camberwell Road, Camberwell, Victoria 3124, Australia
(a division of Pearson Australia Group Pty Ltd)
Penguin Books India Pvt Ltd, 11 Community Centre, Panchsheel Park, New Delhi – 110 017, India
Penguin Group (NZ), 67 Apollo Drive, Rosedale, North Shore 0632, New Zealand
(a division of Pearson New Zealand Ltd)
Penguin Books (South Africa) (Pty) Ltd, 24 Sturdee Avenue,
Rosebank, Johannesburg 2196, South Africa

Penguin Books Ltd, Registered Offices: 80 Strand, London WC2R 0RL, England

www.penguin.com

First published 2008
2

Copyright © Hsiao-Hung Pai, 2008
All rights reserved

The moral right of the author has been asserted

Set in Monotype Bembo
Typeset by Rowland Phototypesetting Ltd, Bury St Edmunds, Suffolk
Printed in England by Clays Ltd, St Ives plc

ISBN: 978–0–141–03568–0

www.greenpenguin.co.uk

Penguin Books is committed to a sustainable future
for our business, our readers and our planet.
The book in your hands is made from paper
certified by the Forest Stewardship Council.

For the struggle of all status-less workers

Contents

Introduction   ix

1. I Do Mind Dying   1
2. Becoming Invisible   26
3. Salad Days   61
4. Dimsum, Cockles and DVDs   90
5. Middle of the Kingdom   120
6. The Zone Six Women   158
7. At the Back of Gerrard Street   187
8. Moving On   222
9. The Status-less and the Status Quo   245

Acknowledgements   261

Introduction

I'll tell you a bit about myself. You don't need to know much. This book isn't about me. My role in writing it is to create a window through which you can look clearly into the lives of a certain, distinct group of others.

You're probably vaguely aware that this group of others exists. The phrases 'cockle pickers', 'Morecambe Bay', 'Chinese illegals found dead in lorry' perhaps ring a distant bell in your mind, reminding you of an item on the news you once heard. Perhaps you've been to Chinatown in London for a quick bite before or after a West End show, and have vaguely wondered about the working lives of the young waitresses or of the wiry men frantically frying in the kitchen, while the portly manager waits at the door to welcome tourists in. You've almost certainly eaten a supermarket bag of mixed salad leaves, bought a bunch of supermarket flowers and opened the door of a microwave.

This book is about the parallel society, the hidden army of labour, that carries on its existence far behind the facade of the British high street. The people in this group are commonly known in the popular media as the 'illegals', but I prefer to think of them as the 'undocumented'. We see them all around us. They flow into Britain, as we know, in huge numbers from many countries of the world; the current estimate is that the 'illegal' population is somewhere between 700,000 and a million. They make a fiscal contribution to the British economy of £1 billion a year, selling their labour all over the agriculture, hospitality and construction industries. Those whose lives I follow in this book are people of Chinese extraction, who have no status as citizens – no 'papers', who have left their loved ones and travelled to Britain for reasons of poverty and who keep their heads down and work themselves to the bone in order to support their families.

I was thirteen when we had to move to Kaohsiung, the second-largest city in Taiwan. My father had a new job as head of Social Affairs in the local government. He was delighted to get out of the constricted academic environment of the university where he'd taught before, but I was unhappy to have to move to a new school. Each morning of those dull adolescent schooldays, we walked along the Love River, which stank of litter and waste water. It was here that I had my first glimpse of routine degradation. Standing by the river, on both of its banks, were tens of heavily made-up women in high heels, each holding a metal box. Their wavy permed hair and eager, anxious faces intrigued me.

'Who are they?' I asked my father.

'They're prostitutes,' he told me. Regulating prostitution was part of his job. Most of the women came from the aboriginal communities, the most deprived in Taiwan. At the time, they were officially known as the 'mountain compatriots' (*shan bao*) by the repressive Kuomintang government. Driven by poverty, they migrated to the cities for work, and almost always ended up in the most degrading and demanding occupations which few Han Chinese (the long-standing ethnic majority) would do.

A few years later we moved back to the capital, Taipei, because my father had been appointed head of the Social Affairs Bureau in the central government. It seemed like a good promotion, but the new job made my father frustrated and depressed. With no welfare system in place, he had no power to implement changes. The atmosphere wasn't always comfortable at home, and it was a relief for me to move out when I was admitted to Fu Jen University on the other side of town.

Here I first came across migrant workers. It was 1989, and the Taiwanese government, due to a shortage of labour in the manufacturing, service and building industries, suddenly opened the labour market to Vietnamese, Filipino, Thai, Malaysian and Indonesian workers. I saw them – anxious, eager, desperate for work – gathering for temporary employment on the building sites around my campus. Their numbers swelled in the years that followed. The work they did spread from the outdoor to the domestic: large numbers of Indonesian and Vietnamese women left their homes and families to work in houses as cleaners and nannies, and I heard rumours about how exploited they were by the agencies. But no one was interested. The country was too busy sorting out its grander affairs, such as 'national reunification versus independence' and the 'national identity'. Migrant workers and the conditions of their working lives were not considered newsworthy.

This failure to address the problem had serious consequences. No discerning person was surprised when a riot among Thai migrant workers broke out in Kaohsiung in 2005. These workers were employed by an agency to work on the building of the city's new subway system. Not only were they owed over-time pay and provided with subhuman living conditions in the 'foreign workers' dormitory' with only twenty telephones between a thousand men and no freedom of movement, they were also (it emerged) physically abused by their supervisors. Beatings occurred frequently. They vanished from the headlines almost as soon as they'd appeared, but at least some of us were aware, now, of the new slave class outside the much-vaunted 'four-group coexistence' in Taiwan – the happy cohabitation of Chinese mainlanders, Fujianese Taiwanese, Hakkas and aborigines – which was encouraged to heal old conflicts.

All this was a far cry from Cardiff (University of Wales), where I arrived as a postgraduate in 1991 to study Critical and Cultural Theory for a year. Having watched the migrants in Taiwan from a distance, it was a shock, in Britain, to be counted among them: an 'overseas student'. From the moment I arrived, I sensed a barely disguised hostility towards the migrant population, a lack of protectiveness towards us. Naturally I made

friends with other 'overseas students', and was told stories of
racial attacks on West Indians and Somalis in the local community; of my Algerian friend's local pub in Catford, south
London, which refused to serve drinks to foreign-looking
customers; of casual name-calling on the streets; of racial
discrimination in restaurant kitchens.

Coming from an ethnically conscious place, with a four-
hundred-year history of colonialism, I was under no illusions
that Britain is a democracy for everyone. When I heard the
English term 'host society' for the first time, I understood that
it involves a process of assimilation. I was well aware, from
the first day, that I am indeed the 'foreigner' (the object of
assimilation). The fact that I was not yet properly 'assimilated'
came home to me time and time again during the fifteen years
that I have spent living in Britain. The experience of trying, as
an outsider, to make a life for myself has given me a lifelong
fascination for the subject of exile.

My MA from Cardiff did not get me a job in 1991. I had my
first taste of unemployment. But I didn't want to admit defeat
and return to Taipei. By this time, I had met my partner John.
Instead of returning with a UK degree to the awaiting career
opportunities in Taipei, I chose to stay and try to find work
with him.

'You are going to regret it,' were the words from friends and
relatives thousands and thousands of miles away. But I wanted
to build my life in my own way, even if that meant poverty to
begin with.

Finding a job worthy of my MA had proved impossible, but
finding low-paid local employment proved easy. There were
plenty of low-paid jobs to be had in the catering trade. Without
difficulty I got a job as a waitress serving cream teas in the north
Devon seaside village of Croyde. I was new to the cream-tea
trade: I didn't even know such a thing existed, or precisely what
a 'cream tea' was. Dressed in a large puffed-out skirt with a frilly
apron round my waist and a bonnet on my head like a Victorian

housemaid, I soon found out. In this strange, uncomfortable costume I was conspicuous, being the only Chinese-looking housemaid in the teashop.

There were whispers that my accent was too strong, and that I didn't take down orders quickly enough. The manageress was alerted, and came to observe me as I served the tourists. Her stare intimidated me, and I performed badly. 'This teashop needs fast, native speakers,' she told me, and I lost the job.

That minor incident gave me a taste of the kind of casual dismissal I was to come across in other people's infinitely darker stories in the years that followed.

Following the cream-tea job, I was given a position introducing and translating books for a Taiwanese publisher. Soon, the desire to write about my own background led me to university again (Durham this time) to study for an MA in East Asian history and politics. Then I started writing articles for the Chinese press, which was fun at first, but palled as I came under increasing pressure to produce a thousand and one congratulatory works about British Chinese success and achievement. I had a feeling that, deep under the surface, there was a world of hardship and struggle which was far more important and needed to be written about. I longed for a job in the mainstream British media. Eventually I got a toe in the door working on an English lifestyle magazine in London – and that was only because they needed a Chinese person on the editorial staff who would help them 'sell' traditional Chinese and East Asian cultures, by repackaging them for the new-age consumer. (The office was feng-shuied by a consultant.) Any probing article suggested by me was politely rejected.

One morning I arrived at the office to hear my colleagues chatting about a news item in the papers. 'That's terrible,' one said. 'Why were they in there?'

The newspaper was passed to me and I froze when I read the headline: 'Fifty-eight Chinese Illegals Suffocated to Death in Lorry in Dover.' As I read the story, I felt my blood heating up with rage. These people were being smuggled by snakeheads into Britain on the ferry from Zeebrugge. (The term 'snake-head', '*she-tou*' in Chinese, is a synonym for people smugglers; the term originated from the image of a smuggler leading the way into the West as a snake's head leads a snake.) They'd paid all their life savings and borrowed heavily for this journey, in the desperate hope of working in Britain to make money to support their families. Like cargo, their bodies were found among crates of tomatoes. This was mid-summer, and the outside temperature was 30°C. The refrigeration unit had been switched off by the Dutch driver, Perry Wacker, who was fully aware of the living cargo inside his truck. Two people survived, deeply traumatized. They described how the trapped passengers had desperately tried to raise the alarm in Zeebrugge, screaming and banging on the locked doors: crying for their lives.

In our magazine office, the news item was just one among many, tossed aside before my colleagues got on with the business of the day: commenting on the most auspicious colours for the walls of your riverside apartment. It was not the place for me, I decided. From that day, I turned my energies towards uncovering the stories of Chinese immigrants.

The Dover ferry news story – like the one about the Thai workers' riot in Taiwan – quietened down pretty quickly, but not before a great deal of printer's ink had been expended in articles about the 'illegals'. 'Illegal immigrants . . .', 'Illegal workers . . .', 'Suspected illegal workers . . .' It was a useful catchword, and its effect was to distance the reader from the event: if these were 'illegals', then perhaps their lives weren't quite as valuable as those of the rest of us.

The British government cleverly diverted attention away from themselves, and their own immigration policy of entry refusal, by blaming the snakeheads. Jack Straw, the then Home Secretary, said, 'The death by suffocation of fifty-eight suspected illegal immigrants whose bodies were found at Dover must serve as a stark warning to others who might be tempted to place themselves in the hands of organized traffickers.' Since then, the standard response from the government to such tragedies has been 'blame the snakeheads and forget about it'.

In the papers, too, I saw there was a pattern of reaction to this kind of event. It went: indifference – debate – indifference. The Morecambe Bay tragedy in 2004, when twenty-three cockle pickers were sent to their deaths by drowning through the negligence of their gangmaster (a commonly used term to mean labour provider, i.e. a company or an individual who supplies casual labour to various industries), was a case in point: before the tragedy the level of coverage of migrant workers' working conditions was minimal; it peaked for a few weeks, then subsided for two years, only reappearing briefly when the Chinese gangmaster was convicted in 2006.

It was the namelessness of the migrant workers that affected me. Because they had no capital and thus no status – it was almost as if they didn't exist. The dead were gone, but I was determined to give the living ones a name, a voice; to look into their lives and tell the world what it's like to be them. I did not foresee what a huge task it would be, involving hundreds of interviews, numerous visits and revisits to innocent-sounding places like King's Lynn, Hartlepool and Thetford; or that, for a short time (thanks to my colouring and ability to speak the language), I would actually take on the identity of an 'illegal' myself.

The homing instinct in humans is strong. Things must be pretty bad in a country if a father or mother decides to leave his or her family for years and live illegally and namelessly in an unknown country, owing a fortune to the moneylender who made the journey possible. What has driven the Chinese to such desperate measures?

Prior to 1978, workers in China had an 'iron rice bowl', a job for life, guaranteed housing, medical care, schooling for their children and a pension to see them through to the end of their lives. State control of all economic production and accrual meant that there was little competition. Wages were low, but then consumption power wasn't an issue as there weren't many consumer choices around. As workers put it, they were 'equally poor': the income gap was small.

But all this changed when Deng Xiaoping and the ruling elite initiated the Four Modernizations Programme and determined to open China to the world economy. He titled the process 'socialism with Chinese characteristics'.

The economic reforms and their consequences, however, turned out to be 'capitalism with Deng Xiaoping characteristics'. (Or, as Chinese workers put it, *gua yang-tou, mai gou-rou*, meaning 'hanging a sheep's head outside the shop, but selling dog meat inside'. Socialism may be on the menu, but capitalism is the food.) This involved a process of dismantling and privatizing state institutions and services on a massive scale. State-owned enterprises (also known as SOE: enterprises run by the state, such as in the production of steel, petroleum, tobacco, alcohol and all essential goods) were the biggest employers in China, providing work for more than 75 million people. The efficiency of these enterprises, some 300,000 of them, was called into question. In order to increase their revenues, make them more competitive and improve the whole Chinese market economy, the central government set out to close them down or sell them off to domestic and foreign companies. This led to, and is still causing, an unprecedented level of unemployment across the country.

Meanwhile, in the countryside agricultural prices and production were deregulated and fell, losing out in competition with international products. The income level of the farming population declined. The result of the bankruptcy of the rural economy was the movement of millions of impoverished peasants and rural workers into the cities since the mid-1980s, after being pushed off the land. Today, 200 million rural migrants are in China's major cities trying to sell their cheap labour.

When China entered the World Trade Organization (WTO) in 2001 things began to deteriorate even faster. The aim of the WTO membership is that China remove all barriers to the operation of international corporations inside the country by 2006. The speed of China's economic development over the past six years has been based on attracting international capital from global businesses. Indeed, China has become the world's factory. For global conglomerates, a repressive state with hundreds of millions of people desperate for work is an ideal place to be. They won't complain if you make workers work for thirteen hours a day and house them in cramped and sweltering dormitories. When China became a member of the rich men's club of the world, life became tougher for the workers and working conditions harder to endure.

The undocumented Chinese workers you'll meet in this book come from three main areas of China that have suffered tremendously from the impact of the opening to the world market. The majority of them come from the province of Fujian in the south-east, and these fall into three groups: impoverished farmers; low-paid service workers and manual workers; and young people with no employment opportunities in Fujian. I asked Geoff Crothall, an activist and editor for the leading labour rights organization, China Labour Bulletin, to give me an update about what life is like for workers in these migrant-sending regions. He said: 'In south-eastern China, from where large numbers of smuggled Chinese migrants in Britain come, although there's technically a labour shortage in many areas, wage levels are low compared to the cost of living, which is increasing rapidly year-on-year. In Fujian, the gap between the minimum wage and the cost of living is the highest in the country. Many factory workers in Fujian and Guangdong don't even make the minimum wage because they're regularly cheated out of overtime payments or have to pay increased charges for food and lodging. Workers are forced to work additional shifts for little or even no additional payment. It's not unusual for factory employees to work eleven or twelve hours a day. And, in extreme cases, workers have died on the factory floor due to excessive working hours.'

The number of people migrating from Fujian to work abroad is high. This is easy to see from the absence of working-age people in some of the villages. However, as few work permits are issued by British authorities to people from Fujian, and ninety-five per cent of asylum applications from this province are turned down by Britain, it's accepted in Fujian now that if you want to get to Britain you must resort to underground means.

The second area from which people migrate to Britain is the north-east of China (consisting of provinces of Heilongjiang, Liaoning and Jilin). The majority of migrants from this area come to Britain on business-visitor or student visas. They work during their stay, and then outstay their visas. Most of them come because they've been forced out of work by the mass closure or slimming-down of state-owned enterprises in the region since the 1980s.

Entering the WTO at the beginning of this century also meant that China was required to speed up even further the restructuring and decline of its state-owned enterprises in order to compete with international markets. China was compelled to dismantle this bedrock of its urban society and keep a large part of its workforce '*xia gang*' – meaning 'off the post' – i.e. unemployed.

The third area from which many recent undocumented workers migrate is China's largest city Shanghai: this is a new group of migrants, whose numbers are growing. They're the industrial workers as well as laid-off employees from the state-run industries, who have been pushed off the fast train of the ruthlessly developing market economy in China.

Despite their regional differences at home, these migrant Chinese workers have one thing in common in Britain: they've broken away from the confinement of the employment pattern that began in Britain in the 1950s. Then, the only employment for Chinese migrants in Britain was in the Chinese catering trade. Now, they've moved into mainstream manual labour. Instead of leading a self-sufficient working life within their own communities (as their predecessors did), and maintaining a pattern of migration independent of the general supply of labour in Britain, these new Chinese workers have become the bottom layer – and the most vulnerable section – of the UK workforce.

They've come to join what I've come to think of as the 'ghost population' in Britain: the almost-invisibles. They arrive with nothing but a longing to improve life for their families. They fully expect to work hard. They know Britain is a First World country (surely that must be good). But they probably haven't been alerted to one vital fact: Britain has not yet installed the basic framework of protection for *all* migrant workers regardless of immigration status. Britain, for instance, has not yet ratified the International Convention on the Protection of the Rights of All Migrant Workers and Members of their Families. Britain has not, that is, signed up to the convention that requires it to grant to its migrant workers freedom from inhuman living and working conditions, freedom of speech, freedom of access to education and social services, legal equality and freedom to join a trade union.

The UN created the International Convention on the Protection of the Rights of All Migrant Workers and Members of their Families – also known as the Migrant Rights Convention – in 1990. It sets minimum standards for the protection of migrant workers, both documented and undocumented, and states that universal human rights should be extended to *all* migrant workers. It needed to be ratified by twenty member states in order to come into force, and this happened in 2003. Now only 37 member states out of 192 have ratified the convention, and if you run your eyes down the list of countries, which include Argentina, Azerbaijan, Belize, Bolivia, Bosnia,

Cape Verde, Colombia, Ecuador, Egypt, El Salvador, Ghana, Guatemala, Guinea, Mali, Mauritania, Mexico, Morocco, the Philippines, Senegal, the Seychelles, Sri Lanka, Tajikistan, Uganda and Uruguay, you search in vain for the UK, the USA, or any migrant-receiving countries in Europe. (Other important labour-receiving countries such as Japan, Australia and the Gulf States have also not signed up to the convention.) The countries who have signed up are all labour-sending countries.

The government shows no intention of changing its position on this issue. As the stories in this book will show, the absence of an infrastructure of protection means misery or even tragedy for undocumented workers.

'Globalization' is a buzzword in China. It suggests the new freedom of choice and movement, the new possibilities for people everywhere to improve their standard of living. But my journey into the world of undocumented workers in Britain tells a different story. That journey began the day I heard about a man called Zhang Guo-Hua.

1. I Do Mind Dying

NEW MALDEN. Zhang Guo-Hua looked at the letters on the station sign as the train pulled in. Yes, it was the right one. Nervously he got out, handed in his ticket at the barrier and walked out on to the pavement of the Surrey town.

He was new to Britain as well as new to New Malden. He'd arrived from Yuhong, a rural district in the Liaoning province of north-east China. As he looked up and down the high street, wondering which way to go, he felt lonely, missing his wife and their eleven-year-old son and eight-year-old daughter. But he was also excited. He was doing this for them.

He'd been a poor farmer all his life. Since the early 1980s, waves of 'reform and opening' initiatives (*gai-ge kai-fang*) were ruthlessly exposing China to the fierce competition of the world market, while encouraging the fast growth of private enterprises. In the 1990s the so-called 'modern enterprise reform' swept across China. Many state-run factories, stores and mines were merged, shut down or went bankrupt, and around 30 million workers were made redundant.

The north-eastern provinces of Heilongjiang, Liaoning and Jilin, known as the 'rust belt' of China for its heavy industries, had a high concentration of state-owned enterprises, which were the backbone of the Chinese economy. Therefore, they were hit the hardest. Nearly five million workers in state-owned factories were made redundant here between 2001 and 2006.

Having been told they'd had a job for life, the workers could not simply be thrown out on to the streets – that would have been a recipe for revolution. So instead many workers were technically 'laid off' with a compensation package based on the number of years each worker had been employed at the enterprise. However, the level of compensation offered to these workers, less than 9,000 RMB (£600) on average, was usually barely enough to live on.

Although some of these laid-off workers were re-employed, most ended up in low-paid temporary jobs and soon became unemployed again. And often, either because of a genuine lack of funds or because of bureaucratic incompetence and corruption, laid-off workers never received their rightful benefits. Geoff Crothall of China Labour Bulletin gave me one example out of the hundreds of such cases he'd come across.

Wang Andong, a seventy-five-year-old former 'model worker' (that is, Chinese working 'hero' who received official recognition from the Communist Party for his decades of hard work) from Heilongjiang, has spent the last eleven years trying to claw back his pension and medical benefits following the bankruptcy of the state-owned machine-repair shop where he worked. As he points out, if he as a former model worker and Party secretary can't get his pension, what chance do other less fortunate workers have?

In the first year of the new century, 20 million people were unemployed in the north-east and mass urban unemployment was as high as seven per cent. The inadequate social insurance 'safety net' wasn't able to maintain a reasonable living standard. Farmers were even worse off than urban workers. Their production often couldn't compete with incoming international agricultural products. Their earnings were around half those of urban dwellers, and the gap was widening. Living became very difficult for Zhang's family. Healthcare, now privatized, became impossible to access. Zhang and his wife, like the majority of the rural population, had no medical insurance. They felt powerless not being able to provide good medical care for their elderly parents and special care for their son who had learning difficulties. They finally decided in 2001 that in order to support his family, Zhang would have to travel abroad to work. Abroad, you could earn ten times as much as in China.

Ten times as much! How could he resist such a prospect? (China's national minimum wage is 5.5 RMB, about 36p per hour, and an eight-hour day would earn a wage of £2.88, if employers abided by the rules – that is, around fourteen times lower than the British National Minimum Wage.) The work might be hard, but Zhang was used to tough physical labour. And if the work was in England – well, England was famous for being a gentle, civilized country.

So here he was, on a bright April morning in 2001, following in the footsteps of thousands of others from the north and north-east of China who were coming into Britain at the time. He had a six-month business-visitor visa (arranged for him by an agency in Shenyang, the capital city of his province), which did not permit him to work. A few hundred pounds in cash, in an envelope hidden among the winter jumpers in his suitcase, was all the money he had. And his mobile phone: his Samsung mobile phone. He was hoping for a job at Samsung.

He turned right and walked towards a parade of shops. Speaking no English, he showed the name on his piece of paper to a passer-by. 'Over there.' The man pointed to an office building. 'S. C. Lim & Co' That was it: the name of the labour provider. Zhang straightened his shirt and walked in. A smartly dressed Chinese woman asked him to sit in the waiting area.

The managing director, Cheng-Zhe Lim, did not shake hands with him when he walked in. He searched Zhang with his eyes and then asked him a list of questions. Heart problems? Health problems? Zhang replied confidently. 'I've just reached thirty-nine and I'm fit and in good health.'

'You're going to work for Samsung,' Lim told Zhang. In return for a registration fee of £100, S. C. Lim & Co would sort out Zhang's documents for him, arrange his national insurance and employ him to work in the factory called Woo One in Hartlepool, a supplier for Samsung. He'd need to pay £150 per month for his rent and food.

The next day, following Lim's instructions, he took a coach

from London Victoria to Hartlepool. ('Har-li-pul. Har-li-pul,' Zhang practised saying it.) Five hours later he stepped out into the cold darkness. The ghostly silence of the place felt like an omen. It frightened him. He waited and waited. Eventually a middle-aged Korean man walked up to him from a distance. With no greeting, he introduced himself as Mr Han. Zhang understood he was one of Lim's men who'd been sent to pick him up. He felt relieved, even at the sight of this unfriendly stranger. He followed Han on to a bus.

Petrol stations, supermarkets, road signs . . . In silence, Zhang peered out of the bus, trying to make it all out. Lorries sped past. The windows were closed, but Zhang could still feel a stubbornly hostile blast blowing at him from the North Sea. This was supposed to be early summer, but it felt like the tail-end of a bleak winter.

Then came long avenues lined with massive industrial estates and warehouses. Zhang gasped. Truly a kingdom of factories!

At last they turned off into a residential road, and Han led him into a semi-derelict house. They climbed the stairs to the second floor. A tiny room was in front of them as they opened the door. A Chinese man, lying on a bed eating roasted peanuts, welcomed him in.

'Four of us share this room,' he told Zhang. But there was only one two-tier bunk-bed. 'This flat was a hotel before,' his new room-mate told him. 'Now it's been bought by Lim. The building's divided into ten rooms, shared by forty of us.' It dawned on Zhang that he'd have to use the same bed as another worker. 'He works night shifts for the next two weeks. So you can use the bed during the night. We change shifts every two weeks. When he gets on the day shifts, you'll be sleeping in the daytime.'

Zhang was soon to realize he was lucky to get a bed at all: when his nephew arrived a few days later, he had to take turns with a co-worker on the sofa. Clearly, Lim was trying to accommodate as many workers as he could to make as much money as possible from the rent.

The next morning, Zhang awoke to a familiar smell of northern baked cakes. 'That reminds me of home!' he said to the man climbing down from the upper bunk.

'Yeah,' the man replied, 'some of the guys make their own breakfast, because Lim doesn't provide it. We pay for all our food, but they only give us two small meals a day. We have to share two dishes for dinner among ten of us, and the food's pretty rough.'

Following his flatmate, Zhang set out to walk to work for the eight o'clock shift. In the dreary morning light, he was now able to see the world of factories around him. SOVEREIGN BUSINESS PARK, said a sign. Red and grey box-like buildings stood next to each other. And there he saw the name: WOO ONE.

Thus began Zhang's six-month working life at the Woo One factory.

Arriving at the building, he took out the photocopied work permit which Lim had sold him for £50 in New Malden, and handed it to 'Supervisor Zhen', the Korean representative recruited by Lim to be in charge of scheduling the workers' daily shifts. Twenty copies of permits were shared between all the undocumented workers in the four plants to which Lim supplied labour. 'Li Ming' happened to be the name on Zhang's permit copy, so he'd be known as Li Ming during his time here. He was told to put on his work clothes and join a mass of Chinese, Xian (an ethnic group in north-east China) and Korean workers on the assembly line. (Lim, he discovered, spoke both Chinese and Korean, and workers from both of these countries flocked to him by word of mouth: he never needed to advertise.)

Zhang had never worked in a factory and didn't know how to use any of the machines. Would someone teach him? The next thing he knew, he was doing the job: putting screws into the plugs of PCs. He had to copy the person next to him.

'It's easy,' said a chubby Korean supervisor named Jin. 'Anyone can do it.'

Hours later, at noon, it was time to have their half-hour lunch break. In the canteen, workers shovelled food into their mouths as if time was running out.

'Have some *dajiang tang*!' Zhang's co-worker said to him. It was thick bean soup, and with it came rice and cabbage from a huge container at the end of the table. The worker beside him told him it was *da guo fan* – food roughly cooked in huge woks for large numbers of people – a throwback to collective dining in China's communes in the 1950s. The worker admitted, 'I didn't know they still had such things in the West. And we'll have the same meal for dinner. If we're lucky, we'll get some thin slices of meat with it.'

All too soon it was time to put the work clothes back on. When the twelve-hour shift finally ended, Zhang dragged himself back to the flat and fell asleep, exhausted, in the bed still warm from its occupant on night shifts.

A few days later, Zhang was moved to a different job: printing on the PC line. It looked much more skilled: there must be training this time. But no: Zhang was put to work at once alongside his cousin (who had arrived in Hartlepool a few days after him; it was common for people to come and join their relatives or friends already working here) and two other Chinese workers. They showed him how to mix different kinds of paint and liquid until the mixture was just right, and then how to press the metal mould into the mix, making a label. The names on the label were so famous! Samsung, Sharp, Sony ... Zhang got to work, hoping he was doing it right.

There were four production lines in the printing department, he noticed: three were for 'foreign' (Chinese, Korean and Xian) workers, and one was for local workers. On each 'foreign' production line, there were three or four workers; on the local one, there were eight. Yet the 'foreign' production line had double the production target of the local line.

Xiao Li, a man from Tienjin in northern China, joined the printing line. He seemed an outgoing, articulate man and he introduced himself to Zhang with a broad Tienjin accent. He'd arrived in England shortly after Zhang, and had followed the same path and been through the same interview with Lim. 'I've never done factory work in my life,' he told Zhang. 'This is physically stretching me to the limit. How come we have less than half the number of workers on our lines, but our production target is 1,500 microwaves per shift, and theirs is only 800?'

Sometimes Supervisor Jin would move Xiao Li, Zhang and other Chinese, Xian and Korean workers to the other side of the factory, where doors were made for Samsung microwaves. Here, the workers had to struggle not only with the work-load but also with the deafening sound of the machinery and the suffocating heat and polluting dust from the burning of plastic in the moulding process. Their concentration had to be absolute. There was not a moment to stand back or rest. Every second counted if the production target was to be met. The workers had had no health-and-safety training, and had no idea about the risks of working with the chemicals used in the colouring process.

Occasionally, Zhang would tell Xiao Li that his blood pressure was getting higher – he often felt weak, dizzy and feverish, and had a faster heartbeat – because of the long hours and lack of sleep. Zhang seemed aware that the work was wearing him out.

'Don't work too hard,' Xiao Li always told him. 'It's not worth it.'

But it was different for Xiao Li. He was a divorcee, with no children to worry about. He told Zhang his story: he'd been a chef at the Sheraton Hotel in Tienjin, earning 1,000 RMB (£67) a month. It was an enviable job for many, but Xiao Li wasn't content with the low wage. So he'd left the job and travelled to Germany on a four-year work permit in 1998. In Germany, he'd been a legal worker, working as a chef, getting a low wage and paying high tax. There was no chance of promotion, and he'd been the victim of appalling racism. 'I was spat on by a German man sitting in a car,' he told Zhang. 'I was furious, and pulled the man out of his car and hit him on the face. For that, I was given a six-month prison sentence. And in the prison, the racism was worse, if anything. My time in that place taught me all about Germany and the West.'

He'd gone back to China, hoping the work prospects there might have improved. But they were worse than ever. 'A lot of people were unemployed. Without connections, it was almost impossible to find a job,' he said. So he decided to use his saving of 20,000 RMB (£1,300) to get a business-visitor visa for Britain. He'd been hardened by his time in Germany; that was why he refused to tolerate injustice now. Zhang sympathized, but he was not so embittered by experience.

Workers who arrived in perfect health at Woo One found themselves becoming ill. Severe weight loss and exhaustion were common. Another co-worker of Zhang's, named Older Gao, also from Tienjin, developed acute asthma after two months. 'My brother's coming to England to work,' he told Zhang, 'and he wants to come to Hartlepool, but I'm not going to let him.' Older Gao didn't want to tell his family the details about working conditions at Woo One, but he guessed they knew: he had to beg them to send him regular supplies of Ventolin inhalers because he couldn't register with a GP in Britain.

Zhang worked alongside these people, quietly, complaining as little as possible, remembering that every hour of work brought an hour's worth of wages to his family. But there wasn't much money to send them after you'd paid your rent, and the hours were long – so long. All the undocumented workers worked a minimum twelve-hour shift each day, but most days they were required to do overtime of four or six hours – sometimes working two shifts of twelve hours in a row. Zhang, Older Gao and Xiao Li watched with envy as the local workers came off their shifts long before theirs were finished, and went home to their families.

'When the orders come in, we're the ones to make sure the demand is met,' said Xiao Li.

Some of the newcomers couldn't take it. A Fujianese man detected the ruthlessness of the regime after his first sixteen-hour day, and left immediately. 'This is not a place for human beings,' he said. 'I don't come here to die.' Workers' ill-health was useful to Lim: he could sack people who were ill and get new workers in, earning new registration fees from them.

'But it's not just Lim, you know,' said Xiao Li. 'The factory likes it that way. Don't forget: it's the factory that puts us on the toughest production line with the highest target. It's the factory that imposes these long working hours. Lim just happened to be there at the right time to make a profit out of us.'

Still Zhang worked on, determined to repress all physical and emotional feeling. Every working hour, he and all the un-documented workers earned £2.31 (£1.80 after tax). Locals earned £4.20 an hour. Differentiated wage levels and working conditions for local workers and the 'international workforce' were open, daily practice at Woo One.

In a twelve-hour shift, Zhang was allowed one half-hour break. During the night shift, he was given ten minutes off every two hours. Sometimes he was made to work for twenty-four hours at a time. From these countless hours of standing up during the interminable day and night shifts, his feet became so swollen and numb that he could hardly walk. He was getting bad headaches. But he couldn't go to a doctor, for fear of his illegal status being found out.

'Just say no to them!' Xiao Li said. 'I do!' Xiao Li was a rebel by nature. He took two breaks on each day shift, regardless of the supervisors' warnings. He knew he'd be sent back to the agency sooner or later. One day the supervisors locked the lavatories so the Chinese workers couldn't use them during work time. Xiao Li asked for permission to use them and was refused permission three times. So he unzipped his trousers and urinated on the factory floor. 'No disrespect,' he said to the supervisor, 'but you pushed me.' The supervisor hit him. He picked up a metal stick and chased the supervisor out of the building.

('I was trained by my father,' Xiao Li told me later when he described this incident. 'He was a martial arts expert. In his time, people thought it was important to know how to fight, because you didn't have other means to protect yourself. Your physical strength was your way to survive in those days. I'm surprised to find you need to defend yourself in this way in a British workplace. If I'd been allowed to really fight, that supervisor wouldn't have survived.')

After this incident he was given a final warning: one more act of rule-breaking, and he'd be sent back to the agency.

Zhang watched his friend with admiration, but still he kept on working. He tried not to get involved in disputes between the workers and the bosses. His sole aim was to earn a living for his family in China. Everything else was insignificant. He hardly saw the town of Hartlepool. A few boarded-up pubs and a petrol station were all that came into his view on the walks to and from work. During September, the workload became even bigger as demand grew but no new workers were brought in. Often Zhang did not see daylight for twenty-four hours.

His nephew noticed that he seemed to have no spirit left.

'Are you sure you have to work tonight?'

'I must. If I say no they'll remember it, and it'll count against me.'

As they changed shifts on the last Sunday of October, Xiao Li thought Zhang looked very unwell. 'Are you OK?'

'I'm just tired,' Zhang said.

During that night shift, Zhang had to tell his nephew and a few fellow workers that he had an acute headache. But he knew the production target was 1,500 completed microwaves per shift. There was no chance of stepping off the production line.

Halfway through the night, the headache became unbearable. For the first time ever, he asked the supervisor for an extra break.

The request was refused. 'Wait till you finish work.'

So he worked on. The night shift seemed so dreadfully long. He exerted all the strength in his body with all his will power, and he reached the target, stamping the Samsung label on the 1,500th microwave just as the shift ended.

His nephew led him back to the house. As they walked, he noticed that Zhang's arms were numb, and he didn't seem able to see. Back at the house, his housemates crowded round and tried to help him. One of the women tried to massage his shoulders, but he was losing consciousness. Like a worn-out machine, he was ceasing to function. He tried to speak, but could not make sense any more.

His housemates got him to the local hospital. A few hours later he was transferred to Middlesbrough General Hospital. There, on 2 November 2001, he died of a subarachnoid haemorrhage.

I first stumbled across the story of Zhang's death by chance a year and a half later. A friend of mine, a Chinese builder in London, mentioned it in passing. He was complaining (with justification) about the hardships of his own working life.

'Poor you,' I said.

'But it could be worse. At least I'm not working up north. I don't want to die like Mr Zhang!'

'Who's Mr Zhang?' I asked. 'I don't remember reading anything in the papers about a man called Zhang.'

'No, you wouldn't have,' said my friend. 'The story was

never allowed out. No one from that place wants to talk about it. Everyone wants to bury it – especially the company.'

'Which company was it?'

'It was Samsung.'

My friend did not know – and it took me a month to discover – that the incident actually took place at the factory of one of Samsung's suppliers, Woo One. To manufacture their parts, Samsung relied upon a group of electronics suppliers: Dong Jin Precision in Peterlee, Young Shin in Billingham, and Chang Jin and Woo One in Hartlepool. Samsung was aware of (but did not shoulder responsibility for) the fact that these suppliers recruited at least half of their workers from an undocumented 'international workforce', as the Samsung personnel department called it when I enquired. The labour provider for all these companies was S. C. Lim & Co, New Malden.

I spent nearly two years piecing together Zhang's story.

First I found out about the impressive public face of Samsung Electronics Manufacturing (UK), part of the multinational Samsung Group with its global turnover of $100 billion. Samsung's site in the UK was opened at Wynyard Park, Billingham, in 1995, six years before Zhang arrived. The Queen herself snipped the ribbon. Locals lined the route to welcome her to the opening ceremony. It was, the Queen said, the best chance the region could have to improve opportunities for local employment in the north-east.

Sure enough, locals were employed: not quite the 3,000 the company had promised, more like 1,500, but this allowed it to be awarded £20 million by the local authorities, which it could invest in training programmes. In Samsung's assembly plant at Wynyard Park, ninety-five per cent of the workers were recruited from the local community. Peter Mandelson, the New Labour politician and MP for Hartlepool after the 1997 General Election, praised Samsung's achievement. 'Who said the economic miracle of Asia's Four Little Dragons was based on cheap labour?' (South Korea, Taiwan, Hong Kong and Singapore are known as Asia's Four Little Dragons; Samsung is the second largest corporation in South Korea.)

What was hidden, from the end of the 1990s to the first years of the new century, however, was a less attractive side of Samsung. Multinational corporate power and greed were at work, and the economic success of the conglomerate was depending on its suppliers' use of cheap migrant labour.

This was what Zhang, and so many others like him, got caught up in. I visited Zhang's co-workers many times between 2003 and 2006; I spoke to them for hours, asking for descriptions of Zhang's daily life in detail, wanting to fill out the bald words of my builder friend: *I don't want to die like Mr Zhang.*

I could now add my own epilogue: 'If someone I love dies, I don't want to be treated as Mrs Zhang was after her husband's death.' For I discovered, as I researched the story and later met Mrs Zhang herself, that she suffered almost unimaginable misery in the months which followed.

There was no autopsy, no inquest, no coroner's report on the unusual circumstances of Zhang's death. Middlesbrough General Hospital simply passed the death certificate on to Zhang's direct employer, Lim, who sent it to the Chinese Embassy, who posted it to Mrs Zhang without translating it for her.

She couldn't read it, but with the help of neighbours, she got its gist. He was dead. She lost consciousness. Her beloved husband was dead. Their children had lost their father. But how could he be dead? He was young, fit, thirty-nine.

(She was not to find out precisely what medical condition her husband had died of until one and a half years later, when I translated the death certificate for her.)

At once, she borrowed money from her relatives and applied for a visa to fly to England for her husband's funeral. Leaving her children in the hands of their grandparents, she came to Britain with her niece. They arrived in Hartlepool on 12 November 2001, to find that the arrangements for Zhang's hasty cremation had already been made without her consent. Zhang's co-workers, horrified by his death, had got together to make a donation of £20 to £40 each, to pay for the funeral and for living expenses for his family.

There was unrest among the workers: they saw what over-work could do to a person, reducing him from a lively, fit father to a corpse. Lim was aware of the anger and agitation. To quieten things down, he made an offer to Mrs Zhang when she arrived in Hartlepool: he would pay her six months' wages in compensation. Naive, desperate for money to support her children, she accepted the offer.

'Making our donation towards the funeral was the least we could do,' Xiao Li told me later. 'But we couldn't be there at the funeral. We were on our shift, and weren't allowed to attend.' Instead, on that bleak November morning two days later, with unswept fallen leaves rattling around the crema-torium, the cremation took place, attended by Mrs Zhang, her niece who accompanied her to England, Zhang's nephew who'd worked alongside him before he died, and by Woo One's English manager and Lim. For the company representa-tives being there was a matter of courtesy. A local priest who had never met Zhang gave a short address, incomprehensible to the Chinese.

As soon as the cremation was over, courtesy vanished from Lim's repertoire. For him the case was closed; for Mrs Zhang, the nightmare had just begun. Lim stopped all contact with Mrs Zhang. She tried to call him; she needed to know the chronology of what had happened, but he didn't answer her calls. All he did was send her husband's ashes back to his parents in China two months later.

From this time on, Mrs Zhang was confronted with an alliance of institutions and private interests that prevented her from gaining justice for Zhang.

How had he died? Why had he died? Middlesbrough General Hospital did not even try to contact her, let alone explain what had happened. The only people who were in contact with the hospital were Woo One's Korean director, its English manager and Lim.

'All communication was conducted between the hospital and the factory,' Older Gao told me later. 'The family was kept out of it.'

By the time I met Mrs Zhang in 2003, she still had not been given access to her husband's medical records.

'But you must keep trying,' I said to her. 'You must write to the hospital again.'

She herself was, by now, an 'illegal', having outstayed her visa, so she was nervous about writing an official letter. But she knew she must if she was to have any hope of seeing the records, and I followed up with a call to the hospital. My own Chinese accent put me at a disadvantage: I was put through to the PR department, and dealt with by an insensitive and uninterested PR officer. Eventually I got through to the records department.

'Sorry,' said the team leader. 'Mr Zhang's name is not in the system.'

'Not in the system? But he died only eighteen months ago.'

To whom could Mrs Zhang turn? I contacted the Health and Safety Executive (HSE). First I enquired about industrial deaths in Britain in general. They were on the rise, the HSE told me; not only in obviously dangerous jobs like construction, but also in manufacturing jobs. Any industrial death, they said, should be reported to them, regardless of the person's nationality and immigration status.

I contacted the HSE in the north-east and homed in on specifics: was Zhang's death reported to them? I was told by Chris Gillies, the Principal Inspector of the HSE, that Zhang's death was not reported to them, and therefore no investigation was undertaken. Well, perhaps it should be undertaken now, I suggested.

They took the matter seriously and began their inquiry. Dr E. M. Gillanders, the HSE's Senior Medical Inspector, took charge of the investigation. She asked for Zhang's medical records from Middlesbrough General Hospital, and found that the records department had spelled his name wrong; that was why his records had been lost.

No apology ever came to Mrs Zhang for this piece of gross mismanagement.

Dr Gillanders revealed her findings to us: Zhang's doctor at the hospital 'was not sure of the relationship between his death and his work'. No one knows why he did not insist on an inquest. Dr Gillanders told me that Dr Clarke, the consultant of the Critical Care Services Unit at Middlesbrough General Hospital, had referred her to Newcastle General Hospital to seek advice regarding the link between Zhang's work and his death. However, to date, the HSE has not produced a report about Zhang's death. His medical records have now been transferred to James Cook University Hospital, as Middlesbrough General has closed down. In October I made a request for his medical records under the Freedom of Information Act, but my request was refused as they said I was not Zhang's personal representative, nor did I have a claim arising from his death.

Later, I asked James Cook University Hospital to comment on the gross mismanagement of Middlesbrough General Hospital regarding Zhang Guo-Hua's death. Simon Pleydell, chief executive of South Tees Hospitals NHS Trust, didn't give his view, but said that the hospital is unable to give any information regarding the circumstances surrounding Zhang's death directly to me without permission from his family.

There was nothing Mrs Zhang could do at the time. Not a legal resident, not an English-speaker, she was powerless.

On top of the misery of not being able to trace her husband's medical records, Mrs Zhang discovered that Lim's promise of compensation had turned out to be an empty one. He never paid up. Instead, he'd offered her a job in another of Samsung's suppliers, Young Shin in Billingham. Mrs Zhang was now the only breadwinner of her family, and she desperately needed an income to support her children in China, so she took up Lim's offer of a job at Young Shin's factory. But Young Shin refused to employ her: they were afraid of being connected with Zhang's death, which might attract attention. She was left with nothing.

'The factory refused to pay the family compensation,' a worker from Tienjin told me, 'because, they said, Zhang was working illegally. That's ridiculous! Everyone knows the factory allows the agency to provide us with false documents so we can work day and night for them. When Zhang was slaving away for them, the factory didn't complain he was working illegally then, did they? Now they use his illegal status as an excuse to disregard his life and death.'

Zhang's co-workers, meanwhile, were still trying to help his family's cause. Xiao Li urged Mrs Zhang to sue the company, but she didn't have the courage.

A few of the workers from the north-east of China where Zhang came from went on a spontaneous strike in the months after the cremation. That was no problem for Lim: he simply dismissed them. But still the atmosphere of unrest went on; the cause of 'justice for Zhang's family' would not go away. So Lim resorted to a more sinister tactic: 'divide and rule'. This involved setting one group of workers against another, exploiting their fear. He told the supervisors to spread the word that 'Mrs Zhang is a bad influence on the workers, because she will attract public attention, which may hinder your job opportunities'. The supervisors hinted to the workers that they'd face possible immigration raids and deportation if they tried to draw attention to Mrs Zhang.

This tactic worked. Sympathetic faces – not all of them, but most of them – gradually turned away.

'I don't hold it against them,' Mrs Zhang said to me. 'I understand why they looked the other way.'

Now she had nothing left. It became clear that Lim and the factory manager were intensifying their pressure to force Zhang's family out of the workplace and the entire area. One day, without any reason, Zhang's nephew was dismissed from Woo One, with no notice period.

'In the end,' Mrs Zhang's niece told me, 'the factory manager told us to our faces that we must leave. They didn't want to invite an investigation from the authorities. We had one more place to resort to for help in suing the company: the Chinese Embassy.'

But the embassy shattered their last hope. 'Zhang Guo-Hua was working illegally,' they said. 'It takes financial strength and experience to sue a company. Can you meet these requirements?'

Indeed she could not, Mrs Zhang realized, once and for all. With no money, no knowledge of the law, no English and no legal status, she'd come to the end of the road.

The following day, she, her niece and her nephew were sent to Hartlepool station by Lim, and seen on to a train. He wanted them out: they had no option but to leave.

Xiao Li, the rebel, had witnessed all this and he was still working at Woo One. Now, he told me later, he bitterly resented the daily monotony and tyranny of the factory. He cursed the machines, detested the Samsung label he had to print on hundreds of thousands of microwaves. He felt an uncontrollable contempt for Zhang's family. Why hadn't they sued? Why had they given up?

He was finding it harder and harder to abide by the factory rules. One day he decided to take a break, right then and there, in the middle of his shift. He just went and sat down at the side, on the floor. Woo One's managing director happened to walk past. 'What the hell are you doing?' he shouted.

Xiao Li knew this was the end. He was right. Lim was told to take Xiao Li off the production line.

His dismissal caused barely a ripple. He was instantly replaced. For the undocumented workers at Woo One, life went on, just as before. Their weekly working hours ranged from seventy-two to a hundred hours. If anything, life became a little worse: the supervisors were more careful than ever to keep an eye on the workers, making sure they had no contact with the outside world. The twenty-four-hour sweatshop regime, and the workers' isolated existence, made them easy to keep an eye on. When I visited in 2004, the Chinese workers revealed that there had been no wage increase despite their continuous demands.

A year after Zhang's death, the HSE served eight notices to Woo One (although it knew nothing about Zhang's story at the time). There were five improvement notices, on major health-and-safety risks such as the lack of ways to ensure safe operating procedures for machinery, risks of injury from entrapment and risks of getting untrained workers to do skilled jobs. There were also three immediate prohibition notices due to risks such as possible access to dangerous moving parts of machinery, which breached the Health and Safety Act 1974 and the Provision and Use of Work Equipment Regulations 1998.

After two years of piecing together the story of Zhang's last months, and of the aftermath of his death, I felt I had a fairly clear picture of what had happened. But there was one man I hadn't yet met. Having heard from so many people about Lim – Cheng-Zhe Lim, of S. C. Lim & Co, New Malden – I was curious to meet the man himself.

The office in New Malden was as unremarkable as any recruitment office – though its darkened windows made it a little sinister. The secretary behind the desk was not welcoming. She was suspicious. 'How did you know about us?' was her first question. It was clearly unusual for a person to visit the office with no introduction or appointment.

I asked to speak to Mr Lim, and after a few minutes of

whispered conversation a wary man appeared from the back room.

'How do you know of my company?' he asked.

I did not divulge to him, yet, the true extent of my knowledge. 'Oh, it's quite well known among the fraternity of Chinese workers I've met.'

Cautiously, he answered my questions. He told me he'd been working with Samsung Electronics for four years, and had an annual contract with their suppliers to recruit 150 workers each year, the number peaking at times of high production. He told me that his company had recently taken over, and now part-owned, Woo One Ltd in Hartlepool.

I found out that his labour-providing business stretched from the construction trade in London to the seafood-processing industry in Scotland and as far as the Shetland Islands, where his small team of Chinese workers processed salmon for export. 'Our company's annual profits are £1.5 million,' he told me.

I asked him about the working hours: I'd heard they were very long and that conditions were harsh.

'The workers want to work hard,' he replied. 'The harder they work the more money they earn.'

I mentioned the matter of an industrial death I'd heard about. Had that been anything to do with working conditions?

He refused to comment.

S. C. Lim & Co dissolved on 29 May 2007, and was incorporated as a company of the same name on the next day, 30 May. Lim's name was conveniently removed from the new company appointment records, while he still manages the company's day-to-day business.

I visited Lim again in February 2008 and put all the allegations to him. Regarding the registration fee of £100, he said: 'It was a fee for our accountant. Workers moved around quickly, to wherever the better jobs are. If the worker found a better job, say, in a salad factory, they could leave us within one to two months. We had 320 workers at that time. But in fact only 147 of them stayed to work. Many of them came and left. My accountant had to deal with them and sort out their tax, therefore I had to charge them £100. This way, they would at least work for six months to a year. After a year, I returned the money to them.'

No workers had actually received the 'accountant's fee' back. Lim explained that was because the workers didn't sign a contract. Yet no worker had ever been offered a contract.

Regarding the claim that Lim's company sold photocopies of work permits for £50 each, he said: 'I never charged workers money for permits. I only sorted out tax for people. If workers couldn't give me their permits within three weeks of starting the job, I'd dismiss them. Some people with work permits asked me if I could sell the documents for them, for as high as £150 per copy. I tried to bargain it down for the workers and sometimes lowered the price to £100 per permit ... Twenty-five per cent of the permits were "borrowed" this way. Mr Han [department head at Woo One] managed the whole thing. The team leaders had a copy [of workers' documents], the permit lender [seller] had a copy, the department manager also had a copy. The team leaders made photocopies and then passed them to Mr Han who then passed them to my office. The team leaders negotiated conditions with the work-permit lender. When the team leaders wanted to keep the workers, they would find documents for them. They would get in touch with the lender, selling permits for £150 or £200. This way, permit copies were reused many times in different factories.' Lim admitted that from 2001 to 2002 his team leaders sold permits to workers on occasions. 'One team leader charged £50. I dismissed him. Another one charged £100. I transferred him to another workplace.'

Regarding the £150 charged for food and accommodation, Lim said: 'The food and rent wasn't arranged by us [S. C. Lim & Co Ltd] at first. If the minimum rate was £4.20, they [Woo One Ltd] would take 60p from us and left us with £3.60. And then they deducted food and rent from this and left us with £3.10 in the end. Later, probably in November 2004, I bought Woo One's flat and took over the management and began to charge workers £150 for food and rent.' As to the hourly rate he paid to workers, Lim said: 'I remember it was more than £1.80 per hour.'

Regarding the overwork that workers believed had caused Zhang Guo-Hua's death, Lim said: 'People weren't forced to do overtime. They all liked to do overtime. But you can't give people overtime work to do only according to their own needs. Zhang wasn't alone. They all did the same work, but no one had the same thing happen to him. Later, his wife told me that Zhang's father had also died of haemorrhage. High blood pressure [Zhang's symptom] was closely related to pressure at work. But there wasn't that kind of pressure ... I didn't actually like them to work overtime because I had to pay them more wages then. I prefer to increase the number of staff rather than making people work overtime.'

As to where the responsibility lies, Lim said: 'I had a contract with Woo One saying how many hours people could work. It was 260 to 280 hours a month. But Woo One always wanted overtime work. I raised the issue with them before. I thought it might have negative effects if there was too much overtime work. They violated our contract. They said workers weren't forced to work, but, when some workers said no to overtime work, Woo One sacked them. I think Zhang Guo-Hua's death had something to do with the overworking. But Woo One wouldn't admit that. The working hours were Woo One's responsibility.'

Regarding Lim's unrealized offer of compensation (equivalent to six months' wages) to Mrs Zhang, he said: 'I never said I was to pay her compensation. I mentioned it to the team leader Mr Jin in the factory that I will ask Woo One for a minimum of three months' wages and a maximum of six months' wages as compensation. I said to Woo One Ltd that, as the death happened in their building, they should be responsible. My lawyer told Woo One that they should be responsible and should have sent the worker to the hospital in time. I asked Woo One if they would compensate on humanitarian grounds but they didn't want to. I asked them for six months' wages as compensation but they refused. So I asked for three months' wages. They refused again. They said I should pay for six months' wages to Mrs Zhang as compensation, and they would pay for keeping Zhang's body in the hospital before the cremation.'

Regarding Lim's dismissal of Zhang Guo-Hua's nephew without notice, he said: 'He [Zhang's nephew] continued to work there after Zhang's death for about fourteen days. But Woo One wouldn't allow it. It wasn't legal. They [Mrs Zhang, Zhang's nephew and niece] were waiting [for work] for two months. Later they felt they had to go. They left voluntarily.'

With regard to unfair dismissal without notice in general, Lim said: 'If they [the workers] violated our rules, such as drinking and fighting . . . then I had to dismiss them.'

During my two years of research into Zhang's story, Samsung Electronics was gradually relocating to Slovakia. The reason given for the move was 'falling prices of electronic goods driven by competition against the cost of production'. The British wage level of £4.50–£5.50 an hour, they said (failing to mention the much lower wage level at some of their suppliers), was too high, compared with the Slovakian wage of £1 an hour. Production at Samsung's new site in Galanta, in the west of the country, began in 2004.

So those glorious employment opportunities, praised by the Queen and Peter Mandelson, were turned to dust. Samsung did not feel any obligation to return the £10.5 million they'd been awarded by the government: they claimed to have reached the required target by employing 1,600 people at the plant's peak time.

Quietly, in the shadow of the great global conglomerate, Woo One in Hartlepool was closing down and relocating to Slovakia as well. Without noise or fuss, the Chinese and Korean workers were laid off, and the factory was closed in March 2005. It was as easy as that to remove all evidence of past events. There happened to be a huge fire at the Woo One site on the very day when it was due to close. The cause of the fire was never established; but Xiao Li is in no doubt: 'The company did this to claim from the insurance company.'

Now it was the Slovakian president Robert Fico's turn to praise the employment opportunities granted by Samsung to his country's citizens. And the impressive statistics were rolled out, proudly boasting: Samsung Electronics has created 3,000 jobs in Galanta, with 2,500 of the workers employed on its 35-acre manufacturing site. Sales have increased tenfold in four years. Galanta (a barren city that has remained out of reach of tourists) is now known as 'Samsung City'. One of every five residents works for Samsung.

And if you look behind the scenes, you find that Korean suppliers have moved in to meet Samsung's needs. Today there are at least eleven Korean suppliers dotted around Galanta, manufacturing PC monitors and TV sets to supply to Samsung Electronics Slovakia.

Woo One has changed its name to Kihwa. The factory is twenty-five miles from Galanta in the town of Surany, and employs between 300 and 500 people, depending on the time of year. I visited Kihwa in autumn 2006. Had the change of name and of location brought an improvement in working conditions? Sadly, I could see no evidence of this. The one thing that had changed was that the Chinese and Korean workers from Woo One were gone. They could not have moved to a different country, having no immigration status to make the crossing of borders possible. Lim had scattered them across Britain to work at other factories or building sites. But, apart from that, the scene at Kihwa was all too recognizable: the same toxic smell of burning plastic, the same gruelling twelve-hour shifts, the workers still not provided with masks to protect them from chemicals in the label-printing process, the same air of resigned acceptance among the workforce. I spoke to Martin, a local employee, who was pleased at least that his wage had gone up from 1.2 euro per hour to 1.9, meeting the new national minimum wage. And at least he had a job in an area where there was not much choice of work. But there was no sick pay at Kihwa, he told me, and no holiday pay written into the contract. 'The company's getting us cheap and not following the rules.' And, as had been the case for Zhang and so many others in Hartlepool, no training: 'you learn how to do the job by following others'.

The sales department of Kihwa are delighted with how things are going. They made a million euro from sales in October 2006 alone. 'Slovak workers choose to work for us,' the sales executive told me, 'because of the good image our company has. People trust us.'

Factories like Kihwa will never be short of staff. As we'll see in the following chapters, there are many more Martins, many more Zhangs, waiting to get on to the production line and go through whatever's required in order to bring some money home to their families. The factories know how to exploit their desperation. The global conglomerates meanwhile, high above the human everyday stories, increase their profits.

Samsung Electronics Ltd, Samsung Electronics Slovakia, Kihwa Ltd (Woo One Ltd today) did not respond to the allegations.

2. Becoming Invisible

Since Dad went to work in England, Mum and I have been missing him all the time. If he stops calling for a few days, we can't sleep well. Dad isn't young any more, and he's alone in a foreign country. It's all because of me. What an unworthy daughter I am! Dad wants me to go to university and have a good life. He's making money for me. We haven't been in a photo together for five years. That's how long he's been gone. When other families are reunited over the New Year, we have only sorrow, and worries for Dad.

— *Yin Yang from Tienjin, the 17-year-old daughter of a migrant father in England February 2007*

Zhang Guo-Hua's death was a shocking testimony to the reality behind the facade of 'multicultural Britain'. Yet before his demise became known to the world, another tragedy unfolded at Morecambe Bay, with more loss of lives. While the whole country was slow to make sense of the deeper causes of the workers' deaths, the British Chinese community remained largely silent. It was almost as if the deaths were not relevant because they were seen as the tragedy of another class.

I resolved to set out on a journey into the hidden world of exploitation to discover what could allow such tragedies to happen. I wanted to give a voice to these workers. How could I gain genuine insight into the lives of the most marginalized group in Britain?

I decided to go undercover: to pretend to be one of these immigrants without official documents and desperate to earn money, and to see where it took me. Having made up my mind, I was impatient to start. I did not foresee that getting into the underground world of employment would take me almost a month.

First, I needed a ticket into that world: a forged work permit. To get a job as an undocumented worker, I would need to buy one of these photocopied permits, either from a dealer or an employment agent. Access is extremely limited, and the dealers and agents are always cautious.

My search began on the street corners of Chinatown in London. A friend of mine, Xiao Yu, an undocumented worker who'd been in England for a few years, told me I might be able to get informal access through one of the street cigarette-sellers there. They might know a contact or an agency I could approach to get hold of the necessary papers.

I wandered westwards from Leicester Square station into Chinatown, where I saw the vendors Xiao Yu had mentioned: women in their forties or fifties selling smuggled cigarettes to Chinese passers-by. I stood near one of them and waited for the right moment to speak to her. 'Excuse me,' I said. 'I've just arrived in this country. I'm looking to buy a piece of *nan-min-zhi*. Can you help me?' (*Nan-min-zhi* means, literally, 'refugee paper', the expression used by Chinese workers to mean 'work permit'.)

The cigarette-seller looked me up and down, then said, 'Go and try the agency there.' She pointed to a narrow alleyway behind Gerrard Street.

It turned out that the agency this woman was pointing to was one of the most notorious Chinese-run employment agencies in town. Just off the row of glamorously decorated restaurants was a narrow path, wet with waste water from the kitchens and nearby noodle factory. I opened a small door, climbed a stinking flight of stairs and reached the door of a company which called itself an 'estate agent'. I walked in and introduced myself to the administrator, a young woman in her twenties.

'I'm looking for any work,' I said. 'I don't have *shen-fen.*' (Workers use *shen-fen* to mean 'immigration status'.)

'This agency gets all kinds of work,' the woman said. 'Factory work, farm work, domestic work like babysitting . . .'

'But I have no proper papers.'

She replied without looking up from her desk. 'You pay us an introduction fee of £200 for placing you in a job, and we'll do all the paperwork for you.'

Before committing myself to this, I consulted some of my Chinese contacts about the agency's reputation. 'Don't go near it,' a Fujianese worker called Mr Li said. 'The agency's not responsible for anything that happens after you've paid your fees. Often, employers sack you after two or three weeks. You've lost the £200, plus you often don't even get paid by the employers. If you come back to the agency for a new job, you'll have to pay another £200 fee.'

Dismissals from jobs occur so frequently, within two or three weeks of jobs starting, that Chinese workers suspect a conspiracy: they believe agencies like this one work with the employers and make a fortune from a steady stream of people looking for work, thanks to unfair dismissals.

'Some of these back-street agencies aren't even registered companies,' said Mr Li. 'We old-timers know they're no good. Only the very new arrivals resort to them.'

So I asked around, looking for a cheaper and more trustworthy option. Mr Gu, a builder in West London, said he could help me. He'd been working in Britain for three years, without documents. He was friendly and approachable, and I was told that lots of Chinese newcomers asked him for help finding work. He'd become well connected over the years. When I asked him for a work permit, he laughed.

'Come to my place. I've got the *nan-min-zhi* you need.'

Bringing a bottle of whisky as a gift, I went to visit Mr Gu. In his smoky living room, which was also the bedroom of his two flatmates, he laid out dozens of work permits on the table

for me to see. These were Home Office IS96 documents grant-
ing the temporary right to work to Chinese asylum seekers
before 2001. 'Back then,' he said, 'you were allowed to work a
little while you were waiting for asylum decisions. Now you
have to eat your own flesh to survive.'

He pointed to the permits. 'They're all photocopies. But
you wouldn't know it. They look genuine, don't they?' He
showed me how to stick on someone's photo without covering
the immigration seal stamped on the original permit. 'Then
you just photocopy it,' he explained. 'And when someone else
needs to use the permit, you stick his picture here and make
another copy. That's how one real permit can be used numerous times. I help my friends make them. We all need jobs,
don't we?'

'How much do I have to pay for one?' I asked.

'Agencies sell them for £50, but I'll give you one for free.
Here you are.'

It was a permit in the name of 'Chen Min' who'd been an
asylum seeker three years ago. I had no idea if it was a he or a
she: Chen Min is a gender-neutral Chinese name.

Now, with my permit, I was ready to be recruited. I
asked my friend Xiao Yu to help me: I particularly wanted to
find employment in Suffolk or Norfolk, as I knew there were
thousands of undocumented Chinese people in the area, con-
trolled by a web of unlicensed agents and gangmasters (officially
known as 'labour providers'). I'd heard that most of the agents
were English, but that there was also a growing number of
Chinese gangmasters (*gong tou*, literally meaning 'leader of
work', as the Chinese workers called them) who'd managed
to penetrate the informal economy, thanks to their grasp of
the English language. Workers without legal status depended
on these men to get registered with agencies and find work
in food-processing and agriculture.

At first I tried registering with the local employment
agencies on my own. I rang them in Norfolk. But I sensed they

were suspicious. It became clear that undocumented Chinese workers could never get jobs directly from the local agencies. The agencies wouldn't take on a Chinese worker without a Chinese recruiter to mediate. This, I came to understand, was because the agencies knew the workers were undocumented. If they used these middlemen, it helped them to legitimize and stay aloof from what they were doing: exploiting a cheap workforce.

Xiao Yu explained that many of these gangmasters had connections with Chinese gangs who ran vast businesses of 'status manufacturing' all over the UK – that is, producing and selling passports to desperate fellow Chinese at a high price. He warned me that it could be dangerous to go near such men. I must prepare a well-thought-out story about who I am, where I come from and why I need a job in the area. Xiao Yu insisted that he make the first call to a Chinese gangmaster he knew of in King's Lynn, in order to protect me from danger. He pretended he was enquiring about work for an unrelated third person.

The man said no. All vacancies were filled. But he gave Xiao Yu the number of another recruiter based in Thetford, by the surname of Lin.

I summoned up courage and rang this man. 'My name is Lin Hong,' I said. 'I'm from Langfang in Hebei province. I'm looking for work. I really need a job.' (Hebei is in the north of China. I'm able to put on a convincing northern accent as my mother comes from a northern Chinese province.)

'What sort of status are you?'

'I have a *nan-min-zhi*,' I replied.

'Good. Let's see. Yeah, we do have work and accommodation in Thetford. But I need to meet you at Victoria coach station first. Meet me there at 8 p.m. on Monday, yes?'

I had two days to get ready. I packed T-shirts and black trousers, and picked out a thick old jacket with two large pockets where

I could keep my notepad and pens – the most precious items in my luggage. Then I set off, with my new name and identity: Lin Hong, a twenty-eight-year-old northern Chinese woman who'd come to England with a student visa and outstayed it by a few months. A woman with no relations or permanent residence here, no bank account and no authorized status; I was what is known as an 'illegal'.

I arrived at Victoria coach station an hour early, and rehearsed my lines over and over in my head. The tension was hard to bear. At eight o'clock, at the coach terminal for Thetford, Mr Lin appeared.

'So you're Lin Hong.'

He looked at me from head to toe. Was he suspicious already? He took out a packet of Marlboro from his yellow coat pocket, and began to question me in detail.

'I worked as a kitchen porter in south London for a month after my visa ran out.' I poured out my memorized story.

'But why did you leave that job?'

'My boss sacked me. Then a friend introduced me to a babysitting job.'

'And why did you leave that?'

'Because I'd heard about work in your area. I heard it was better paid.'

He lit a second cigarette. I went to get two cups of coffee from the station café, and passed one to him. He looked surprised at the generosity. He dropped his inquisitive manner and relaxed a little. Perhaps I'd convinced him. The next minute, he hurried me on to the coach leaving for Thetford, and we took our seats at the front.

As we drove eastwards out of London, Mr Lin started talking. All the way to Thetford, he told me stories from his past.

'My parents were poor farmers outside Fuqing. My father overworked me. He had a terrible temper. He used to punish me whenever I made a mistake. One day he beat me so hard that I ran away and swore never to return. I went to work in other provinces, and got involved in all kinds of risky business. Printing fake currency, things like that. Once I was shot at in a police chase. Later I was smuggled into Taiwan, with the help of local snakeheads. But the police in Taiwan are strict. I was arrested and deported after three months.'

He continued with his story. 'During these last five years in England, status manufacturing has been a large part of my income. Many Chinese need me to help them. They come to me to buy passports.'

He looked cheerful, waving his hand around as he spoke. I noticed his Rolex watch. Then, without emotion, he moved on to the Morecambe Bay cockling tragedy.

'My girlfriend was one of the victims in my team,' he said. 'It was a shame.'

A shame? Surely it must have been worse than 'a shame'. I couldn't help asking, 'How did you know her? Where was she from?'

'A nice woman, she was, in her twenties, from Liaoning in north-east China. Ah Hua, her name was. I was in London that night. I did ask her to go with me to London, but she wanted to stay to work. Always hard-working, she was.'

Later I was to hear from Ah Hua's friends that she was actually in her forties and came from a different province. They told me she'd been working at the food-processing factories in Norfolk. When the peak season was over, she'd been persuaded into cockling by Lin. I also found out that although Lin kept referring to the drowned cockling team as 'my team', he had not in fact been the boss in charge of that team. It became clear that he was a man of raging ambition, full of boasts. 'I'm going back to Morecambe Bay,' he told me. 'I'm going to set up my own cockling business. Soon.'

The coach's windscreen wipers swished backwards and for-wards. Lin started to play games on his mobile phone. It rang, and he chatted to someone in Fujianese, not knowing I could understand a little of it.

I made out these words: 'Listen, I'm bringing a girlfriend with me.'

It was 11.30 p.m. when we arrived at Thetford coach station, and climbed down into the darkness and wind. We walked for twenty minutes. I tried not to show my fear. What was I walking into? As a status-less person, my destiny was in his hands.

'Here we are.' Lin unlocked the door of a dingy four-bedroom house on the outskirts of the town. 'Everyone's asleep. Be quiet.'

He showed me into a room three metres by three: a shared bedroom. The bare white walls shone out in the dark. Three men were sleeping on mattresses on the floor, lined up against a double bed. Lin threw his bag on to the bed. I froze.

'Where do I sleep?' I asked.

Lin pointed to the double bed.

The thought of what he intended to happen in the next hour overwhelmed me. I didn't have time to think out a response. I panicked.

'But you told me on the phone I'd have a bed.'

'Listen, miss, it's all full here, OK? I'm doing you a favour, OK? There, now, in you get, and get some sleep.'

'I want a bed for myself,' I hissed. Would my investigation have to end before it had properly begun? Would I have to run away from this situation? No. I must not admit defeat. If I were truly an illegal person desperate for work, what choice would I have but to stay? Therefore I must stay.

'Give me my own bed,' I repeated. Lin wouldn't listen, and started to get undressed. There were footsteps on the stairs.

'You see, you've woken up my brother,' said Lin. His 'brother' turned out to be a more experienced recruiter, from the same Fujianese town as Lin. The two men had sworn brotherhood. In this house in Thetford, Lin's brother was known as Lao Lin (which means older Lin), and Lin was known as Xiao Lin (younger Lin).

At this moment, to my intense relief, one of the men on the mattresses woke up. 'What's happening here?' he asked. 'Who are you?'

'My name's Lin Hong. I've just arrived.' I pointed to a small space beyond his feet. 'May I sleep there for the moment?'

'Sure,' the man said, moving his mattress to make a bit more space for me. Lin didn't utter a word, and went to sleep in his double bed. I had no bedding, only my thick winter jacket to get me through the night.

'Who forgot to flush the toilet? Who was it?'

I was woken by an ear-splitting female voice. People were walking up and down the stairs, opening doors, making breakfast before their morning shift at the duck factory.

As I sat up, Lin appeared at the door, dressed. 'You have to pay £30 per week for your bed, you understand?' I nodded, refusing to look him in the eye.

I climbed the stairs to the bathroom. It was tiny, without a washbasin. I had to brush my teeth over the bathtub. Some people used their own plastic tubs as basins. Every half-minute, there was a knock on the door. 'What are you doing in there? Taking drugs?' It was that harsh Chinese female voice again. 'You're only allowed three minutes in the bathroom.'

I later found out that this was Miss Chio, the fiancée of the English landlord. She laid down the rules in this household.

As the workers left for the morning shift, I went into the tiny kitchen. My room-mates, three men from Shanghai, were having breakfast. One, named Zhang, was having tinned spaghetti with baked beans ('It's cheap and tasty,' he said) and the other two, Qin and Tan, were having rice soup, and picking marinated Chinese cucumbers out of a jar with their chopsticks.

Lin walked in without saying good morning. 'Don't touch rubbish like that,' he said to me. He got out his wok and some fresh squid. He chopped some onions and Chinese cabbage, and cooked them all with noodles. 'Here: your breakfast,' he said, putting a plateful in front of me. 'Fujianese seafood noodles.'

The men from Shanghai stared in amazement. 'Lin never cooks breakfast for anyone,' they told me later.

It was obvious Lin was trying to please and impress me. I was just wondering why this might be when he came and asked me for a registration fee of £200 up front, in order to get me registered at the local recruitment agency. Most people needed to wait till they received their first set of monthly wages before they could pay this fee. Keen to get a job, I paid him the full fee at once. I could see he was pleased as he counted up the notes.

But the prompt payment didn't speed up the job-finding process. Lin said he'd take me to the employment agency late that afternoon. It was clear he was deliberately taking his time. He knew I badly needed work. I'd told him I now only had £40 left. He was playing the control game. He wanted to see me yield to the pressure of financial desperation and become obedient to him like the other workers.

It was imprisoning, this feeling of being totally in the power of this man and his brother if you wanted to find work. They were our gateway to earning money – our only gateway. If we wanted to get a job, we could not get on the wrong side of them. Lin sent Zhang, Qin, Tan and I into town to do shopping while he went off to King's Lynn for a few hours to 'sort out status problems for people' – in other words, to sell passports to Chinese people for £400 to £700 each.

So off we went into the town centre. We were not the only migrants in the town: we passed quite a lot of others, and I sensed the discomfort of the locals in our presence.

My room-mates knew where the cheapest shops were. 'You can afford to eat meat, if you know where to buy it!' said Zhang. They led me into a quaint butcher's shop. 'Look, they have pigs' tails, pigs' ears. Anything the English don't eat, they sell it really cheaply.'

Carrying the large bags of rice and noodles ordered by Lin,

we walked back to the house. The sense of freedom when Lin and his brother were out was palpable. We sat around in the kitchen and chatted. My Shanghainese friends told me they'd arrived three days ago, recruited by Lao Lin. 'He's a more vicious recruiter than Xiao Lin,' they said. 'He's ruthless. He's given us two weeks to pay the registration fee before it rises to £250 in the third week. He knows damn well we're new and we can't get shifts as easily as the others.'

I asked them to tell me about the bossy woman with the ear-splitting voice.

'She's supposed to be the fiancée of a guy named Adam, our simple-minded landlord. He pops in every two weeks, to pick her up to go out. He has no idea she sleeps with Lao Lin in the double bed upstairs. They're a pair, those two. She helps Lao Lin collect the registration fees from us. And she takes a share of the weekly rent, which has just increased from £25 to £30 a week.'

I looked at Qin's face and noticed how thin he was, how anxious. 'With all these profits Lao Lin's making,' he said, 'he's still on my back every day. I only have £60. I need to work right away to pay back the registration fee to him. The so-called registration fee that never guarantees you work. I'm waiting for them to give me a shift. I'd take all the work they'd give me.'

Zhang, Qin and Tan had all been construction workers in Shanghai. Their brown, lined faces and their rough, wrinkled hands showed their trade. They told me how bad things had become in Shanghai in the last decade. They'd all lost their jobs in their mid-forties, joining hundreds of thousands of un-employed in the city. 'There was no safety network any more,' said Zhang. 'The state support we got when we were laid off was tiny – not enough for one person to live on, let alone a whole family. People asked why we left a booming city like Shanghai. We wouldn't be here if we had swimming pools at home, would we? The only reason the three of us left our homes is poverty. We all have families to feed. I have a son at the university, and I want the best education for him. He's bright. I want him to find a good job after university.' Zhang's voice mellowed as he spoke about his family.

'Now I'm in England, struggling to find work, I understand how the migrant workers in Shanghai must feel. They travel in their millions from the interior provinces to Shanghai for work. They're far away from their families too. And they do the most menial jobs and suffer from the worst treatment, the lowest pay, the worst housing. The city can't do without them. They make up a quarter of the Shanghai workforce. But in spite of their hard work, they have no status in the city.'

Zhang, Qin and Tan told me they'd been in Britain for a year, but they'd never been settled anywhere for long. The search for work had moved them on, from one city to the next. The recruiters and employment companies had total control over their fates.

'First we got a job at a flower farm near Plymouth,' Qin said, 'via a Malaysian Chinese gangmaster. Picking daffodils. It took three hours to pick a hundred bunches, for which we were paid £3 – that's £1 an hour. And we couldn't even be sure the gangmaster would pay that. When the daffodil season was over we had to move on. We got in touch with another Chinese gangmaster based in Lancaster. He told us there were cockling jobs in Morecambe Bay, and said he'd provide us with beds and three meals a day. It sounded like a good deal, and we travelled straight up. It turned out the house was crowded: ten Chinese men in a small room. And the meals were inadequate: three dishes between ten of us. Cockling turned out to be incredibly hard work. We got £5 for a bag of cockles. The maximum I could pick was three bags a day. It was backbreaking. My health deteriorated.'

'We were lucky to leave before the tragedy,' said Zhang. 'The people who drowned in Morecambe Bay weren't fishermen. They knew little about the sea. The bosses didn't give a damn. The local buyers just set huge production targets, and the Chinese bosses insisted the targets were met. The cockle pickers died because the demands on them were unreasonable in unsafe circumstances. Something like that would never happen to the local cocklers.'

Qin went on with the story of their year in Britain. Could it get any worse?

'Then we worked like hell on a flower farm near Birmingham for two weeks – and we were paid £15 each. The gangmaster refused to pay us any more than that. We were powerless. Then we went to work for an English company in Coventry, putting adverts into magazines. Twelve hours' work a day – and the middlemen made unexplained deductions from time to time, so we never knew how much we'd get or when we'd get it. We worked for sixteen hours on Christmas Day, for which we didn't get paid. It was tough. We depended on our jobs to pay rent and buy food, and of course to send money home.'

'What d'you think you could have done to stop this kind of exploitation?' I asked.

Qin shook his head sadly. 'The greatest sickness in the Chinese culture is our deep-rooted habit of enduring exploitation, enduring slavery. Think about it! If we all had the courage to down tools and expose the situation, it could work. But, instead, we compete against each other; some of us turn into oppressors ourselves – and we become more and more defenceless.'

Zhang and Tan nodded in agreement. 'And we always have our immigration status to worry about,' said Zhang. 'How can we speak out if we have no rights?'

There was nothing to say. The four of us sipped our green tea in silence.

At five o'clock, Lin reappeared from King's Lynn.

'Let's go and get you a job,' he said to me. We walked into

the town centre and arrived at the agency: Pertemps Recruitment East Anglia. The building was small: you wouldn't guess it was a major recruitment company for the food-processing industries in Norfolk, one of 203 branches in the country with over 25,000 workers on its books – many of them undocumented workers from Brazil, Eastern Europe and China.

I followed Lin into the office. He looked relaxed, as if he was trying to prove just how comfortable and powerful he was in this place. The office was crowded with workers waiting to be registered or allocated jobs by the two English-speaking Portuguese administrators. Our turn came. I was nervous, rehearsing my answers to any questions they might throw at me. But the administrator asked nothing. She just keyed in my details from the photocopied work permit, and there I was, registered on the company's computer, under the name Chen Min.

Lin had no idea I could understand English, which meant he didn't know I could tell that his relationship with the agency was far from harmonious. The administrator, Alexandra, mocked his accent and spoke to him with contempt in her voice.

'That company's hard to please,' he said to me as we left the agency. 'You always have to share things with them.' I took that to mean he resented having to keep Pertemps appeased and having to share his profits with them, while trying to make a profit from us. (Lin said he wasn't the first to recruit workers for the agency. Pertemps started getting jobs for Chinese people in 2001, and, according to Lin, initially it was via a man in his late twenties from Hubei province. Just like Lin, this Hubei man spread the word among the Chinese migrant community that 'money's easy to make in Norfolk, and there's nothing like this in London'. So waves of Chinese new arrivals came into the area.)

Still I was without work. 'Will you take me to the agency again?' I asked Lin on the third morning.

'Fine,' he said. 'And this time we'll go prepared.'

He led me into the agency for a second time. As he approached the administrator he handed over some presents. The administrator took them and passed them to Alexandra, who was sitting next to her.

'Alexandra will look after these,' she said. Alexandra took the presents without a smile, and put them under her desk.

My jaw dropped at this open bribery, but before I could gather my senses, I found she was booking me a job for that afternoon, at Grampian Country Pork, the largest poultry and meat manufacturer in Britain. I was speechless.

'What did you give her?' I gasped, as we left.

'Oh, this and that, with maybe a bit of cash inside as well. You really don't know a thing about England, do you? You need to feed these *guilao* [literally 'ghosts' – the term used by many Chinese to refer to Westerners] with little presents from time to time – cigarettes and money, anything. Then they'll guarantee you work. It's the norm here.' He seemed carried away by the success of his bribe. He was so smug that he decided to go off and relax at his favourite casino nearby. 'Come in with me,' he said.

I followed him in and observed him closely. With the 'registration fees' I'd paid him three days ago, he was able to indulge himself in the casino for the whole afternoon. This, I saw, was the place where he came to forget about the world around him. I felt his control over me loosening a little, and dared to ask, 'May I go for a quick walk?'

He was so absorbed, he didn't hear me.

'May I get some fresh air?' I asked. He waved his hand at me. 'Go!'

So I had twenty peaceful minutes to myself on a bench in the churchyard off Thetford's high street, before my first shift began.

A minibus picked us up: ten of us, the lucky ones who'd got work that afternoon. I was the only Chinese. The others were from Brazil, Portugal and Eastern Europe. More were picked up along the way. We drove for an hour to Grampian's largest site at Little Wratting in Suffolk. I asked my fellow workers if they knew where we were going, exactly. North? South? No one knew. All they knew, all they needed to know, was that they were being sent to Grampian to work. Three Brazilian women took out their lunchboxes; others tried to sleep before the long shift. Outside, we passed pretty cottages, family houses, gardens with swings for children.

Eventually the minibus drove through the great metal security gates of Grampian. The harsh factory buildings made my fellow workers sigh with dull foreboding. The bus stopped next to two lorries bound for Sainsbury's. No one uttered a word. It was as if we were an army of soldiers getting ready for combat. I saw some of my Chinese housemates waiting in a queue to leave work. Qin was among them. He waved at me. His face looked pale. He was shivering with cold.

We were told to stand in a queue and wait for instructions. And there, on a huge sign above the grey block in front of us, was the famous Sainsbury's slogan: 'MAKING LIFE TASTE BETTER'.

For once I almost wished I couldn't understand English. Making life taste better! The glibness of the slogan shocked me. Life could hardly have tasted worse for most of the workers in this queue.

We were sorted into teams. I was told to work in the Sainsbury's butchery unit with some of the Eastern Europeans and one Scottish woman. We put on uniforms and caps and were taken across the wet, slippery butchery floor to the unit to join a team of local workers.

There was no instruction or training. Within seconds, I was machine-cutting pork, learning how to load meat into the cutter by copying my fellow workers. Then I was told to separate the good meat from the bad meat. Which was which?

For the second hour we packaged the cut-up pork, taking it from a vast, stomach-turning mountain of raw meat. For the third hour we put the packages into cardboard boxes and refrigerated them.

It was hard to adjust to the fast pace and the monotony. When your mind can't catch up with the speed of your body, you switch off your mind: it becomes disengaged from your physical being, and you feel your body becoming a cog in a machine. But then tiredness sets in, and you are reminded you're not a cog, but human. I felt drained and stiff from standing in the same position for three hours. I felt sick at the sight and smell of so much blood.

The precious half-hour break passed in what felt like ten minutes. It took three minutes to go upstairs and take off our filthy uniforms before being allowed into the canteen. Twenty-seven minutes left. I was parched, and needed a large glass of water. Twenty-four minutes to go. Some of my fellow workers were slumped on chairs, their eyes shut. The Scottish woman was smoking, looking out of the window. She told me she was from Aberdeen, and had come south to look for work. 'I went to the agency, just like you people did,' she said. 'But I didn't need anyone to lead me into the agency. It's more difficult for your people, isn't it? You aren't legal, are you?'

The bell went. Back into uniform, back to meat. And the work got harder. Now we were made to unload large chunks of frozen pork ribs, each weighing about ten kilograms. I found it hard to manage. We worked non-stop as box after box of ribs was sent to us. The supervisor was nearby, keeping his eye on us. All the workers kept their heads down.

During the fifth hour my feet became numb and I had backache from lifting the heavy ribs. A Polish worker told me they were going to Sainsbury's, Tesco, Marks & Spencer and Waitrose. I later found out that Grampian processes 3.6 million pigs a year at this site in Suffolk. We were a tiny part in this process: each of us no more than a replaceable cog.

During the second break I was too exhausted to have a cigarette. I shut my eyes for a while. Then it was back to heaving frozen ribs for two more hours. By this time I was struggling to keep up with the pace. Thankfully my body was on a kind of auto-pilot.

At 11.30 p.m. the shift finished. We were all too tired and cold to talk. We went to the gate to wait for the agency minibus to collect us. It was raining as we stood there, waiting in the dark.

'Why are they always doing this to us?' said one of the Brazilian workers. 'The agency bastards deduct £2 a day from our wages for transport, but they're always late.'

Half an hour later the bus rolled up. Workers were dropped off at various places during the long drive home. We got back to Thetford at 1.30 a.m. I had no strength to gather my thoughts or take notes. I went to my mattress and fell asleep.

I had earned £28.42.

Three hours later I was woken by noises in the kitchen. Five of my housemates were up, getting ready for their 6 a.m. shift at Kerry Foods' duck-processing factory in Redgrave, near Diss. Bleary-eyed but curious, I got up to join them in the kitchen.

'Hi, I'm Feng,' said a bearded man with a thick central China accent. He was packing home-made steamed buns into his lunchbox. 'I always make my own food. A habit from when I was a child. I grew up on a farm in Henan. A true peasant!'

'What's it like at Kerry Foods?' I asked him.

'It's a tough place,' he said. 'The agency wouldn't send you there if you'd just registered with them. They'd wait to see how good you are, how fit. The factory-floor supervision's harsh, believe me. I got a bad muscle injury there from lifting heavy equipment. I couldn't register with a GP, so I had to rely on my own medical knowledge and my Chinese medicine. It took me more than a month to get better.'

A man in spectacles introduced himself as Lao Zhou, and told me more about Kerry Foods. 'Its annual sales are over £2.5 billion. But they don't want to be too extravagant towards their workers. So they found us – the Chinese. We get £149 after tax from the agency for a forty-hour week. Not extravagant at all.'

He pierced one last bun with his chopsticks and stuffed it into his mouth. 'Come on, guys, time to go! We don't want to miss the minibus, do we?'

The Shanghainese men and I were not so lucky – or unlucky – to get work every day. For newcomers, Pertemps organizes shifts just for the day, so you have to turn up each morning, hoping for work. We got there at ten and were told to come back at noon; at noon we were told to come back at two. At two we were made to sit in the waiting room with a group of Chinese workers from another house, but still no shifts came our way. 'Sit there!' 'Go away.' 'You stupid.' I constantly heard the administrators speaking to the Chinese in this abusive way. They had no idea I could understand them. 'That idiot,' one administrator said to the other, 'he thinks he's in charge of sorting out the shifts here.' She was talking about a Chinese man who'd been returning to the agency every two hours, desperate for work.

Lin, meanwhile, was trying to lure me up to Morecambe Bay to help with his proposed cockling business. 'It'll only cost £6,000 to get all the equipment. I'll need fifteen workers, the type who'll be able to put up with the hard work – and I'll provide them with documents, accommodation and transport to work. D'you want to come with me? You can be my accountant. All you'd have to do is count up the bags. We'll get £12 per bag from the English buyers, and give the Chinese £6 per bag. Easy money!'

It was clear he wanted me to be more than his accountant. He was planning some kind of mutually profitable relationship. He asked me if I wanted to return to China. When I said, 'Probably not,' he said, 'I can give you a good life here.' My housemates told me he'd been looking for a partner ever since his girlfriend died in Morecambe Bay.

'Look at that couple upstairs,' he said to me. He was talking about the fifty-year-old woman from a village in Hunan who'd begun a relationship with the Shanghainese man she'd met on the double mattress they shared when she first arrived in Thetford. 'She gets what she wants. She gets her food paid for. And he gets what he wants! It's normal, understand?' He tried to put his arms around me. I moved away.

Supper in the house was in three or four sittings. Lin, Lao Lin and Miss Chio went first. Then I joined Zhang, Qin and Tan as they cooked the pig's tail we'd bought the day before, with soy sauce and mounds of rice. Then it was the turn of Lao Zhou and Feng. They always cooked together. They liked the same cuisine: wheat-based buns and bread, dumplings, and egg and tomato soup. 'It's cheaper to eat together,' they said. 'We spend £6 a week each on food and household goods. You can live on that amount if you know where to shop.' I watched Lao Zhou as he made dough, cut it into pieces, and stuffed the pieces with minced vegetables. 'Hey, Langfang girl, you know how to make our northern buns, don't you?'

I thought quickly. 'My mum didn't allow me into the kitchen when I was a child.'

'You're an unusual Langfang girl!' said Lao Zhou. 'I thought they all knew how to cook.'

'Mahjong! Mahjong! Who's going to come and play?'

Zhang was calling from the front room. All the housemates were gathered there, talking, smoking and trying to pick up a bit of English by watching *Coronation Street*. The mahjong table was laid out, ready.

Zhang looked excited at the prospect of playing mahjong all night. He had his roll-ups and his old jar of Buddhist Tieguanyin tea. 'Come on, then, who's going to join me? Feng? Good. Anyone else? Qin? Great. Now we need one more. Anyone for mahjong?' He called up the stairs. That proved to be a mistake.

Slowly down the stairs came a plump man in a dressing gown. 'I'll play.'

It was Lao Lin. Everyone went quiet. Zhang looked crestfallen. He sat back, lit a roll-up and said nothing. I knew he hated Lao Lin: the man who'd recruited him and was now charging him interest on his registration fee to push him to pay up.

'I thought you wanted to play,' Lao Lin said.

So the game started. Who could say no to Lao Lin? I watched the game, and watched the recruiter's face. Suddenly he turned and looked at me. 'What are you staring at?'

'Nothing,' I said. I slipped back into the kitchen.

Lao Zhou followed me a few moments later. 'You've got to be careful with Lao Lin,' he said. 'He used to be a close ally of the gang leader Guo-Hua, who's based around here, until they fell out over profit-sharing. Guo-Hua's gang goes around charging protection fees from all the Chinese newcomers. No Chinese house in the town can avoid them. A few months ago, they came to rob this house.'

'This house?'

'Yeah. That's why we always keep the doors and windows locked, even when we're in. Nine of them broke in. They all had knives and two of them had guns. "Take out your money! Put it on the table!" they ordered. We were terrified. We took all the money out of our pockets. I had to take out the £200 in mine. One and a half weeks' wages. But that didn't satisfy them. They tied us up and searched us. I had twenty weeks' wages hidden in the wardrobe, buried in my old clothing. I was dreading losing it. But amazingly they didn't find it. They robbed £250 from Feng. He was so depressed, because he'd been just about to send the money home.'

I listened to the story, horrified.

'Lao Lin had fallen out with Guo-Hua a little while before the robbery. These scum, they swear brotherhood with each other and then fight bitterly over who gets more money! And the English employment agencies rely on such men as these! You know what it's called: "the coexistence of two paths, black and white". The dark criminal world needs to cross into the open, daylight recruitment world to be able to make profits, and vice versa.'

'What happened after the robbery?' I asked.

'We couldn't report it to the police, of course, for fear of arrest and deportation. Luckily Guo-Hua was arrested recently in another robbery and put behind bars. That'll keep the peace for a while, till he gets out.'

And still the game of mahjong went on, quietly, in the front room.

The only soothing thing in this house – in this whole life of ours – was sitting in the kitchen watching Lao Zhou make his delicious northern pancakes. But it always seemed to be accompanied by bleak or tragic stories.

The next evening Feng spoke about their friend Ah Chao, whom they'd shared a house with briefly while he was working at Grampian. He'd been recruited by Lao Lin. 'A quiet person, Ah Chao was. Never spoke about himself much. The work at Grampian dried up, and he went up to Morecambe Bay, desperate for more work. He wanted to prove himself.'

Ah Chao's body had been almost beyond recognition when it was found near Morecambe Bay, days after the cockling tragedy. He'd only lasted a week.

'Isn't it lucky,' Qin said, 'that no one in this room was cockling at the time? That we're all alive, talking and eating here?'

'Well,' Lao Zhou replied gravely, 'death may not be a bad thing for Ah Chao. Living was more unbearable for him. He was heavily in debt when he was cockling. At least death brings freedom.'

After supper, Lao Zhou took his Chinese-language map of Britain to show everyone. He told us he'd paid 20,000 RMB (about £1,300) to get a six-month business visa to the UK.

Once that had expired, he'd set out on his life as an un-documented worker, and he pointed to all the places he'd worked in, from a Chinese kitchen in South Wales to a flower-processing factory in Devon. He talked about his Buddhism: his outlook on life was a passive, meditative one. There was no point, he believed, in taking action against oppression.

'That's the problem with your kind of ideology!' retorted the sceptical Feng, with a twinkle in his eye. 'You find your own inner comfort and forget about other people's misery!'

Both men were trying hard to learn English. They knew it was the route to more freedom and control of their lives. 'If you don't speak the language, you get bullied,' said Lao Zhou, 'especially by the foremen at Kerry Foods.'

'No work today,' said the administrators at Pertemps the next morning. Zhang and Qin had come in with Lin and me. I felt my patience wearing thin. These women had been paid, they'd been bribed, and still they drove us away. I looked at Alexandra with fury in my eyes.

'You have to wait,' she said quietly. 'You're new.'

Lin had to drag me from the office. Zhang and Qin looked demoralized from so much fruitless waiting. As we wandered down the high street we saw some of our fellow workers outside the bank where they cashed their money from Pertemps. These workers didn't have bank accounts there, but arrangements were made with the bank so they could hand in payslips to cash their pay from the agency's account. They were comparing their payslips. Unsurprisingly, they'd received less than they'd expected.

'Look, they didn't pay me overtime!' said Mr Li from Shanghai, who lived in another house run by Lin and Lao Lin. 'I worked thirty-eight hours and they only paid me for thirty-four. How can they not pay me?'

Lin came up and explained the agency's rule: you don't get overtime pay if you work less than forty hours a week.

'But we do shift work!' shouted Mr Li. 'It's not a full-time job!'

I suggested to Mr Li that we go into the agency to sort this out. As I was going in, Lin grabbed my arm.

'Who do you think you are? No legal status, and you think you can just walk in and make a complaint? You look after your own job first! Mind your own business. Remember, you're illegal!'

It seemed as if I'd seriously transgressed Lin's rules. He refused to take me back to the agency that day. 'You're finished,' he said.

On the way back to the house, more gently but more threateningly, he said, 'Let me put it this way. My job is to get you jobs. OK? So don't make my job hard by getting on the wrong side of the agency. Last time, when a Chinese man was about to make a complaint to the agency, I told him I can make anyone disappear, just like that. You can be thrown into a river and your parents in China would never find out what happened.'

Lin's words didn't frighten me, because I knew something that he wouldn't like the workers he recruited to know: I found out that Lin had only been paid £125 for the previous week's forty hours' work at Kerry Foods. Apart from being given more regular shifts than others, he wasn't given any financial reward by the agency for his recruitment activities. Despite the fact that he was our formal gateway to work and that his income came largely from charging Chinese workers heavy fees, Lin was only a rung above us. He was at the bottom of the entire underground recruitment chain. Those who benefited on a large scale from our cheap labour were the employment agency and the factories to which our labour was supplied. Lin played no part and had no say in our wage disputes with the agency.

Back at the house, I mentioned to Feng the incident at the bank and Mr Li's shock at the unpaid overtime work. Feng told me:

'That's so common around here. Some of us haven't been paid for a whole week's work. When we demand our wages from Pertemps, they just say they got our names wrong. During the Chinese spring festival last year I did two days' overtime work on a Saturday and Sunday, and wasn't paid a penny for it. I went into the agency to complain. They checked on their system and insisted I'd only done one day's work. They said I'd get paid the next week. I thought to myself: they've tricked me; but one day's pay is better than none. So I told them I'll come back next week. But, when I returned, they denied all memory of that promise. The agency administrator simply said they don't owe me anything. I was furious and shouted at them and at the English manager. But there was nothing else I could do. We're Chinese. We're illegal.'

To avoid attention from Lin, I asked a Shanghainese man upstairs to change his sleeping place with mine. I moved up to share a room with Lao Zhou and Feng. To my intense relief, Lin decided to take a trip to London and Liverpool over the next few days, to organize his new cockling business.

Lao Zhou, Feng and I lay on our mattresses, talking till the small hours. They said they'd like to take me somewhere they loved in Thetford – a place they named 'the observation point', high up on a grassy hill.

'It's the only place where I can find peace here,' Lao Zhou said. 'You can look down on the world below you. You feel freedom in that fresh air on the hill.' Feng suggested we take a picnic at the weekend. 'We can bring our lunchboxes. Maybe a bottle of something . . . and we can drink under the blue sky. Ah, I can't wait!' He pulled open the curtains and looked out of the window at the stars, like a child dreaming of an outing.

When no work came the next day, Zhang began to get seriously worried. 'We were never warned about this irregular pattern of work, when we called up Lao Lin,' he said. 'He told us there'd be no shortage of work. Now we've paid half the registration fees, we have no option: we must stay. Every time we go to a new place, we have to pay a new set of registration fees. We're in a trap.'

We wandered the streets of Thetford. I noticed, once again, how close, yet how distant, we were from the locals going about their daily lives with their shopping bags and their dogs on the lead. Such a tranquil life, theirs seemed. The two worlds crossed each other without the locals knowing anything of ours.

Zhang sighed. 'I'm going to make enough cash to go back to China at the end of the year. I don't want to stay any longer than I have to. Life is hell here. Hi, Mr Lai!'

We passed a Shanghainese friend of theirs, who lived in another house. 'Hi. No work today?' We shook our heads. 'Listen,' said Mr Lai. 'You have to learn their way of doing things. You'll need to bribe the agency girls with cash if you want to speed up your work arrangements. That's how you build up their favouritism towards you. A friend of mine just paid them £100, and he got loads of work.'

'Only one problem,' said Zhang. 'I haven't got £100 to bribe the bastards.'

The next day we arrived at the agency at 10 a.m. and were told, as usual, to come back at noon. All night I'd been thinking about Mr Lai's advice. Now I decided to give his idea a try. I wrapped a £20 note round a packet of cigarettes. A small present for the first go, I thought. We went back at noon and I handed the package (wrapped in a plastic bag) to the administrator Alexandra. She accepted it without a shadow of embarrassment, and other members of staff and the English manager saw her do this.

'All right,' she said.

I went back to the waiting area and sat next to Qin. He shook his head with resignation. 'I wish I had the cash to do that. It's the only thing that works here. Whatever we have in

China, they have here: bribery, back-door connections, you name it. It's an ancient capitalist country, after all.'

The bribery worked. I was given two morning shifts for the next two days, at Grampian Country Pork. Zhang, Qin and Tan were put on the shifts as well.

As I walked home I found Qin sitting on a bench, reading a Chinese newspaper that a friend had brought to him from London. It was his connection with the outside world – with home. Home was never far from his mind. He spoke to me about his ten-year-old daughter.

'You have no idea how much I miss her,' he said. 'She was closer to me than to her mother. I always took her side. Once her mum was really telling her off, because she'd just broken a plate. I stepped in. "Look," I said to my wife, "our daughter is a person of action; a person of action makes mistakes." My daughter looked at me with so much thankfulness in her eyes.

'When I was leaving for England, it was hard to explain to her why I had to go. It was for her, of course. I want her to have better opportunities in her life. It's tough in China. It's competitive. Education is something you need to plan and pay for these days. It's easy for middle-class parents. My wife and I are in a different category. We can't afford to buy her reference books or to pay for private tuition to prepare her for a university in the future. Besides, a university education costs between 100,000 to 200,000 RMB nowadays. I left home for her. How do you explain to your child that you're leaving her because you love her so much?'

Feng was depressed that evening too. He'd developed a constant backache from the physical labour at Kerry Foods. And the job wasn't even secure. 'Once the peak period's over, we'll be waiting for shifts every day like the Shanghainese boys. What'll I do then? If I return to China, things will be even worse there. I don't have the power to change anything – not here, not in China. We're poor dispensable farmers. Who cares about our lives? And here we have the recruiters on our backs. I feel the blood being sucked out of my body.'

At least we did have work the next day, I reminded him. We'd better get some sleep. Feng took sleeping pills out of his suitcase and swallowed them. But I still heard him turning all night, unable to sleep for worrying.

At 4 a.m. I heard him getting up. He and some others were preparing to go on their morning shift at Kerry Foods. I couldn't get back to sleep, so I got up to get ready for my morning shift at Grampian. Feng was in the kitchen preparing his lunchbox, and offered me some of his buns to take to work. 'I had such a bad night,' he told me. 'I couldn't sleep, thinking about my working life and my purpose for being here. The thoughts were going round and round in my head. I was reliving those days in King's Lynn when the Chinese recruiter took us there to work in the food-processing factories. We lived ten to a room, like dogs. No – dogs have better lives. Then when I arrived here in Thetford, I realized that things were hardly better. The first few nights I was just crying in bed. Working like a machine, getting bullied by the agency people and the factory supervisors, coming home every day just to sleep and get ready for the next day's work . . . It's like being a robot. I ask myself, what will all this bring?'

He paused for a moment, then said, 'You know, I shiver when I hear news about those workers who died at Morecambe Bay. Because I know that could happen to anyone – me and you, people without status. I can't help crying for those people.'

It was time for him to go to work. 'Look after yourself on your shift today, sis,' he said. I started to get ready. Zhang came into the kitchen for a quick cup of green tea, and packed his lunchbox.

No minibus appeared at 6 a.m. That was predictable. Qin pulled his jacket round him, lit a roll-up and smoked it, shivering in the cold. The bus drew up at last. An hour later we arrived at Grampian. I was put in the washroom with Brazilian and local workers, loading decontaminated Sainsbury's containers. The room was humid and the lack of fresh air made me constantly sleepy.

Without the others noticing, I chatted to one of the local workers in English.

'How d'you like the job?' he asked.

'It's not too bad. Definitely better than cutting and packaging meat in the butchery.'

We got talking, and I asked him how much he was earning here.

'Not much,' he said. 'Only £240 a week, take-home pay. What about you?'

I told him we were earning at best half that amount, for doing the same work.

He looked shocked, standing there open-mouthed with a Sainsbury's container in his hand. 'I'm sorry to hear that, I really am. Yeah, the agencies round here do have quite a bad reputation.'

The half-hour break was the most cheerful I'd had yet: Zhang, Qin and Tan hurried me to the factory shop to buy cheap meat for the week. 'It's a bit old, but not too bad,' Zhang said. 'Look: bargains!' We bought ten packets of pork stuffing for £1, twenty packs of sausages for £1, and a large box of corned beef for 50p. The thought of the good meal we were going to cook that evening made the next part of the shift pass more quickly. When it ended at 3 p.m. we went outside to wait for the minibus. Yet again, we waited and waited, freezing cold and tired. Half an hour passed, forty-five minutes. A Portuguese worker rang the agency to ask where the bus was. 'Just wait,' came the reply.

Eventually it came, an hour late.

That evening the whole house smelled of fried English sausages cooked in soy sauce, and of English pork stuffing with rice. We shared the results of our culinary experiments with everyone in the house. Later Feng made Chinese pancakes and stuffed them with corned beef for everyone's lunchboxes tomorrow.

The next morning, the minibus didn't turn up at all. Half an hour late, a four-seater car arrived, driven by one of the workers, a Brazilian man. 'No bus today,' he said. 'The agency said I had to drive you to the factory.' We squeezed ourselves in. I could hardly breathe. The car was far too small for six.

In the Grampian washroom, our job for the day was to take labels off Sainsbury's dirty containers and load them on to the conveyor belt to be decontaminated. We had to work fast. I tried to keep count: thirty containers per minute, 1,800 per hour. Every now and then we came across a packet of liver, bacon, or chicken jalfrezi in one of the containers. Tan wanted to take them home. I had to tell him they were no good – long past their sell-by date. It was painful for Tan to see these things being thrown away.

'It's pay-day!' said the Brazilian driver as we walked back to the car.

Zhang was excited. 'The first thing I'm going to do with my money is pay off the registration fees to Lao Lin. I'll get some peace then.'

The Brazilian driver sang songs in Portuguese all the way back to Thetford.

'No need to be so cheerful about it,' said a female Brazilian worker from the back seat. 'It's only small money we'll be getting.'

The driver paused, then continued singing. Small money, yes, but it made living possible.

We drove straight to the agency. It was crammed with workers of all nationalities, queuing to be paid. Most of them, like us, had just got off their shifts. The place was steamy with sweat. Names were called out. Pay packets were handed over. Zhang watched. He was getting nervous. At last, his name was called out, and Qin, Tan and mine. Zhang opened his payslip.

'There must be a mistake,' he said. 'It's so low: £23.60 for an eight-hour daytime shift!'

Alexandra, the administrator, heard the angry noises. I looked at her, and she said to me (knowing by now that I could speak some English), 'Chen Min, go and tell them the tax is heavy because this is your first week. You're new people, OK?'

Zhang, almost in tears, spoke to the administrators in Chinese. 'Tell us, how come the tax is so high? What have you done with our wages?'

Qin went up to join him. 'We're paying tax with the National Insurance numbers we gave you. You know full well they're from other people's old work permits. We only have your word for it that the tax goes to the tax office. We have no idea how you sort out our tax. These calculations on our payslips might all be fake, for all we know.'

He waved the payslips in the administrators' faces. The English manager looked away, busying himself with another matter. The language barrier was used as a shield to fend off the workers' anger.

'There's nothing we can do, is there?' Qin turned to me. 'We can't get into their accounts, can we?'

I put my hand on his shoulder, trying to calm him. It was true: there was nothing we could do. The office was gradually emptying. We decided to go back to the house.

Later that evening, Feng came into the kitchen. I looked up at him. He had a warm smile on his face that gladdened my heart. He took out a box of chocolates and a packet of cigarettes from his compartment in the kitchen cupboard. 'I bought these for you after work today.'

To my look of puzzlement, he said, 'Listen. I'm going to give these to the director of the agency. I'm going straight to the top. If you give presents to the administrators, they just play games with you. If I give these to the director, I can guarantee she'll arrange regular work for you – at least for a time.'

I couldn't believe it. Tears were pricking my eyes. Here was a man whose days and nights were spent worrying about how to send enough cash back to China to feed his family – and he'd spent two hours of his own wages on these gifts to help me to get a job.

How was I going to break the news to him that I was actually leaving the next morning?

I couldn't find any words. This was the end of my under-cover work, and I had to leave. But I'd become another person. I'd lived the life of an undocumented Chinese worker, and I'd changed into a woman with a completely different background and life experience. I'd shared joy and sorrow with my fellow workers, and I was beginning to treasure their friendship.

'Feng,' I said eventually. 'Thank you – thanks so much. But I'm leaving tomorrow. I've got a job in a Chinese restaurant in London – a regular job.'

Some of the others had come into the kitchen, and heard what I said.

'You're joking!' Feng said. 'She's teasing, isn't she?'

Lao Zhou knew I wasn't. 'She's serious,' he said. I could see the sorrow in his face.

I poured out glasses from the bottle of whisky I'd bought to say farewell.

'Let me tell you,' Feng said, 'life isn't easy in London. You could be running into all sorts of trouble. Look – take this.' He tried to press £30 into my hands, which he'd fetched from his suitcase. 'This will help you get food and transport before you settle into the job.'

'No, Feng, I can't accept it. I really can't.'

He was insulted. He felt it his duty to help me. 'OK. But if it doesn't turn out well, sis, do come back. Will you promise us?'

★

None of us slept. We sat up through the night, talking about our memories and our dreams. 'I've always wanted to see the landscape of Scotland,' Lao Zhou said. 'The forests, the lakes, the mountains – I've heard about them.'

'Maybe one day,' said Feng dreamily, 'we could all just travel, with a camera and a tent. That would cost us nothing! We could see the world.'

At 4.30 a.m. it was time for Feng and Lao Zhou to leave for their morning shift at Kerry Foods. As we said goodbye, I thought to myself that I'd probably never see them again. I packed my bag, and said farewell to Zhang and Qin. I walked out of the house and turned to look back at it once, twice, three times, until it was out of sight.

I was going back to the normal world, the one with comfort and opportunities. I was leaving my friends behind in another world, the one where exploitation and casual inhumanity are commonplace. They had to continue to trudge their lonely path in that dark world below.

The following response was published in the *Guardian* on 27 March 2004:

Agency [Pertemps Recruitment East Anglia] denies that staff accepted gifts.

In a statement released through its lawyers, Pertemps confirmed that 'a Mr Lin is a temporary worker with Pertemps ... and ... has apparently recommended the agency to others of his acquaintance'. It said it had 'no knowledge of any fee being charged by Mr Lin from his fellow workers'.

The statement also 'categorically denied' allegations that Pertemps staff accepted cash and presents. In the case of the Chinese purses allegedly containing bribes from Mr Lin, the staff concerned had provided written statements denying the allegations. They had also denied accepting any gifts from the worker called Chen Min. According to the Pertemps statement, Chen Min had left a blue plastic bag containing cigarettes and a £20 note on an office desk. 'These items were duly returned to Chen Min when she next visited the office a few days later.'

Contrary to the agency's statement, I had never received the 'gifts' (cigarettes and a £20 note) back from the agency staff. Referring to the photocopied work document that I'd used, Pertemps said that it worked 'closely with the immigration department which has reviewed Pertemps East Anglia Ltd procedures and been entirely satisfied with the same'. Pertemps' solictors said in March 2004: 'You continue to make generalized allegations regarding "out of date" and "obviously photo-copied" documents. These allegations are denied.'

Alasdair Cox, of Grampian Country Foods, said employment agencies used by the company were audited and checked to ensure they met with legislation.

Whilst the recruitment agency in question is refuting the allegations made against them, we are treating this issue seriously and are carrying out our own investigation to ensure that they, and we, are complying with the required employment legislation.

He added:

As the very nature of this work is temporary, in some cases a matter of a few days, a health-and-safety test is provided by the supplying agency before they enter the factory. No workers would be allowed to operate cutting machinery without the appropriate training being provided.

Kerry Foods said in a statement:

To augment our locally recruited workforces, Kerry Foods has contracted with Pertemps Recruitment in East Anglia to provide tem-porary and permanent staff to some Kerry Foods plants in accordance with a written code of practice. Kerry Foods to date has no evidence of any breach by Pertemps of this code of practice. Workers at all our plants are employed in accordance with the strict conditions of our code of practice.

Sainsbury's said:

Whilst we do not employ these workers directly we take this issue extremely seriously. We have worked very closely with all our suppliers, including Grampian, to ensure that they are aware of the potential issues surrounding temporary labour.

Sainsbury's is a responsible employer and would terminate contracts with any supplier proved to have seriously breached employment law.

In February 2008, Pertemps denied the allegations. Pertemps' solicitors said:

We would like to make it clear on behalf of our client that these allegations are entirely without basis, wholly untrue, and our client takes great exception to them. Our client had a proven track record in actively encouraging and assisting migrant workers of all nationalities. Our client has previously lobbied Members of Parliament in order to improve the circumstances of Chinese migrant workers generally and in this action was strongly supported by its Chinese migrant workforce.

3. Salad Days

When I wake up in the morning, I don't know where I am.
My feet are light and my head is heavy. The wall in front
of my opening eyes is white and empty. Then I remember:
I am here, in another's country.

– A salad-processing factory worker from north China
August 2007

As the bus turned out of the village with its thatched cottages into winding lanes lined with hedgerows, an expanse of green unfolded before Gao Jun's eyes. Fields of lettuces were glinting in the sunshine on this windless May day. Gao Jun's first thought was – Sussex is beautiful. His second was – there must be a lot of work around here.

Through the open window of the bus a sweet scent wafted in. Gao Jun breathed in and shut his eyes with pleasure. 'English grass!' he said in Chinese to his companion Ren Xiang, who'd come to pick him up from Gatwick Airport. 'I like the smell.'

Gao Jun, who was thirty-six, had never seen countryside like this. He'd grown up in poverty in Tienjin in northern China, and had rarely been out of the cramped confines of urban struggle. He was used to suffocating crowds and their day-to-day intrusion on his privacy. Those crowds were forever scrutinizing, competing, commenting. They submerged your being, day in, day out.

To be here, in this calm place, seemed like a dream, as he said to me. 'Only yesterday I'd been in that stifling urban world. In this country, everything – the fields, farmhouses, gardens, lanes – seemed full of such civilized comfort and affluence! I felt as if I was in a film. I looked up at the cotton-wool clouds and thought we must be under a different sky. I felt I was being embraced, blessed by the blueness. It was the most carefree moment of my life. Two girls were sitting in front of us on the bus. They kept staring at me – maybe because I'm unusually tall for a Chinese person. One of them had a pierced nose. A nice face she's got, I thought to myself. The texture of porcelain, the colour of peaches. What a shame she has to damage it with that piercing!'

Gao knew the British had a reputation for kindness and good manners. He told me he'd read a story in a Tienjin paper about a Chinese student in London who'd got lost and had asked an older English man for directions. The man had not only helped her to find her way home, he'd also spent the day showing her around the city. What a civilized people the British must be!

'The next stop's ours,' Ren told him. 'Langmead Farms.' He hurried Gao off the bus, explaining that they were near the seaside town of Selsey – famous for summer holidaying and sightseeing, not so famous for lettuce-harvesting, although Langmead Farms has thousands of acres of land in the area.

'Caravans – there are so many caravans!' Gao said as Ren led him round to the back of the farm buildings. 'I'd heard of these things, but I've never been in one.' There were clothes hanging on washing-lines: this sign of domesticity made him miss with an aching pang his wife and young son whom he'd left behind in Tienjin. But he'd see his brother today.

One of the caravans had a red-and-white flag sticking out of the roof. 'Polish workers live in there,' Ren explained. 'They like us Chinese. We get the day off on Sunday, and sometimes we get invited to their caravans for a beer. The Brazilians' caravans are far over there,' he said, pointing to the left. 'I'm pretty certain they're just like us – no papers. I think their agency got them Portuguese work permits. No one here talks about papers or status. But if you go out of this little circle of foreigners into the local world, then you'll have some explaining to do.'

Gao was astonished by the diverse origins of the farm workers. His ethnic group in China, Han, makes up ninety-two per cent of the Chinese population, and he'd never spoken to anyone outside it.

'I feel nervous. How will I communicate?'

Ren told him not to worry. 'Foreigners find a way of understanding each other. We use a lot of body language. We'll find our fingers and hands very useful. And we'll be working in teams, in our own language group. Here's our caravan!'

Gao peered in through the window and saw a young Chinese woman washing dishes. She glanced out through the ragged curtains and waved at Ren. Her name was Xiao Yun. She'd come with Ren to Selsey from London. Gao entered the caravan and was surprised. He'd been told it was for five people. It looked more like for two. The threadbare cushions were stained with cigarette tar. 'No five-star hotel, is it?' Ren said.

I met Gao Jun and Ren Xiang in 2002 and followed their life in Selsey from May 2002 to summer 2004. Shortly after Gao Jun's arrival I visited them at the caravan site. I, too, was surprised by the cramped living conditions. Ren told me he'd seen worse. When he'd arrived in England he'd been picked up by two Tienjin men who charged him £200 for the pick-up, and took him to a flat in Leyton where he had to share a ten-square-metre room with six others. 'There were no beds or sheets. I slept on my luggage. The Tienjin contact said to me, "That's what it's like in the UK." Selsey is paradise by comparison.'

As Gao stood shyly in the caravan, Xiao Yun came out from the kitchen and asked him if he'd like some north-eastern dumplings. Hungry and thirsty, he accepted the dumplings gratefully and ate them fast, washed down with Chinese tea. Just as he finished, his brother, Older Gao, walked into the caravan. The two men embraced each other. Older Gao was almost in tears. The brothers hadn't seen each other for over a year.

'But look at you,' Gao said. 'You've lost so much weight. What has living here done to you?'

The Chinese workers had been sent to Selsey by an agency named the Chinese and English Culture Service, based in London. Since the beginning of May, they had been arriving for the lettuce harvest. Each of them had paid £50 for photocopies of work permits and a registration fee of £200 to Huang-Hua, the boss at the agency.

'That registration fee,' Ren told me as we sat talking in their caravan, 'was only for getting us work once. If the job ended and we needed another, we'd have to pay a new fee. And we had no idea how long this work was going to last.'

I found out that Huang-Hua was not only the boss at the agency: he's also the general secretary of the Democracy Party. This is what attracts so many Chinese migrants to him. The Democracy Party is thought of by the Chinese as the 'elite in exile' – a political party formed of exiled Chinese from many different backgrounds, many of them intellectuals, who embrace Western-style democracy as an alternative to the ruling power in China. What the newly arrived migrants don't know, however, is that members of the Democracy Party in Britain use the vulnerable status of undocumented Chinese migrants to broaden their party membership and make profits out of them at the same time. The workers, desperate to find jobs, become victims of an absurd hypocrisy: the supposed opponents of China's repressive state are oppressing Chinese workers abroad.

Ren told me how he'd got his job and his papers. 'A group of Democracy Party people were getting passers-by to sign their petition in Chinatown. I was curious and went up to have a look. I got talking to them. Huang-Hua, a thin guy wearing glasses, asked me if I was working, and we exchanged phone numbers. Later he phoned me and said he could find work for me and my friends – he said he ran an employment agency. Of course we jumped at the chance: as a newcomer you'll jump at any opportunity, won't you? He soon made the arrangements and we were picked up at Chichester Station by someone from the farms.'

Later I interviewed the bespectacled Huang-Hua and asked him about his supply of labour to the farms. 'Langmead Farms was happy to employ our two teams of Chinese workers and to accept the reproduced permits,' Huang-Hua told me. 'When there's a high demand for labour, which can't be met by the supply of Eastern European student workers on the Seasonal Agricultural Workers Scheme [SAWS], the farms tend to use our Chinese workforce. This is the case everywhere in the UK, with all the farms we work with.'

Ren and all the Chinese workers understood their role only too well in this system. It was to fill the labour shortage when the SAWS quota was full, and to work in places where it was difficult to recruit locals.

'Look at all these British farms and growers,' Ren said to me. 'Unemployment's low in this area. They're finding it hard to recruit local workers. And, anyway, locals wouldn't work so hard for such low pay. So how are the growers going to meet the needs of their market? Easy: they employ us! There's no way people like us can get on to the SAWS scheme. They only issue a tiny number of permits to people from China. It would be almost impossible for any of us, the *lao-bai-xing* [ordinary folk], to get on the scheme – especially if we're middle-aged and don't have the language skills.'

To verify Ren's point that legitimate work routes for Chinese workers into Britain's seasonal agriculture are extremely limited, I talked to four main SAWS operators, who recruit on behalf of British farmers and growers. (SAWS is administered on behalf of Work Permits UK by contracted operators.) One of them, Concordia (YSV) Ltd, which recruits for Langmead Farms where Ren and Gao worked, said they hadn't recruited from China for five years. 'Even before that, the number of recruits from China was always low. There's always been a problem with recruitment from China: there's always the concern about people overstaying their visas.' Another operator, HOPS Labour Solutions, told me, 'We haven't recruited from China in the past three years [2004 to 2007], due to a government decision to stop recruiting from there.' The two others I spoke to, Friday Bridge (International Farm Camp) and Sastak Ltd, said they had never recruited any Chinese workers at all. I made a Freedom of Information request to the Border and Immigration Agency (BIA), under which SAWS is run, to release figures of the number of Chinese nationals whose applications to the scheme have been approved in the past few years. The BIA's records show that, in 2004, when the SAWS quota was 25,000, the number of Chinese workers approved was only 675. Between January 2005 and October 2007, when the SAWS quota was cut down to 16,250 per year, Chinese nationals have ceased to be selected, and there have been *no* Chinese workers admitted on to the scheme.

Ren said there wasn't any way for Chinese workers in China to get into direct contact with a British employer. 'We would if we could. Who in their right minds would go through a middleman and pay £200 each time we get a new job, if we could get in touch directly with British growers and work openly and legally on a proper permit? It makes me sick to hear agency people like Huang-Hua saying they want to "improve employment opportunities for our compatriots". As if he cares about us! This is how it works: we sell our cheap labour for them, and they may one day help us with our status. If we join the Democracy Party, we might have a chance with our asylum application. The only drawback is if we make an asylum claim as the opponents of the Chinese regime, we'd certainly never be allowed back to China again.' (As the majority of un-documented Chinese workers plan to return home after a few years of working in Britain, very few of them have opted for applying for asylum as a member of the Democracy Party.)

Chinese and English Culture Service Ltd said: 'We charged a registration fee of £200 each. But we refund £100 to those who were made redundant by the company after two months [of working] even when they received holiday pay from the company. We have never sold any documents to anyone. All workers brought a copy of [their] work permit themselves.'

On Gao's first morning of work at the farms, he was woken at six to get ready.

The sound of people talking in other languages wafted in through the caravan windows. 'I couldn't wait to be in the green open space I'd admired the day before,' he told me. As they walked out into the May dawn, the lettuce fields looked beautiful. Hundreds of migrant workers of many nationalities emerged from the caravans.

The workers were split into teams. A young Malaysian Chinese, the only one who could speak some English, was chosen as Gao's and Ren's team representative. Ren explained to me that there was a set target. 'We must pick fifteen piles of lettuce a day. Each pile is about ten boxes, and each box has twenty lettuces in ten bags. We harvest, select and label the crop, then pack them into boxes. We have twelve hours to reach the target. It's hard. But if you keep at it steadily, you can finish before sunset.'

The Chinese workers bent down to pick and cut lettuce. Gao copied them. One lettuce, two lettuces, three lettuces . . . Ren had already reached ten. Gao said that he had worked in a state-run car plant in Tienjin, but he'd never had to work this fast.

Gao told me that the car plant had closed down, like many other state-run workplaces all over the country. 'I would have liked to keep the job if I could, even though I was earning just 1,400 RMB [£93] a month, not enough to live well in a big city like Tienjin. Living expenses were going up all the time. The money they paid us for laying us off – it's called *mai duan gong ling* [literally, "buying off one's working years", which means workers are compensated according to the number of years they have worked] – wasn't enough to live on. So I used up my life savings, and borrowed a lot of money, to get myself a business-visitor visa for 70,000 RMB [£5,385] to come to England.'

Ren said that he was from the city too. He'd worked in the clothes industry, and then run his own photo studio for a while, before making a loss. 'We're not used to this kind of work. But I've trained myself to be fit since I came to England. It's the only way you can last in a job.'

Gao noticed some of the Eastern European workers strolling into the fields, late for work.

'Those Eastern Europeans have a different way of working,' Ren told him. 'They get up later than us, work more slowly than us, take a few more breaks than us, and reach the target later than us. That's how they like to do it.'

'Can't we be like them?'

'Well, the boss wouldn't like it if you were always late starting and late finishing. You'll see for yourself.'

During the third hour of lettuce-cutting, Gao was finding it hard to keep going. Bending down for hours was tough. He was impressed that Xiao Yun was keeping going better than he was. Every now and then she stood up to stretch her back, then got straight back down to work.

They heard car engines, and looked round. Jeeps were driving into the fields, and well-built Englishmen with guns got out. 'They've come to shoot rabbits,' Ren explained. 'Not for eating themselves – they wouldn't have a clue how to skin them. Just for sport. They sell them to the local butchers around here. The farm makes extra money by doubling up as a shooting playground.'

By noon, Gao was exhausted. The sun's heat on his back had

made him dehydrated. Ren handed prepared buns to everyone in the team. 'I wished I could go and eat my lunch in the caravan,' Gao told me. 'I needed to sit down in the shade, but the half-hour break didn't allow time to walk to the caravan and back. The farms didn't provide us with shelter. We just sat down where we were to eat and drink. I saw Ren sitting down next to Xiao Yun, asking how she felt. I envied their solicitude for each other. She was a divorcee from Shenyang, I knew, with a ten-year-old son in China.'

Fifteen minutes of the lunch break to go . . . Gao lay down in the field and shut his eyes. He was too tired to watch the clouds. Ren nudged him awake. 'Time to get back to work. We're still far from the target! The pay's piecemeal. If we don't pick enough lettuce, we won't get paid enough!'

Ren said that the Chinese workers were paid about 5p per unit. 'Each of us cuts about 700 lettuces a day. That makes each of us £35 in a twelve-hour day. It works out at just under £3 per hour.' As found, migrant workers on the farm, including the Chinese workers, were being paid around two-thirds of the agricultural minimum wage (which was £4.77 per hour before 1 October 2002 and £4.91 after that date), and were not entitled to overtime pay like local farm workers.

The hours passed; Gao summoned all his inner resources to get through the day. The Chinese teams worked the fastest, reaching the target at 5.30 p.m. As they left the field, the Ukrainians were still at work.

'If we keep on at this pace,' Ren said cheerfully to his co-workers, 'the farm will be impressed, and they might keep us for longer and employ us again next harvest season.'

There was good news the next morning as they walked into the fields to start work. The farm manager told them they were permitted to catch rabbits if they wanted to. There was an excess of rabbits on the farm, apparently.

The Chinese workers were excited at this news. Xiao Yun

was already thinking about cooking them. She said meat was expensive in England, so if they caught a few rabbits each week, they'd be able to have a good diet on a low budget. 'But the problem was,' Gao said to me, 'we urban Chinese had no idea how to catch a rabbit. We had to ask for help from the workers from rural areas in the north-east of China who had hunting expertise.'

The rural workers were delighted to help. 'It's time for us peasantry to show our force!' they said. Catching rabbits was easy for them. 'They're stupid animals. When you surround them, they don't move. You can just catch them by hand. Or you knife them once, and they're yours.'

That evening, straight after work, the rural northerners went rabbit-hunting. It didn't take them long to return with two large rabbits, still alive. 'That was a real morale boost. I hadn't eaten any meat for days,' said Gao. But he had no idea how to kill one. Zhen Yi, one of the rabbit hunters, said that was easy too: you just cut its throat with a sharp knife, hold it upside down to drain the blood, then peel the skin up from where the knife went in.

'I couldn't bear to watch! So I went out for a walk around the farm,' said Gao. 'Then I saw the Ukrainian workers strolling back from their work. Half an hour later I came back to the mouth-watering smell of meat cooking in soy sauce. On the barbecue fire, Xiao Yun was making a rabbit stew. Near us the Ukrainians were setting up their barbecue, and we Chinese invited them to join us.'

The rumour spread across the caravan site: 'The Chinese caught rabbits for supper.' Lots of people came to try the Chinese rabbit stew. 'The joy was shared,' Gao said. 'Everyone was so impressed.' A young Ukrainian woman did a vigorous thumbs-up sign for the stew, and Gao tried to explain to her how it was cooked, using a few words from his tiny English vocabulary and all four of his limbs.

As they sat and ate, people chatted about work in the

simplest form of English, and seemed to understand each other.

'You like job?' the Ukrainian woman asked Gao.

'No, no – difficult,' he replied. 'You – how old?'

'Twenty-two,' she answered, using both her hands to gesture 'two'. 'I am student. Going back to my country after work finishes.'

A Ukrainian man in his early twenties told Ren he'd been made to drive a tractor on his first day of work with no training. It had upset him. 'They want to save costs. Our safety – they don't care.' Ren told him that he, too, had been made to drive a tractor on his first day here.

Everyone started to tell their stories about their first week in England, separating back into their own language groups as the stories got more convoluted. Ren told the Chinese about his first day. 'I was supposed to be going to a building job, but I had no idea how to get to the workplace in Tottenham. The Tienjin man whom I'd paid £200 to pick me up didn't help. He just said, "When you're abroad, you've got to find your own way. No one's going to help you." So I left the flat at Leyton at 5 a.m., allowing two hours for the journey. I asked for help in my broken English. And people told me so many different things. I kept changing buses. I got totally lost. I arrived at the workplace at nine. No one was there. They'd gone to work at a building site in the area. I stood there dumbly, knowing I'd lost the first opportunity I'd had in England. Then it started to rain, of course. I took shelter in a phone booth. "Stop raining," I said to the sky. "Can't you see I'm in trouble?" But it took no notice. There was nothing to do but start the journey back to the flat. But which bus? Someone told me to get on to a Number 73, so I did, and stayed on to the last stop. I had no phone: only a piece of paper with the address of my flat on it. I got on another bus, and found myself in a place called Walthamstow.

'From a phone booth, I managed to phone my wife in China. But when I heard her anxious voice, I couldn't bring myself to tell her I was lost and alone. "I'm fine," I said, "and work's fine." Her voice made me feel stronger. I kept going, from bus to bus, and got back to the flat in the evening. And you know what? No one asked me about my day.'

Gao didn't know whether to cry or laugh.

'But I got something from that day,' Ren said. 'Now I'm the London bus expert. I give handy tips to every Chinese newcomer.'

Xiao Yun came to sit next to Ren, taking his arm in hers. She told everyone that she wouldn't know how she'd have managed without Ren's help.

Gradually, during our talks together, Ren and Xiao Yun told me the story of how they'd got together. Ren had been sent to pick her up at the airport. From the first moment they'd met, he'd felt emotionally attached to her. There was something about her independent spirit that attracted him. They found comfort in each other at their most depressed moments.

'England was so far from being the country I'd imagined,' Xiao Yun said. 'I was shocked by its harshness. Ren helped me through the first dark days.'

'I never thought I'd be the type to *da-huo* [have a temporary partner],' said Ren. 'People do things like that because they're far from their wives or husbands. They don't know when they'll be going home – it could be months, or years – and they truly need someone, emotionally, mentally, physically or even economically. It's certainly easier to live here if you share your living costs. It's easy to get into that way of thinking. It's particularly difficult for men. The ratio of men to women coming to work in England is about twenty to one. With Xiao Yun it just happened. It wasn't something I planned. She stayed with me in a crowded flat in Vauxhall when she first arrived. We shared a room with four men on mattresses. I knew she wanted to be with me. We talked all the time. But there was no room, no privacy. One day she led me into the tiny bathroom of the flat. And there we became lovers.'

'Ren's more than a lover,' Xiao Yun said to me. 'He's my best friend here. He's made me feel hopeful in this cold, unfriendly country. He told me that the best way for me to solve my status problem is to get married to someone with a passport. Then I'll never have to worry again. I'll have a future. But I told him that for the moment I preferred to be with him.'

The 'rabbit dinner' was the talk of the farm the next day. It became an addiction on the caravan site, bringing people together, giving them a social life to look forward to in the evenings. The hunters went out each night. The Ukrainians gave hunting a try, too, and the Bulgarians. But no one did as well as the Chinese.

They were doing too well, it turned out. A month later, the farm manager appeared again. Rabbit-hunting was banned. There were now too few rabbits on the farm. No one had imagined the workers would be such effective hunters without guns.

The next day was the weekly pay-day. In the farm office, the names on the photocopied work permits were called out. 'Li Shang Ming!' That was the name on Gao's permit, sold to him for £50 by the agency. 'I was handed a sealed envelope, and opened it. It was cash, £100 for the week,' Gao told me. 'There was a payslip inside, stating deductions for tax and £30 for rent. I went back to the caravan, trying to calculate how the wage came to be so low. I couldn't work it out. Anxiety was spreading across the caravan site as people came back with their pay packets.'

Ren came back and announced that he'd heard from the Ukrainian workers that it was even worse down at the salad factory twenty minutes away. They told him it's a family business, run by the same boss. Apparently the deductions are even bigger there.

This was small consolation. I could hear the growing sense of uncertainty among the Chinese workers when I talked to them on the night of the pay-day. 'How long are we going to do this for?' Gao asked repeatedly. No one had any idea. 'The farms don't tell us. But harvesting work doesn't last for ever. That's one thing we know.'

Everyone had to live with this uncertainty. But no one was willing to leave before they were told to. They'd all paid £200 to the agency, and were determined to earn as much as possible to make that worthwhile.

So the summer went on. The migrants worked for eleven or twelve hours a day, six days a week. Many of them developed asthma from breathing in the liquid that sprayed out of the lettuces when they picked them. Yet they had no choice but to continue with the work. On their only day off, some did food shopping and cooking, some just slept to get their strength back. For months, Gao had no access to a newspaper. Occasional calls to his wife in Tienjin became his only access to the world beyond the farm.

One day in late summer, I visited them on their day off. Gao took me for a long walk. The team came with us. We walked to the beach, three miles away from the farms. Here, the Chinese workers could temporarily put their status and the farm work out of their minds and merge into the local scene. We strolled to the western end of Selsey Bill.

Gao loved watching the sea. 'If only I could just sit here for ever, watching the waves. I thought about my fifteen-year-old son and my family on the other side of the world. If things had not been so bad in China, I wouldn't have come this far. Not that things were much better here.'

'Do you regret coming to England?' I asked.

He paused, and said: 'At the moment I have yet to see any reward for this self-imposed separation from home and family.' But how long would it take? He had no idea. He didn't want to say at this point that it had been a mistake. He must be patient; time would tell.

Meanwhile Xiao Yun and Ren were thinking, more practically, of supper. There were seafood stalls all along the beach. Xiao Yun nibbled some crabsticks she'd bought, throwing bits to the seagulls. Ren was more interested in getting some fish to cook in the Tienjin way. After twenty minutes of hard bargaining, he managed to get the price down: £2 per kilo for a large crab. They decided to splash out and share the cost. 'When did you last eat crab?' Ren asked.

'It was at my son's birthday dinner,' Xiao Yun answered quietly.

And, lying limply on the beach, was the perfect accompaniment: seaweed.

'Nice thick pieces,' said Xiao-Yun. 'No one picks them up here.'

'These could lower our daily food budget,' said Ren to me as they all bent down to pick up seaweed and stuff it into a carrier bag, attracting amused looks from the locals.

'Better stop,' said Ren. 'We're attracting too much attention. We don't want anyone asking questions.'

Yes, it was only temporary, that blissful forgetting of their status.

That night, the Chinese team won lots of praise again. They cooked the seaweed with soy sauce and sugar, and Ren prepared a Tienjin steamed crab dish. The Poles loved it, and offered the Chinese some of their meat stew and potatoes, cooked with roadside herbs.

Harvesting lasted well into the autumn. November came. Days were getting short and cold. The Chinese team, shivering as they arrived for work, were spoken to by the farm manager.

'The harvesting work has come to an end. You are expected to leave the caravan site as soon as you can.'

The Malaysian Chinese team leader translated the manager's words.

'But you didn't give us any notice!' Gao shouted out in

Chinese. The manager glanced at him briefly and ignored the incomprehensible babble.

'Where do you expect us to go?' Gao carried on. 'The farms promised us work. They can't just throw us out with no notice.'

But he knew deep down, as did all the Chinese workers, that the farms could do exactly that. With no papers and no status, the workers had not a leg to stand on.

They went back to the caravan and talked to the Malaysian Chinese interpreter. 'Please,' Ren urged him, 'talk to the manager. Ask them to transfer us to other sites.'

A meeting was agreed for the next morning. All evening, the members of the two Chinese teams sat together discussing the demands they would put to the management. First: continued employment at other Langmead Farms sites. Failing that: employment at Natures Way, the nearby salad factory where many migrant workers were sent when farm work came to an end.

Morale high, they walked into the manager's office the next day and laid down their demands.

'We have no vacancies for you,' said the manager, 'not here, not anywhere else.'

'But you promised us work,' the interpreter said. 'You said there was a lot of work. You gave us no notice. Please.'

The manager, with a bored expression, looked down at his papers, then said, 'Fine. You can go and work at Natures Way Foods, the salad factory. We're sister companies. But the pre-condition is that you must be employed by Advance Recruitment, an agency we work with. Please contact the manager of the agency, Anatoly Bespaly. This is his phone number.'

'Can't we contact the salad factory directly?'

'No. Contacting Bespaly is the only way you can get work in the factory.' The manager saw them out.

★

'We'll have to contact the agency,' Gao told me. 'We have no choice. We can't afford to stay without work.' The Malaysian Chinese interpreter made the first call to Anatoly Bespaly on the team's behalf. They knew nothing about him except that he was originally from Estonia and had been supplying labour to the salad factory for years.

Bespaly agreed to take them on immediately. No documents were needed. He arranged to pick them up that evening in two minibuses.

Gao packed his bag and said goodbye to the caravan, which was even more cigarette-stained than it had been when he'd arrived in May. But he was fond of the little place. Maybe he'd be back next year.

In the dark, the Chinese workers looked out of the minibus window at their anxious reflections. They were being driven to the town centre of Selsey. What would they find there?

When the minibus stopped at the corner of Church Road, seven of them got out. The driver pointed to the first-floor flat above a garage. He rang the bell for them. A chubby European man with light-brown hair opened the door, and introduced himself as Arunas, Bespaly's manager. The Chinese workers followed him up the narrow staircase.

There were three rooms in the flat, to share between nine people: seven Chinese and two Russian workers. There was no furniture, just a TV in one of the rooms.

No longer shy about his broken English, after months of practice with the Ukrainians and Poles in the caravans, Gao went up to the two Russian men in the kitchen and introduced himself.

'I Gao. Where from?'

'Russia,' they answered. 'You Chinese?'

'Yes. We work salad factory.'

Arunas came into the kitchen to talk about money. 'Listen. Each of you pays £45 per week for your bed here. It will be deducted from your wages. I'll give you a call tomorrow about your shifts.' He left. The Malaysian Chinese worker was being sent to another flat, so the Chinese no longer had help in communicating with the Westerners.

The two Russian flatmates looked at the Chinese with sympathetic grins, and gave them each a glass of vodka. Ren retaliated by giving them a cup of Chinese tea. On the table were some plastic boxes of salads. They caught Gao's eye. 'Products we make in factory,' explained one of the Russians.

'You make by hand?'

The man nodded. 'Each box different salads.'

'*Guilao* eat these, just like this?' Gao asked Ren.

'Of course! *Guilao* love these. They don't always have hot lunch like us. They have raw salad meals.'

The Russian man told Gao that they also made salads with croutons for McDonald's. Sometimes they got to take salad meals home. Most days they had these for breakfast.

Gao asked if he could try some. He then took his chopsticks out of his suitcase, opened one of the salad boxes and tried a few mouthfuls. 'It's quite tasteless,' he said, frowning. 'I prefer my Treasure Mountain cigarette.' (But when I visited him later, he had got used to these salad meals and persuaded me to have one.)

The Chinese workers met their boss for the first time when he visited unexpectedly. Just as the two Russian men were about to leave for their night shift, they heard a key turn in the front-door lock, then heavy steps on the stairs.

'Must be Bespaly,' one of the Russians said quietly, sitting up straight as if for an inspection. The Chinese workers came to understand that the name 'Anatoly Bespaly' was much-feared by migrant workers around here. Every now and then he would pay an unexpected check-up visit. Normally he kept away from the workers. He delegated to Arunas, who in turn delegated to a 'link person' who could speak the language of the particular group of migrants. As I found out in the months that followed, Bespaly's hierarchical system of supervision

enabled him to keep his distance from workers and their complaints about pay and conditions.

He walked into the room. 'Who the fuck is smoking in
here?'

Gao froze. He understood the word 'smoking'. He didn't
dare speak. Bespaly glared at him, walked around the flat,
looked into each room, nodded to the Russian men, and left.
No one knew why he'd come, but they all felt unsettled. Gao
found it hard to get to sleep that night in the freezing bedroom.
Bespaly's aggressive face kept coming into his mind.

He was woken by the noise of the Russians returning in the
morning. He got up and went into the kitchen. They were
drinking from a bottle of vodka, and asked Gao if he wanted
some.

'Too early,' said Gao.

'No, no, you sit, you drink with us.' Gao accepted a glass,
not wanting to seem rude. 'That's right. Drink up!'

'Drink to the demise of Bespaly!'

Gao realized that drinking was as much a common language
among them here as their shared contempt for Bespaly and the
factory.

While following Gao's story, I talked to Russian, Chinese
and Bulgarian workers in this Selsey flat from 2003 to 2006 and
found out more about Bespaly. They told me that he was a
worker himself six years ago, a line operator at Natures Way.

'He liked his job and got so comfortable with the bosses that
he decided to set up a business recruiting workers for them,'
said one of the Russian workers. This, I learned, is how most
non-local gangmasters start off: working on the production
line. They learn to speak the language, and start to see the business potential in recruiting workers: they establish contacts in
this country, and already know lots of workers from their own
countries. Bespaly isn't the only gangmaster supplying workers
to Natures Way (the others are the Portuguese-run JD and
Passion Café and the English-run ERA), but he supplies the

largest number. He also sends workers to do loading in the area. His agency, unusually, recruits workers from a wide range of backgrounds: Chinese, Russians, Portuguese, Bulgarians, Iraqis, Kurds, Afghans and others. Over the years his name has spread from the nascent migrant communities in Sussex to those in Kent. The words 'Anatoly Bespaly has work for you' are frequently on people's lips. He owns a large house in London as well as other properties around the country.

There are thousands more like Bespaly all over Britain, some local, some from abroad, the workers in Selsey told me. 'This kind of thing [gangmaster profiteering] is very normal in England. But English people don't know.'

I tried to check Bespaly's credentials. His company name 'Advance Recruitment' is printed on workers' payslips. As I discovered later, it is not a registered company. I asked Bespaly himself to confirm his company's name. In his heavy, husky voice he told me it was registered as 'Advance Employment Service' with a London branch and a growing trade in Kent. But I found that this was not registered either. Despite the underground nature of his business, it has expanded: today Bespaly has offices in Latvia, Lithuania and Estonia, recruiting young men and women to work for him in England.

The first day, Ren and Gao told me, went by uneventfully. Arunas did not telephone the new Chinese arrivals to tell them about their shifts as he'd said he would.

On the second day the bedroom door was opened at 6.50 a.m. 'Get up! Get up! Go to work!' It was Bespaly, shouting at their bedside. There was a sudden demand for them to cover for absent workers. Gao dragged himself out of bed and got dressed quickly. None of the workers complained. They needed work. By 7.20 they were gathering outside Natures Way factory with crowds of others, ready to get on the day shift, which started at 7.30. Thus began the first of many twelve-hour working days at Natures Way.

The first thing that amazed Gao was the huge number of his

co-workers – 400 of them. 'Never – not even in the car plant in Tienjin – had I worked with so many people.' The Chinese workers were led into the hand-cutting department, where migrant workers cut and washed lettuces, cabbages, carrots, spinach and other vegetables. The local workers went into the machine-cutting department.

'The people in the tougher hand-cutting department are all foreign, like us,' Ren told me. 'Many different countries. Like us, many of them don't have legal status.' He also said that local workers work half the hours migrants do.

Gao saw Arunas sitting at his desk wearing a suit: Advance had its office inside the factory. 'You'd better keep on the right side of him,' the Chinese workers were always told by other more experienced migrants. 'He's the eyes of Bespaly. He sorts out all the shifts.'

I asked Bespaly about the contract between Advance Recruitment and Natures Way. He reluctantly told me that it was renewed every six months, for the supply of a hundred workers. However, I found that Advance was recruiting more than 150 workers, exceeding the required number. As Gao and Ren realized later, Advance was getting more and more workers into Selsey, to fill up six flats, with no guarantee that they would have work. 'It's all about profits. The more workers Bespaly recruits, the more cash he can make from their rent and transport,' they said.

The Chinese workers began to feel uneasy with all these incoming workers. 'No one knows if they're going to have work the next day. Now we're taking turns to get on the shifts,' said Gao, 'You feel lucky if you get work. That's why you see some people working for fifteen days non-stop. They can't refuse. They don't know how long the work will last.'

'We thought things were harsh for us at the lettuce farm,' Ren said to me, 'with our low pay – two-thirds of what the locals got. But at least daily work was guaranteed. We need regular income to send home. That's more important than anything.'

Workers' asthma problems, which had started at Langmead Farms, continued at Natures Way. Older Gao (who had in fact developed asthma from his previous work in Hartlepool) and Zhen Yi suffered particularly badly. Gao tried to explain his older brother's problems to the English supervisor, using hand gestures and imitation coughs. But the supervisor didn't understand, so Gao had to stand by and watch his brother coughing and gasping for breath as he washed the lettuces.

'You can get sick with these little lettuces,' Ren said. 'But who's going to care? Natures Way is making around £8 million per day from these salads. It's sold at over £1 a packet at Tesco and other supermarkets. One of the Russians told me.'

Indeed, Natures Way is the second biggest food manufacturer in Britain. It was formed in 1994, in response to a request from Tesco, and started to supply the supermarket with lettuce from its sister company Langmead Farms Ltd, which covers 6,000 acres of land in Chichester, as well as a further 1,500 acres in the south of Spain. From 1996 to 1998, during the time when its migrant workforce began to grow, Natures Way's turnover grew from £1 million to £10 million. Today it has sites in Selsey and Runcton, and annual profits of £175 million. Its salad products are transported to every Tesco store in Britain. It also supplies Morrisons, McDonald's and Sainsbury's, as well as the European markets.

Apart from the low pay and long working hours, what workers found hard to cope with was the low air temperature in the salad-processing departments: about 5°C. Almost every worker wore a woollen hat under the required cap. The job was static, spent standing in one place, so there was no way to keep body temperature up. Standing in the cold for seventy-two hours a week gave Ren a headache. Xiao Yun, also, was suffering. 'I'm always longing for the half-hour lunch break to come,' she said, 'so I can go outside to get some warmth.'

The workers were given fifteen minutes off every three hours to get warm. (This was less time than the Bulgarian and new EU workers that were employed later.) By the time Xiao Yun took off her uniform (this was compulsory) to go outside for a break, there were only ten minutes left. And she had to come back five minutes early to put the uniform on again in time to start work.

Some of the workers complained to the factory about the low working temperature, but their concern was ignored. After two weeks at Natures Way, Gao developed a fever. It became so bad that he couldn't walk very well. When his friends went on their night shift, he stayed in. He decided to have a hot bath, hoping it would make him better. In the bathtub of the tiny bathroom, he felt his muscles loosening in the warm water, and his temperature going up. He thought he was about to faint, but fell asleep. Four hours later he woke up in a tub of cold water.

'I am cold,' he said to himself, in Chinese. He heard his voice echo round the bathroom. 'Then I remembered I wasn't at home,' he said to me. 'Never have I felt so alone, so cut off from the world. I sat in the cold water for ten more minutes before getting out. As I dried myself my thoughts turned to the fake name I'd adopted: Li Shang Ming. I tried to imagine being called this by my wife and son and my parents. I felt so guilty. Your name is a gift, given to you by your parents. It should be cherished. Changing it is a violation of the natural bond between you and your parents. Why was I doing this? I asked myself. I felt I was an unfilial son as well as an irresponsible father.'

Gao was not alone in this feeling of guilt. Every other Chinese worker here was using a fake name, in and outside of work, in order to avoid the risk of exposing his or her status. Sometimes the older members of the team would forget their fake names, or blurt out their real names by mistake. Adopting a false identity was hard. You needed to make yourself believe it, so it became easier to live with, Gao had learned.

The next night, still not better from his fever, he struggled back to work. He couldn't afford to be off sick. Then pay-day came. Bespaly came to the flat and handed out the envelopes of cash, without any expression.

Everyone laid out their cash and payslips on the kitchen table to calculate whether the pay was correct. 'They always play tricks with your wages,' the Russian flatmates said. Gao put his cash on the table. His weekly wage was £85.91, after a national insurance deduction of £13.99 and a rent deduction of £45. (He showed me the payslip when I visited.) It didn't leave much to send back to support his family. The Chinese workers later found out that Bespaly had a reputation for using any excuse to lower workers' wages, and if Bespaly paid you sixty hours' wages for sixty-three hours' work, then you should be grateful.

It wasn't easy to send or save cash, either. Without legal status, the Chinese workers weren't able to open bank accounts. Bespaly exploited this fact: his men, like Arunas, charged £50 for opening bank accounts for newcomers. The Chinese workers couldn't afford this fee. There were no Chinese banks in Selsey. They had to send the money through the help of Chinese friends who could use banks for them in London.

The banks charged a fee each time you sent money to China, so Gao wanted to find a safe place in Selsey to keep his hard-earned cash before sending it home in a lump sum. His supervisor at Natures Way, a Portuguese woman, offered to help him save his money (nearly £1,000, earned over several months) in her bank account. Naively, he accepted. When he asked for the money later, she denied it had ever been entrusted to her. He begged her to give it back, but she ignored him.

'I'm going to sue you,' he said to her eventually, knowing it would be impossible to do so. He reported the matter to the factory's management, but they told him it was nothing to do with them. The supervisor had exploited his lack of status and his inability to speak English – and, according to other Chinese workers, this wasn't the first time she'd done it.

This betrayal came as an appalling shock to Gao. During one of my visits, he asked me to intercede with the Portuguese supervisor, and try to get the money back. I went to visit her in her flat, but she shut the door and refused to speak to me.

Gao was to find out later that the blatant theft of twelve weeks' wages was not the worst thing that could happen to an 'illegal' at Natures Way. During his months at the factory he heard about other supervisors, such as the Georgian one who was violent and abusive towards his Kurdish workers, hitting them and shouting at them, trying to make them work like machines. Bespaly's men were no better. Ren returned to the flat one day, and told everyone what he'd seen. 'It was Bespaly's link men: I saw them beating an Iraqi man up for demanding wages owed to him. They just went for him and kicked him. Everyone was scared. I watched, wanting to help the guy, but other people told me to leave.'

Another supervisor, a heavily built Bulgarian called Mario, was notorious among Bespaly's 'link people' for his bullying tactics. The Bulgarians hated and feared him. The factory liked to refer to him as a 'community go-between', but the workers referred to him more accurately as 'Bespaly's running dog'. Bespaly did not have a Chinese 'link person' working for him. Had he tried to find one? The Chinese didn't know: it was a mystery. Gao, ever patriotic, thought he knew. 'No Chinese worker would take up that kind of position,' he said. 'Bespaly wouldn't be able to find a traitor like that among us.'

When I visited Gao, Ren and Xiao Yun in the summer, their Portuguese co-worker Pedro offered them a lift in his rusty second-hand car to a car-boot sale in Chichester. Gao got on well with Pedro: they joked together and tried out their basic English vocabulary during their working hours. Gao asked him what a car-boot sale was.

'Lots of cheap, good things. You'll like it.'

Pedro had legal status – hence the second-hand car – and it was clear to Ren, as they parked the car and walked towards the car-boot-sale field, that Pedro fancied his chances with Xiao Yun. 'Maybe it'll be good for her,' Ren said to me, 'to go out with that guy.'

'Won't you be upset?' I asked.

'Of course I will. But I've got no right to tell her that. From her first day in England I've been telling her she should find a way to sort out her status. If she can find someone good, someone to marry her and help her with her status, I'm not going to stand in her way.' He lit up his Red River.

Coming upon the field full of cars displaying their wares, Gao was as excited as a boy in a toyshop. Instantly an object caught his eye: a camcorder for sale, price £4. It must be broken, at that price. Gao couldn't resist picking it up. He pressed a button and a light came on. He focused on the slim, almond-eyed Xiao Yun and Pedro standing next to her. They posed, smiling. He pressed the 'record' button. It worked! He turned the camera towards Ren: good old Ren, with his deep wrinkles on his worn-out face. The wrinkles seemed to deepen each time he squeezed out a smile for Gao. He'd never looked at Ren this closely.

He couldn't leave without buying the camcorder. 'I'd always wanted to record what I saw, but didn't feel good enough at writing to keep a diary,' he said to me with a smile. Filming would be his form of diary-keeping. He'd send a tape home to Tienjin, to show his family what life in England was like. (But how much should he show them?)

From that Sunday afternoon, Gao's life became magical to him, in spite of the grind of the twelve-hour shifts. He always had his filming to look forward to. The next Sunday he sat on the beach for hours, filming local children playing in the water. Some passers-by even said hello and nodded at him. Later he walked down the high street and filmed ordinary life: local shoppers, a mother pushing a pram, strolling tourists, an old couple having tea in a cosy low-beamed tea-house. It was almost as if he was making himself part of the scene, merging into it, by filming it. He wanted so much to be part of the community around him. He walked down a footpath into the country where he filmed cyclists wearing helmets (no one wore them in China). Then he came to a country pub with a statue of a man on the roof. (If he could have read English, he would have known that this was Captain Morgan, after whom the pub was named.) He climbed up the scaffolding on the building opposite in order to film the statue at eye level.

Should he go inside the pub? He'd never gone into one before: he'd felt too nervous about being asked questions. But this camcorder had changed everything for him. It had given him a purpose, as well as something to hide behind. He walked in. The pub was almost empty: three men were sitting up at the bar chatting to the barman. They turned and looked at Gao. Did they think he was some weird Japanese tourist whose camcorder needed replacing? He didn't care. They carried on talking, and he focused on them, recording their conversation.

The pub was next to a caravan site, and when Gao came out at 7 p.m. he saw Portuguese workers returning to their caravans after work. He'd heard from Pedro about Portuguese people working for the Portsmouth-based catering agency Passion Café Foods Ltd, who sent them to work at Natures Way and housed them in caravans. So this was where they lived. With his camcorder he focused on them dragging themselves back to the caravan site. He'd heard that they had to pay a heavy fee to the agency's branch in Portugal to work here, as well as £60 a week for a bed in the caravan. Why, as EU members with no need to get a visa, were they getting such a bad deal? He didn't understand. His camera paused on an exhausted face.

Indeed, these workers, as well as Eastern European workers from the periphery of the EU, were (and still are) badly exploited. While there has been a growing tendency for retailers to demand flexible labour in order to be able to produce work at short notice, gangmasters have kept their labour costs down by recruiting migrants with little experience – and therefore low expectations – of the employment environment in Britain.

Work continued at Natures Way throughout the year, into spring 2004. As summer approached again, the Chinese workers hoped they'd soon be able to return to work on the farms. But things had changed. The Chinese-run agency was no longer able to supply Chinese workers to Langmead Farms. The farms no longer needed undocumented workers to fill their labour gap. Now they could use authorized cheap labour from the new EU countries: Poland, Latvia, Lithuania and Estonia.

The talk of a crackdown on illegal working was in the air as employers got ready to welcome the new EU workers. It was time to leave. Ren began to make calls to his friends in London, asking them about vacancies on building sites. Gao knew he had to look elsewhere too. He knew Bespaly would keep them on as long as he could, to make best use of their cheap labour and rental income, but when the time came he'd get rid of the most visible 'illegals' to keep himself safe.

Gao and his brother would have few people to turn to in London. They could follow Ren, but they knew nothing about building work. Where should they go?

This second eviction had the effect of disillusioning and hardening Gao. 'I no longer felt the urge to film objects and happenings around me. Nothing seemed worth recording through a lens. Everything seemed tawdry and mean. I thought, What's the point in preserving memories of this ugly existence?'

As he departed from Selsey to search for work elsewhere, he decided at the last minute to leave the camcorder behind in the flat. Bulgarian workers would be coming in that day to take the place of the Chinese. They'd probably delete everything on the camera, but who cared?

★

The Bulgarians, not yet members of the EU, and mostly with-out documents to work as a result of the British government's visa restrictions on them since 2004, turned out to be prone to exploitation by labour middlemen, just like the Chinese. They, too, were to find mystifying deductions on their payslips after seventy-two-hour working weeks. Some of them had their wage cut to £3 an hour by Bespaly, whom they nicknamed the 'Mafia boss'. Their legal status since Bulgaria joined the EU in January 2007 has still not guaranteed their entitlement to basic rights – thanks to rampant gangmaster abuse, and the lack of enforcement of the legislative protection that should be theirs.

The Bulgarians, in their turn, were laid off without notice in summer 2004 when more and more Polish, Latvian, Lithuanian and Estonian workers arrived after them. Life in Selsey was not much better for these new arrivals, even though they were members of new EU countries. They paid hefty registration fees and were not guaranteed daily work. I visited the flat in Selsey in 2005 and 2006 and saw Latvians and Estonians return-ing exhausted from their night shift to the bleakness of housing with poor facilities and salads past their sell-by date. These workers will carry on toiling away here until some kind of justice comes to their aid, just as the Chinese and Bulgarian workers did before them.

Anatoly Bespaly did not respond to the allegations. Natures Way Foods strongly denies the allegations made. 'Between 2003 and 2004 Advance Employment Services [Anatoly Bespaly's company] supplied our business with agency workers. We have strong systems and procedures in place to manage our labour providers. We carry out announced and unannounced audits and work closely with the Immigration Authority to ensure the highest standards are maintained and our labour providers operate good practice. We managed our labour providers in this way in 2003 and have continued to do so since.'

Langmead Farms Ltd said they were not able to respond in time.

4. Dimsum, Cockles and DVDs

They told me the money would be better up here. And I've always wanted to be near the sea. So I came. But a third of my money goes to the boss. And the sea isn't as blue as I'd imagined.

— a Tienjin woman working as a cockle picker in Morecambe Bay
November 2003

As the coach pulled away from Victoria station, Ah-Hua looked out. It was raining. He watched the drops sliding down the window, blurring the edges of the red pillar boxes. 'I'm going to be OK,' he said to himself in Fujianese. The bus driver made an announcement, incomprehensible to Ah-Hua except for the word 'Manchester'. That was where he was going.

He opened his small suitcase and took out the box of tea-marinated eggs he'd made for the journey. He started peeling one of the eggs. Doing this always reminded him of the parting at the very beginning of his journey. His wife had made him a picnic of these eggs when she'd come to see him off at the bus station at Fuqing. That precious snack had only lasted him for the first two days of the three-month trip, when he'd been smuggled from China to England. But he'd never forget the fragrant taste of the tea leaves and strong soy sauce he'd consoled himself with for those first two days.

He was going to a new life in Manchester! He wanted to think of the 'new life' in the abstract. But in his pocket he carried a crumpled piece of paper with an address on it. The address, in Chinese characters, was of a real place, the place he was being sent to: a restaurant in Manchester's Chinatown. The address had been given to him by Boss Yu. Ah-Hua might be going to a faraway city, but he couldn't get away from Boss Yu, the London-based snakehead who'd met him on arrival in England. He still owed Boss Yu and his associates £10,000.

I was living in Manchester in 2005 while training at the *Guardian*'s Manchester office, and I met Ah-Hua two years after he'd taken this journey north. We had many conversations, some in a pub and some in the flat where he was lodging. He told me his story, from the distant days of Fuqing to the more recent days in Manchester.

He'd been a casual builder in Fuqing, a city in Fujian province, from where the majority of the estimated 70,000 Fujianese Chinese people in Britain have migrated. In Fuqing he had no regular income. He was earning 500 RMB (about £38) a month at best. His wife was earning the same amount, working full-time in a shoe factory.

They lived in an old farmhouse on the outskirts of Fuqing with their eleven-year-old son and Ah-Hua's parents. They could not afford a house of their own, and were living a hand-to-mouth existence, barely above subsistence level. Their son often came home from school talking about the parents of his classmates who had improved their standard of living by working abroad, especially in the UK. These parents were able to build new houses for the family and could afford after-school lessons for their children to give them a leg-up to a good career.

Ah-Hua and his wife were tempted by the idea of working abroad. They thought about it for several months. Finally they made up their minds: Ah-Hua would set out first, to England. He knew of a local snakehead who'd been around for years and, it was said, successfully smuggled more than twenty people from Fuqing to Western Europe each year. Ah-Hua approached him and asked him to arrange his journey to Britain. The man's required fee was 200,000 RMB (around £15,400 at the time), as Ah-Hua had expected. The price was high – cripplingly high. It was equivalent to thirty-four years of his total annual wages in China. But his choice was a stark one. He could either stay put and keep his family in poverty for the rest of his life, or he could try to borrow 200,000 RMB to come to Britain, try to pay back the loan in three or four years, and start a better life. If the journey really was the route to a whole new life, a new future for the family, it would be worth it. Ah-Hua agreed to pay the entire fee on his arrival at the destination country.

Why was he resorting to a snakehead? He had no alternative. It's practically impossible for a Fujianese solo traveller to be granted a visa by the British government because in the last three decades or so there has been a higher percentage of Fujianese among Chinese asylum seekers coming into Britain. With increasing reluctance from the British government to receive asylum seekers since the mid-1990s, the level of refusal has been high. There's an assumption among the British authorities that Fujianese people, whether applying for asylum or for work permits or student visas, are 'bogus' and potential 'over-stayers'. Therefore these people's legitimate route of migration has been narrowed down – much more than those of travellers from other provinces. If you are from Fujian, being smuggled in is almost the only option left open to you.

From the moment of agreeing to the fee, Ah-Hua set about trying to raise funds by borrowing from his relatives. Many others from Fuqing do the same: borrowing is common practice in his province. His relatives trusted him and were willing to take out their savings to help him. They believed that some day in the near future, he'd be earning a large income and improving the life of his extended family at home. How proud they would be to have played a part in making this possible!

But Ah-Hua's relatives were ordinary working-class people, just like him. They didn't have much to lend. Ah-Hua had to turn to a moneylender to borrow some of the fee – but he could only borrow a limited amount because the interest rate was so high. In the end, he was only able to gather half the required fees for the journey. The knowledge that he wouldn't be able to pay off the fees to the snakehead on arrival made him hesitate about going. To arrive in a strange country saddled with a huge debt: that would be hard. It was his pride that finally made the decision for him to leave China. He felt this was something he had to do for his family. To retreat back to poverty at home would be cowardly. 'I'm a man for my family,' he said to himself. 'I'll do what I have to do.'

Within four weeks, the snakehead had made all the travel arrangements. The day of departure came – that day with the tea-marinated eggs, and the heartbreak of waving goodbye through the bus window. Ah-Hua was sent on the journey with three other men from his hometown. They were instructed to travel north-east to Shenyang, where they were picked up by a local snakehead contact. From there they took a train to Harbin, and waited there for several days to get on a plane to Moscow with Chinese passports the snakeheads had prepared for them. Ah-Hua didn't even have a chance to look at 'his' passport, because the snakehead was carrying all the documents with him.

When they landed in Moscow they were taken to the railway station and boarded a train to Kiev in the Ukraine. There, the local snakehead who picked them up housed them in a flat already occupied by twenty others.

'On that first evening,' Ah-Hua told me as we sat at a pub table in Manchester, 'we were given packets of instant noodles for dinner. But no saucepan to boil the water in! So we had to eat the noodles dry. Then the local snakehead told us that "access" wasn't frequent, and we'd have to wait. The only way to get across the Ukraine through to Slovakia is by crossing the mountains. The common route into Western Europe used to be via Romania, but now the number of local snakeheads there has decreased. The snakehead kept telling us we had to wait. I had no idea that the waiting would last for three weeks.'

Ah-Hua only heard that the Ukraine is notorious as one

of the harshest countries to be smuggled through once he'd started the journey. Often, travellers have to climb mountains in the snow, with local snakeheads (some of them corrupt police officers who take a share of the profits) leading the route across the borders. When Ah-Hua and his fellow travellers were finally led on to the mountain, they were given only a few slices of bread to last the night. 'But we were much more fortunate than some of the other travellers, those before us, who were provided with nothing to eat but grass. Some people froze to death or drowned while crossing rivers. A pregnant woman died, we heard. And a man from Fujian was badly injured when he fell, and because he hadn't been able to seek medical treatment he had to have his leg amputated after the crossing. There was no choice but to get through these mountains under cover of night, to avoid getting caught. Once you start this journey, there is no turning back. You have to make it through this darkness, or you lose your life.'

Ah-Hua would indeed be counted as 'lucky'. Some Chinese migrants (I have since found out) spend six months waiting to be smuggled across the Ukraine only to be led to their death on such journeys.

A month and a half after leaving Fuqing, Ah-Hua and his co-travellers, after crossing Slovakia in a van, arrived in the Czech Republic. Here they were picked up by a Chinese snakehead who told them to call their families in China and pay half the agreed fees, as they were now over halfway to their destination. 'It won't be long now,' Ah-Hua told his wife on the phone, after asking her to pay the 100,000 RMB (£7,692) he'd managed to raise.

In fact they would be waiting in the Czech Republic for another month. Just as he was beginning to lose hope of ever getting to England, he and his co-travellers were put into the back of a lorry driven by a local man, heading for Holland. Squeezed into a tiny space among twenty others at the back, Ah-Hua closed his eyes and dreamed about England. He was nearly there! He'd find himself a job – maybe in a restaurant, or a factory or on a building site. He'd be earning ten times as much per hour as he'd been earning in Fuqing. He'd work night and day to pay off his debts.

In Holland they were picked up by yet another Chinese man and taken to another overcrowded room, where they were stuck for another month, with no word about departure. During this time Ah-Hua wrote letters to his wife, reassuring her that he was nearly there and that everything would turn out fine. But he never sent the letters. The Chinese men and women weren't allowed to leave the flat alone. Ah-Hua sneaked out a few times and wandered around a few street corners, but he never found a place to buy stamps.

At last the great day came: locked in the back of a lorry, the travellers were loaded on to a ferry and transported to Dover. As they felt the lorry rumble off the ship on arrival, they could only imagine the White Cliffs. Two hours later they were let out and found themselves blinking in the grey day-light of a London industrial estate. They were met by the local snakehead contact, whose name was Boss Yu. It was here Ah-Hua had to make the confession he'd been dreading: that he was not able to pay the second half of the agreed fees. He knew he'd broken the rule that once you enter into an agreement with a snakehead you stick to it – whether it be paying the fees up front, or (as is more usual) paying a deposit in China and getting the rest of the fees paid by your family the moment you arrive in the destination country.

Boss Yu called the snakehead in Fuqing, who ranted at Ah-Hua on the phone. 'I know how to deal with the likes of you!' He told Boss Yu to put Ah-Hua on a job himself, so they could monitor him closely and make sure he paid them back regularly and fast. But Boss Yu didn't have any vacancies in London at the moment. He told Ah-Hua he was going to send him to work at a restaurant in Manchester's Chinatown, and that he'd have to pay the unpaid fees with interest.

That was how, two days after his arrival in Britain (where he was housed with fellow travellers in a flat in East London), he found himself alone on the coach to Manchester. Running out of credit on his mobile phone, he called his wife. 'I got us into this trouble, and I'll get us out!' His wife told him over the crackly line that she and the family had hardly enough to survive on. 'Be patient,' he told her. 'I'll work my hardest and you'll see how quickly we pay off the debt.'

Six hours after leaving London the coach arrived in Manchester. Boss Yu's contact was waiting to pick him up. Without introducing himself, he led Ah-Hua across the street. Ah-Hua was impressed by the tall buildings and wide roads but he wasn't given time to look around. A few minutes later they walked through an ornate Chinese gate into Chinatown. Ah-Hua took the crumpled piece of paper out of his pocket and looked for a restaurant of the same name.

'Don't bother,' the man said, pointing to a large restaurant with golden dragons round the window. 'We're here.'

Customers were crowding into the restaurant. Inside, the tables were filling up with families impatient for their weekend dimsum feast. Ah-Hua was pleased to see such enthusiasm among Westerners for Chinese food. He was led to the back of the restaurant to meet Mr Cheung, the manager. He bowed on meeting him and reached out his right hand for a handshake, but it didn't come. Instead Mr Cheung said, 'Saturday afternoon's a busy time for us. I'll take you to the chef and he'll show you what to do.' Mr Cheung was from Hong Kong and spoke Mandarin with a heavy Cantonese accent.

Ah-Hua was led into the kitchen at the back of the restaurant. A wall of heat and steam hit him as he entered. The chef was flipping beef and bamboo shoots in a wok. The assistant chef (known as the *chao fan mien*, which means 'frying rice and noodles' – his main task) was living up to his job description on the other side. Ah-Hua felt dizzy. It must be the heat and the airlessness. 'Over there,' the chef said to him. 'Stir-fry those.' Ah-Hua read the characters on the order. The dish was Singaporean fried rice-noodles. The *chao fan mien* was getting too busy with his noodle-frying, Ah-Hua was told, so Ah-Hua would have to help him.

He'd hardly cooked in his life, and certainly not in a restaurant. He'd expected to be washing up, or carrying things. Boss Yu hadn't told him much about the job, except that his wages would be around £120 a week, if he passed the trial. The trial? What if he failed? Then he'd be unemployed and heavily in debt. The thought terrified him. He set to work, trying his best to look competent and experienced.

Frying vegetables next to him was a young man called Chen, from the island of Pingtan off the coast from Fujian. He was known in the kitchen simply as *you bao* – 'fryer'. The name, again, was apt: he fried non-stop, everything from Cantonese dumplings to banana fritters. Over the noise and sweat of frying, he found time to be friendly to Ah-Hua and to show him the best method for stir-frying.

In between orders, the head chef had time to look at Ah-Hua and speak to him. Ah-Hua noticed how tired and unshaven he looked. 'Your job,' he said, 'is to help out in here: chop, fry, wash up, clean. When the restaurant closes, you'll have time to talk.'

From that moment till midnight, Ah-Hua worked as hard as he could – harder than he'd worked on all the building sites of Fuqing. He wanted to pass this trial. At midnight Mr Cheung came up to him and asked him how old he was.

'I'm thirty-two.'

'You look very thin and young. You did OK. You'll stay.'

He'd passed the trial!

'Thank you, Mr Cheung! Thank you!' Ah-Hua bowed gratefully. Then he carried on mopping the floor, hardly able to contain his sense of relief. How would he have been able to face Boss Yu if he'd failed?

'You work from 11 a.m. to midnight, six days a week,' Mr

Cheung instructed. 'You're off every Monday. You'll some-times be asked to do deliveries.'

'Deliveries?'

'Yes. You know how to ride a motorbike?'

'Not really.'

'Well, many of our delivery staff don't when they start. But they learn soon enough!' Mr Cheung patted Ah-Hua on the shoulders. 'Fujianese boys learn fast, don't they?'

Mr Cheung spoke from experience. He's a successful restaurateur, who came over from Hong Kong in the 1980s and has built up a business envied by his rivals in Manchester. He uses lots of workers from Fujian province. Traditionally, the Fujianese used to migrate to South-East Asia and the United States, where they formed (and still maintain) a pattern of chain migration through their long-established networks. But in the past two decades they have recognized a need for their labour in Western Europe, and have broadened their route of migration accordingly. The number of Fujianese migrants into Europe, and particularly Britain, has been growing steadily since the 1990s to fill the labour shortage in the Chinese catering trade as well as the construction industry. Their willingness and their cheap wage have made the Fujianese highly employable, despite their lack of status.

On his first night Ah-Hua was the last to leave the restaurant, at half-past midnight. Mingled with the sense of relief at the prospect of regular employment was a foreboding sense of entrapment. His lodgings had been arranged for him: a mattress in a four-metre-square room in a flat in Longsight, a Man-chester suburb a few miles' bus-ride away. Apart from four mattresses, there was nothing in the room but a poster of a young, heavily made-up Chinese woman wearing designer clothes and posing on a Mercedes. He had no idea who the landlord was. He was told to pay his weekly rent to Boss Yu's contact in Manchester.

To his delight he discovered that Chen – only 'Fryer' during working hours – was one of his room-mates. He offered Chen a Seven Wolves cigarette from Fujian, and they got talking. They found the instant common ground of so many Chinese migrant workers: poor working conditions. Chen told him he'd got his job not from Boss Yu but from an agency in London's Chinatown. He'd been naive. 'I didn't know anyone then,' he told Ah-Hua. 'I wouldn't have resorted to one of those agencies otherwise.' He told Ah-Hua he knew about Boss Yu and his kind. Half the kitchen boys in Manchester's Chinatown were tied to jobs arranged by creditors like Yu.

In spite of the depressing subject of their conversation the two men were soon laughing together about the absurdity of their, and others', situations.

'I haven't laughed like this since I left home,' said Ah-Hua.

'Well, if you can't cry, you've got to laugh,' Chen said. 'Or you'll get very sick in this country.'

Later, while visiting Ah-Hua at Longsight, I met Chen, and he told me his own story of the journey he took to Britain. 'Things were getting tough in Pingtan, and it was hard to find a job. So I went to find work in Fuzhou city [the capital of Fujian province], and started selling seafood. I did that for a few years. But more and more people were selling seafood, and my sales declined. I came to Britain at the beginning of 2000 – I arrived just before the Dover tragedy. It could have been me suffocating in the dark at the back of that lorry. I paid 250,000 RMB [£22,700] to come here. I had to borrow heavily from moneylenders to raise the funds. The snakeheads arranged everything for me. I travelled with two others from Fujian. First we had to take a bus to Guangzhou in southern China. Then we were flown as tourists to Thailand, where we were picked up by a Thai snakehead who housed us for two weeks. They put us on a plane to Hong Kong. From there we flew to France, led by a French snakehead. We were using fake passports produced by the snakeheads. They kept the passports, to prevent us from running away. We had nothing but our plane tickets. In France we were picked up by a local snakehead and taken by train to London. All through that train journey we didn't speak to the man because he was French and we couldn't speak a word of the language. We were led by the local snakehead in each country: led like sheep. We had to put our faith in each one, totally. That was scary. In London, the French snakehead led us on to the underground – the famous London underground! – and handed us over to a Chinese snakehead. In this man's house we had to call our families and tell them we'd arrived safely and they should pay off the fees.'

The day after he arrived in Britain, Chen applied for asylum. That proved to be a pointless waste of time. 'They kept me in a detention centre for a week. It was a really bad place. I didn't speak the language and no one understood me. The staff were quite rough. They never wanted to help you with anything. Within a week, my claim was rejected. I shouldn't have bothered. If your land has disappeared because the government's building an airport on it, and you're not getting any compensation because the local officials took all the money, then you certainly haven't got a case. If you're persecuted for your religion, you still haven't got a case – if you're from Fujian!' Chen laughed. 'The best thing you can do is not to apply for asylum, and never ask for their mercy, but just disappear and depend on yourself. I've learned that.'

I asked him whether he'd paid off his debts to the moneylenders in Fuzhou.

'No, not yet,' he said. 'I've been paying the debt for five long years since I arrived here, and I still owe them 70,000 RMB [£4,600]. I borrowed on an interest rate of two and a half per cent. They put a lot of pressure on my family to pay back the loan. They call every now and then to remind us. So far the pressure has only been verbal. But I need to show the moneylender I'm serious about returning all the money soon. Almost all my earnings go to paying the debt. But the jobs have paid so little! First I had a leafleting job for a Chinese takeaway in north London. They paid me £120 for seven days a week. Meals were included but I had to pay £20 a week for accommodation. This kitchen work's not much better. I'll need another long year in full-time work to pay the debt off. I hope I can keep this job for a year.'

On his second day in Manchester Ah-Hua experienced his first of many gruelling thirteen-hour shifts at the restaurant. He and Chen took the bus to Chinatown, got off at Piccadilly and walked down Prince Street. It was here that Ah-Hua had his first glimpse of an intriguing new side of Manchester life. Two Chinese men and a woman walked past, and Chen asked them how they were doing.

'Not very well today,' one of the men said. 'The *guilao* are all having their Sunday lie-in.' Ah-Hua saw that the man was carrying a pile of DVDs.

The other man put his heavy rucksack on the ground to have a rest. 'But on a good day you can easily make £60 a day,' he said to Ah-Hua. 'And good days aren't rare.'

Ah-Hua had heard rumours of a new-born Chinese pirate-DVD trade in British cities, but this was the first time he'd actually met a seller. He asked the man where he'd got his discs. The man was evasive. 'That way,' was all he said, with a vague wave of the arm.

'Why wouldn't he tell us where he'd got the discs from?' Ah-Hua asked Chen.

'Those guys work for big people,' Chen told him. 'It's better that you don't get to know who's behind the street sales. Sometimes it's safer not to know things. You don't want to get involved in that.'

Sunday in the restaurant was busy. Ah-Hua spent the first two hours, from 11 a.m. to 1 p.m., defrosting and chopping vegetables and meat. At one o'clock, lists of orders started to pour in. The *chao fan mien* took order after order without a second's break. Ah-Hua watched him move his wok up and down mechanically. Sweat ran down his forehead. He never spoke, and his face displayed no emotion.

'I could tell,' Ah-Hua said to me, 'that he was holding in his resentment of the job.'

Ah-Hua and Chen were given stir-frying jobs to do. 'Hurry up! People are waiting!' the chef raised his voice above the noise of the fan and the frying. 'Quick! These two orders! Quick!'

'The chef's voice reminded me of my boss on the construction site in Fuqing,' Ah-Hua told me. 'I never asked him, but I knew from his accent that he came from my hometown. But that didn't bring us together. He only spoke to me when he was shouting at me to hurry up. I later found out that he's the one who liaises with Boss Yu. He's the one who puts Boss Yu in touch with the restaurant. They're not exactly friends, but they have a working relationship. The chef takes an under-the-table commission from Boss Yu for placing people like me in the job. It's an open secret. And it means that the chef's as ruthless as Boss Yu himself.'

After six hours of non-stop work, Ah-Hua and Chen were given half an hour off to have their dinner in a quiet corner on the second floor of the restaurant. Then Ah-Hua was told to do his first delivery to customers in Lower Cambridge Street. The chef gave him verbal directions and an English map that he couldn't read, and off he went, revving up cautiously. He was careful not to be run over by a bus like the untrained Fujianese man in London he'd heard about, who'd been told to do deliveries by his employer and had been permanently disabled in the accident. Half an hour later he found the address in Lower Cambridge Street. It was a friendly gathering and they gave him a generous tip of £2, which Ah-Hua hoped they wouldn't regret on discovering the food had gone cold. He found his way back to the restaurant, and as he'd expected the chef shouted at him. 'Where the hell have you been?

We've been slaving here and you've been off cruising around on your bike!'

After a few days of this work, ending at half-past midnight each night in a bus ride of exhaustion, Ah-Hua and Chen were starting to discuss their options. They realized that they didn't really have any. Both were in debt. Boss Yu's plan was that Ah-Hua would pay off all his debt in two years. 'Two long years,' Ah-Hua said. 'There's nowhere to run. Wherever I go, Boss Yu will find me.'

Chen advised him not to even consider running away. People who ran away and were caught – well, it was better not to think about what happened to them. Ah-Hua understood. He knew he'd have to stick it out.

And so he did. A year and a half later, thinner, worn out, but now an expert fryer and motor-scooter rider, he was still to be found in the kitchen of the same Manchester restaurant, working from 11 a.m. to midnight six days a week. Boss Yu's contact in Manchester came to his flat to pick up the fee every month. Ah-Hua's meals were provided by the restaurant and he didn't have any expenses apart from the £20 weekly rent. He'd been able to save up most of his monthly wages of £480, and had been paying £380 a month to Boss Yu. Now he only had about £3,000 left to pay. He'd be able to do that in eight more months at the restaurant.

But right then, in mid-June 2004, a new opportunity presented itself. An acquaintance of his called Ah-Qiang, who came from Fuqing, called him and told him there was lots of well-paid cockling work at the north end of Morecambe Bay.

For every Chinese person in Britain, the name Morecambe Bay has only one association: death. How could Ah-Qiang be suggesting such a place? The Morecambe Bay cockling tragedy, when twenty-three workers (twenty of them from Fujian) had been drowned, had happened only four months ago.

But Ah-Qiang reassured Ah-Hua. 'He told me that things

had really quietened down there now,' Ah-Hua told me. 'He said people were more aware of safety. He told me that hundreds of Chinese workers were returning to the area. But the thing that really decided it for me was when Ah-Qiang said there'd be *no one above my shoulders*. No one! He promised, "You'll be able to make much quicker cash, and you'll be your own boss." It made me realize how sick, how completely sick I was of being bullied, shouted at, slave-driven by the chef here. The thought of being able to set my own work targets – I couldn't resist.'

The very next morning, Ah-Hua announced to Mr Cheung his decision to leave the restaurant. Mr Cheung told him he'd have to give a week's notice, but Ah-Hua didn't mind. The knowledge that he was about to leave completely changed the job for him. He sang his favourite Taiwanese pop song as he worked. In the evening he called Boss Yu, who'd already been notified of Ah-Hua's job change by the restaurant. Boss Yu made an arrangement that his contact in Liverpool would from now on collect regular payment from Ah-Hua.

So it was time for another coach station, another box of tea-marinated eggs – and another farewell, this time to Chen, Ah-Hua's only friend in England. Maybe events would bring them back together one day.

He was excited to be going to Liverpool, the city of the Beatles. Ah-Qiang met him at the coach station and led him through the streets (which one did the Beatles live in, Ah-Hua kept wondering) to the Kensington area.

'It was run-down,' Ah-Hua said to me. 'I was surprised by how depressed it looked. We arrived at a terrace of houses. Some of them were totally deserted. Ah-Qiang took me into one of the houses. He showed me into the front room, and I couldn't believe it: there were nine mattresses on the floor, and a crowd of people. I just sat down on my mattress. I didn't feel like saying a word.'

The next morning he and fifteen of his flatmates were

transported by minibus on a hundred-mile journey to More-cambe Bay. They reached the coast after an hour and a half and then drove along the bay for another fifty minutes. 'I watched the sunlight glitter on the sea,' Ah-Hua told me. 'It looked so peaceful! So different from what I saw on the news the night of the tragedy!'

At last the minibus stopped by the bay near Askam-in-Furness, to the west of Morecambe Bay. Everyone got off and put on their yellow jackets and Wellington boots. Other teams were arriving in their minibuses and vans. The workers walked out on to the sands. The hundred-strong crowd gradually broke up into groups of two or three. The tide was down. To Ah-Hua it looked as if the sea had been drained away by pulling out a plug. All he could see was miles of brown sand as far as the horizon. Underneath his feet lay the cockles which had engendered the corporate greed and human desperation that had led to the horrifying events of that February.

He knelt down and started to dig with his rake. There were lots of cockles, but they seemed small. He dug and dug, and loaded the cockles into a sack. Within an hour, he was exhausted and stiff. The midday sun was fierce, and the skin on his face felt dry. Then he remembered what Ah-Qiang had told him: 'There'll be no one above your shoulders.' It's true, he thought, and stood up to stretch. No one was going to come after him to push him to work. But (as another worker had grimly reminded him on the minibus) if he didn't keep going under the burning sun or the pouring rain, he'd be begging on the streets.

So he continued to dig. At the end of the day, he was paid £15 for three bags of cockles. The price for these cockles was lower, he was told, because their quality was inferior. He wasn't pleased. He'd earned the least in his team. This was less than the wages he'd been earning in Manchester's Chinatown.

He had a foreboding of a terrible new pattern of his life,

which went like this: you move on in order to try to make things better, but, always, things actually get worse.

When they arrived back at the flat in Liverpool they saw some English graffiti on the wall of the house: 'Fuck off, Chinkies.' Ah-Hua couldn't read the words but his flatmates told him they were hostile gestures from local youths, who had nothing to do with them but just hated them anyway.

In the overcrowded kitchen of the flat that evening, the conversation was depressing. People were worrying about the police, who'd been seen rounding up Chinese cocklers on the bay. There'd been a police raid on the beach. They'd broken up a fight – a fight not between rival teams of cocklers, but between the bodyguards of the different teams. 'Cockles aren't very good quality these days,' one of Ah-Hua's flatmates explained to him. 'Too many people are cockling, you see, and the bay's been exhausted. We have to keep moving around, looking for better cockles. The ones here, in the northern part of the bay, are pretty small and don't sell for much money. Some teams have bodyguards to stop rival teams from coming to the same bay. These guys are causing a lot of trouble on the sands. The English newspapers don't understand. They think it's us, the cocklers, making trouble here. We're peaceful people, just working here for a living. We don't want violence.'

Inferior cockles, overcrowded accommodation, long daily journeys, threats from locals, in-fighting on the beach . . . why hadn't Ah-Qiang warned him about all of this? Ah-Hua felt he might have made the wrong decision to come to Liverpool. But he couldn't turn back now. The kitchen job was gone, and he must face up to the reality of life on the sands. He must keep earning: Boss Yu's contact would be calling by in three weeks' time to pick up the month's cash.

He went back to work on the beach the following day, and knelt on the sand for hours without a break, digging cockles frantically. He earned £25 that day.

As he collected his money that evening, he saw a Chinese man sitting alone on the beach, having a break. He went up and spoke to him. The man was Gao Jun – the same Gao Jun whom we last saw leaving Selsey and the salad factory behind him. He told Ah-Hua what had happened since. He'd been persuaded by a contact from Tienjin to move to Morecambe Bay to work as a cockle picker. He'd travelled by coach from London Victoria to Morecambe, only to find that his Fujianese cockling boss was going to cram him, along with twelve others, into a semi-derelict hotel room above a run-down pub in a back street of the town. The worst thing, he told Ah-Hua, was that there was not even much work around. This was because of the raids the police were conducting at the moment. 'The boss is terrified and won't let us out to work. So now we can only work a day here and a day there, and we spend most of our time in the hotel, waiting for the bad time to pass. I don't know how long we can last like this, trying to make a living and hiding ourselves from the authorities and the public all the time.'

Inevitably (in this new pattern of life Ah-Hua had found himself in) things got worse. Two days later he heard that a team of Chinese cocklers had been arrested on their way back from Morecambe Bay to Liverpool. They'd been taken away and detained. One of them, a thirty-year-old from Shenyang, was being kept in a cell at Caenarfon police station in North Wales. He'd come to England only four months ago to work to raise funds for his father's medical treatment. Like Ah-Hua, he'd only paid off half the fee on arrival, so the snakehead had been on his back ever since. They'd arranged for him to work as a cockle picker so he could be monitored and chased up for regular payment, but he'd been arrested a week into the job. Others arrested in the team had been sent to Oakington detention centre near Cambridge. They claimed asylum immediately. Phone calls were being made between Ah-Hua's flatmates and the detainees who were asking for help.

Ah-Hua felt extremely unsafe. Would he be next? The thought of being arrested was terrible after all he'd gone through. He only had £3,000 left to pay off, and he'd be a free man. He certainly couldn't afford to get deported: deportees without documents were heavily fined on arrival back in China, and Ah-Hua hadn't even paid off the fees for coming.

His fear was shared. All around him, his flatmates were talking on their phones, making arrangements to leave. A few were trying to go back to work in Chinese restaurants and takeaways in London. Some were looking for jobs in Birmingham. One or two were looking for local Chinese-restaurant jobs in Liverpool. The team was dispersing.

Ah-Hua called his friend Chen in Manchester. Chen was well connected: if there was a job going, he'd know about it. But Chen told him the restaurants were full at the moment: they weren't recruiting. He said he'd look out for any vacancies, but couldn't promise anything. So Ah-Hua waited. And as he waited he seemed to feel the police net closing in on him. On the local news he saw there'd been another fight: the hired bodyguards of a team of Chinese cockle pickers had attacked their rival team's van and injured the workers with their rakes. Speeding away from the incident, the van had collided with a lorry, slewing across the carriageway and landing on its back. Three of the van's passengers were in a critical condition in hospital. Ah-Hua was frightened. Although his own team hadn't been involved in the incident, he couldn't help feeling as if his own undocumented status was being exposed. Rumours were flying around: the police were coming. Chinese whispers were intimidating the entire cockle-picking community in Liverpool.

Ah-Hua no longer felt safe walking the streets. The sound of a police siren made him want to run for cover. He had nightmares at night.

'Then I knew it: I had to get out of that place,' he told me.

'I couldn't risk getting deported. That would be worse than anything. I couldn't let it happen to me.'

At six the next morning, while the others in his room were still asleep on their mattresses, Ah-Hua left the flat and the cockle-picking world behind him. He felt guilty and exhilarated, like a deserter. Without turning back, he jumped on the coach back to Manchester.

'I never thought I'd be so pleased to see Manchester again,' Ah-Hua said to me. 'As I got off the coach the air actually seemed lighter. No local people staring! No policemen spying!'

But also – no job. He had to go back to the restaurant in Chinatown to beg for work. 'Mr Cheung, the manager I'd worked under for eighteen months, spoke to me as if I was a total stranger. He told me there was only casual work in the kitchen, and he'd call me if I was needed.'

Once again, Ah-Hua felt the sweat of fear on his forehead. In two weeks' time Boss Yu's men would come to visit. What if he couldn't pay them? That wasn't an option. He'd have to find the money somehow. As he walked along Prince Street, the encounter with the Fujianese DVD sellers on his first day flashed through his mind. '*You can make £60 on a good day. And good days aren't rare!*'

He called Chen and asked him for the phone numbers of some of the DVD sellers he knew.

'Chen warned me,' Ah-Hua told me. 'He said, "Didn't I tell you, you don't want to be doing that kind of work. You'll be working for the wrong people." But my debt gave me no choice, you see? I told him I'd take responsibility for my decision. Reluctantly he gave me some numbers, and I dialled one. I got through to a Fujianese man called Lin Yun.'

Lin Yun turned out to be an approachable, straightforward man in his mid-thirties from Fuqing, just like Ah-Hua. He warned Ah-Hua that DVD-selling was a dodgy world to go into. But Ah-Hua insisted he was desperate for a job. Lin Yun agreed to introduce him to the *piantou* (head of films) – the man in charge of making the DVD copies. He took Ah-Hua to a second-floor flat in Longsight.

'These people move around a lot, but they're here for the moment,' Lin Yun explained. A tall Chinese man with dyed light-brown hair opened the door. Three Chinese men were sitting in the room, smoking. They looked Ah-Hua up and down, searching him with their eyes. 'So why d'you want to do this?' one of them – the *piantou* – asked. Ah-Hua could tell from the man's accent that he was Fujianese, but he couldn't place which town he was from.

'I need the money. I'll work hard.'

The *piantou* stood up now. 'It's got to last, you understand? It's not something you pick up and drop the moment you want to.' He spoke in a bored, mechanical way, as if he'd said these words hundreds of times before. 'This isn't a game. It's a business.'

Ah-Hua nodded. But he was puzzled. He'd always thought 'pirate sales' were something you could choose to enter and leave as it suited you – a gap-filling 'black job' when you were in between jobs.

He'd soon find out how mistaken he was.

The *piantou* opened the door and went into the next room. Ah-Hua saw towers of DVDs in there, reaching to the ceiling. He could also see dozens of DVD burners and printers. The man came out of the room and handed him a pile of DVD copies. 'Take as many as you need,' he said. 'You buy them for £1.75 a disc, and sell them for £3.'

On Lin Yun's advice, Ah-Hua paid for fifty discs. Before leaving the flat, he asked the *piantou* where in Fujian he came from. 'From Dong Bi village,' the man replied.

As they left the flat, Lin Yun told Ah-Hua that Dong Bi wasn't just a village. 'Dong Bi is known as the biggest gang in Manchester. They've been dominant in this city for seven or eight years now. They also operate in London.'

Ah-Hua didn't like the sound of this. Was he, yet again, finding out alarming information just when it was too late?

'Running the DVD trade is only one part of their business,' Lin Yun went on. 'They also charge protection fees, they profit from high-interest loans and they bodyguard whoever pays them. You name it, they'll do it – anything to make a profit. They're ruthless. Some of them are operating in Fujian too. The local authorities in Dong Bi know about the gang and have done nothing, apparently. People say you can get away with murder in Dong Bi if you have cash. Just bribe the village chiefs!'

Ah-Hua pointed out sadly that corruption happens in most villages in China. 'Tell me which local officials can't be bribed!'

As they walked back to the centre of town, Lin Yun went on to explain how the Dong Bi gangsters find victims among Chinese people without legal status – like them. He told Ah-Hua how he'd come into the DVD-selling job. He'd managed to pay off the snakehead's fee of 250,000 RMB on arrival in England six years ago, but he still owed money to the moneylenders back in China. For the first five years he'd worked himself to the bone as a kitchen porter in Manchester's Chinatown. He'd been so good at the job that he'd been promoted to assistant chef. He'd worked twelve hours a day, six days a week for £140. Then a year ago a Fujianese friend had called him and told him he could earn much more working in a restaurant in Lancaster. So he went to Lancaster – but it was terrible there. The chef charged him an introduction fee of £150, and then bullied him so much that it was impossible for him to stay. So, six months ago, he'd come back to Manchester – only to find that all the restaurant jobs had gone.

'Only six months ago,' he said to Ah-Hua, 'people were being chased out of Chinese restaurants and takeaways on to the Morecambe Bay sands. Now people are coming this way again, just like us, moving back after being chased away from Morecambe Bay. And the Dong Bi gang comes in to exploit this situation. They know very well we have no choice.'

Neither Lin Yun nor Ah-Hua was aware of the true financial context of their job. The pirate-DVD-selling trade in Britain is worth about £500 million a year. At the bottom of this massive trade, run by organized criminals, Lin Yun, Ah-Hua and 10,000 similar sellers across the country make just enough money to survive. DVD-selling is in fact seen as one of the most 'typical' Chinese jobs around. Any Chinese-looking person with a rucksack on his back could be mistaken for a DVD seller. I have experienced this on the street myself numerous times. 'DVDs?' many passers-by have asked me.

Ah-Hua described his first day of DVD-selling: 'I was very self-conscious. I spoke hardly any English apart from "thank you", "sorry", and "three pounds". At first I followed a few footsteps behind Lin Yun. "DVD! DVD!" he called. I noticed that about one in five people stopped. I started to call out too. "DVD!" A young man stopped to look through my copies, and he asked for two! He gave me £6! That cheered me up. It didn't seem hard at all. Our morale was high.'

They walked on, through the Arndale shopping centre, looking for customers. 'Some chubby teenaged girls came up to us, and asked us what films we'd got and how much they were each. "T-r-ee pounds," I told them. They said they hadn't got the money. They said they'd pay us back tomorrow. We were quite intimidated. The girls were ten centimetres taller and ten kilos heavier than we were. Lin Yun just nodded hesitantly, and handed the DVD over to them. They walked off, laughing their heads off. I asked Lin Yun, "Why did you do that?" and he said, "Listen, I know these kids. They pick on Chinese people. If you say no to them, you'll regret it. Let them take it. It's only one copy."

'"But if we did that all the time," I said, "we wouldn't be

making any money at all."' So we decided to go somewhere else. And we had much better luck. In St Patrick's Square I managed to sell fifteen copies in an hour. £45, just in one hour!'

Lin Yun congratulated Ah-Hua at the end of that first day. 'You did well. But you'll have to keep it up.'

Ah-Hua asked him what he meant, exactly.

'Well, as I explained to you, Dong Bi controls the trade. They'll pressurize you into selling more and more.'

From the next day, Ah-Hua and Lin Yun got up early each morning in their different lodgings, took the bus into town and worked from street to street, from pub to pub, for seven or eight hours a day. With a map in their hands, they learned to find their way around the city on foot. They built up regular contacts to whom they sold dozens of copies. They also paid a pub landlord to allow them to sell DVDs inside his pub, where they became acquainted with the locals. Occasionally, they'd get complaints from customers who weren't happy with the quality of the copies. Sometimes they were chased by boys trying to rob them of their DVDs, and once they were spat at by passers-by. Undeterred by all this, they managed to earn more than £40 a day each. And, every day, Ah-Hua counted the number of weeks to go till all his debts would be paid off to Boss Yu.

They carried on working through the summer and autumn. 'Sales went up and down,' Ah-Hua told me. 'On good days, when the sun was shining and people were out, we could earn up to £70 a day. On bad days, when there was trouble from local youths, or there were too many police around, we could make about £40. And at last – the day came! I prepared my final payment of £460 for Boss Yu's man, and handed it over. "You're clear," he told me. I felt like a new man. I called my wife to tell her the good news. She brought me back to reality. The snakehead's fee was paid, but we now had to begin to pay off the loans, on an interest rate of two and a half per cent per month, to the moneylender in Fuqing from whom we'd borrowed money for the first half of the snakehead's fee. My wife had been struggling to pay back some of the loans with her tiny monthly wages, but the interest rate had gone up faster than she could cope with.'

At virtually the same time as this bad news came a dwindling in Ah-Hua's rate of DVD sales. Lin Yun was experiencing the same thing. A variety of factors seemed to be causing this. It was partly that customers were getting tired of the poor quality of mass-produced DVD copies. Also, since May 2004, there had been a tightening up of the immigration controls laid down in Article 8 of the Asylum and Immigration Act, 1996. Restaurant and takeaway employers could now be fined for employing 'illegals' and failing to check up on their employees' papers. So they'd become reluctant to take on undocumented workers – which meant that more and more of these people, desperate for jobs, had taken up the illegal job of selling DVDs on the streets. Competition among sellers was growing. On top of that, there seemed to be more police on the streets, which made the doubly forbidden trade – both illegal and conducted by 'illegals' – extremely difficult to carry out.

It was obvious that Ah-Hua should leave and find a job elsewhere, but he soon found there was no easy way out. One day he arrived at the headquarters to pick up some DVDs, and overheard two sellers from Fuqing telling the bosses they intended to leave the trade and go back to working in restaurants.

'A Dong Bi gang member stopped them from leaving,' Ah-Hua told me. 'He said to them, "It's your choice, but, if you leave, the consequences will be your own responsibility." The men had some knowledge of Dong Bi's reputation. They decided to stay in the trade. It was at that moment that I understood the kind of trouble I was in.'

The new dark pattern of his life seemed to repeat itself yet again. Within days, fears for his safety became immediate. As he was picking up some DVDs a gang member confronted him. 'How come you're taking fewer and fewer copies now, when you come here? Where have your customers gone? Are you actually selling?'

Ah-Hua replied nervously that he didn't know the exact reason – it was just getting harder to sell.

'Well, try a bit harder,' the gang member said, with a calm voice which nonetheless terrified Ah-Hua.

Living under the control of the gang became a huge weight on Ah-Hua's shoulders. Selling ten copies a day wasn't good enough for Dong Bi, but the sales wouldn't go up. Ah-Hua and Lin Yun relied mostly on regular customers in town, such as the owner of a corner shop and two middle-aged men in a pub who had a penchant for erotic films and kept asking for them. But the number of regulars was declining.

As the days went by, Ah-Hua's trips to the *piantou* in Long-sight became journeys of fear. He continued to hear stories of sellers being attacked by gang members, and he dreaded being attacked himself. How could he get out of this trap?

Then, one day in autumn 2005, his wife told him on the phone that the moneylenders had called for payment. 'I knew I had to do something to push up my earnings,' he told me. 'The news about the moneylenders left me no choice. I'd have to leave the DVD trade. I wasn't selling enough copies.' He knew no one could help him but himself. Should he run away to another city? But he'd heard about sellers who'd run away, and he knew what happened to people like that. You couldn't run away from Dong Bi. He decided that the only way out was to confront the gang members and tell the truth.

It was Ah-Hua's worst trip to date, that bus journey to Longsight to break the news. He arrived at the *piantou*'s head-quarters and informed the gang members that he intended to return to work in the restaurant trade. He waited for coercion, but it didn't come. He left the flat.

That night five Dong Bi gang members knocked on his

door. As he opened it, they pushed their way in. They beat him up till he lay helpless on the floor. He felt blood running down his face. Then they dragged him out of the flat, bundled him into a car, blindfolded him and drove off into the night. He had no idea where he was being taken. He thought he heard one of them say 'Mo-s-ton', the northern suburb of Manchester. It was only when they locked him up in their flat half an hour later that he realized he was being kidnapped rather than killed.

'I was in that flat for three weeks,' Ah-Hua told me. I could see the anguish in his face as he spoke of it. 'My hands were tied behind my back. I had no contact with the outside world. I couldn't even reach into my pocket to see if my mobile phone was still there. The gang gave me water and fed me with scraps of their leftovers. I was losing all sense of the world around me. I kept hearing the name "Yu Jian" being mentioned. I got the sense that this guy was the leader of the Dong Bi gang. Then one morning a gang member came up to me and said what I'd been dreading more than anything else in the world.

'"We know your family in Fuqing. Pay us £12,000, or your family will be in hell." It was my nightmare come true. How could they have located my family? How could we possibly afford this money?'

Of course, they'd located the family very easily from Ah-Hua's mobile phone. They pushed the phone to his ear. 'Call your family now. Tell them to find the money.'

'So I was coerced into asking my wife to borrow more money from the moneylender. When she heard I'd been kidnapped she cried desperately on the phone. The burden of keeping the family above subsistence level was bad enough. The thought of borrowing more money was too much to bear. She became uncontrollably upset. I tried to reassure her, but I'd run out of words. I felt as hopeless as she did. I felt so guilty for bringing my family into this state of despair. But my wife knew she mustn't collapse and give up. She was overcome by fear:

fear of losing me, fear for the safety of her son and family, fear of losing everything we'd fought for so far. We had to fight on. Within a week, she managed to borrow £7,000 from the moneylender in town.

'I told the gang members that was all we could get. I begged them to be satisfied with that. They beat me up again. But I simply had no more to give. They decided to make do with the £7,000 and to let me go. I left the flat, half-dead after that ordeal. But I couldn't report the kidnapping to the police for fear of deportation.'

Shortly after this, Lin Yun (who had also dared to tell the Dong Bi gang that he was intending to leave the DVD trade) was attacked and robbed. Later I met Lin Yun, and he told me what had happened to him.

'I was living in a flat in Longsight with seventeen other Fujianese. We'd just arrived home from a hard day's DVD-selling in the street, and we were confronted by five gang members who pushed through the door with guns, knives and sticks in their hands. They said, "We've come to take protection fees. Take out all your money, each of you, now!" No one dared resist. Everyone knew these guys could do real harm. Everyone took their day's earnings out of their pockets: £60, £40, whatever we had. I'd only earned £30 that day. Then they said, "All the cash in the house, on the table, now! If we search the house and find more, you'll lose your leg." On hearing this, one of my terrified flatmates opened the wardrobe and took out his £200 from the bottom drawer. Others took out money from their suitcases. "Well done, everyone," the gang member said. We watched him count out the cash. It came to £1,000. He put the money in his pocket and said, "Now you're all covered. Well done."

'I thought he'd finished, but then he turned to me. "Come over here, Lin Yun," he said. "Listen here. You've pushed us over the limit." I was dreading what was coming next. "Put £3,600 on the table. This is a penalty for you." I told him I

hadn't got that amount of money. I said I'd stay in the trade –
I wouldn't try to leave again. "You think you can get away
with it that easily?" the man said. He raised his eyebrow to the
other gang members and said, "Teach him." They pulled me to
the middle of the room and beat me up, right in front of my
flatmates. "This lesson is called *sha ji jing hou* [killing a chicken
to warn and set an example to the monkeys]," the man who
gave the order said, clapping his hands as the men kicked me
and spat at me.

'I was left with deep bruises on my arms and legs. I couldn't
walk for two weeks. I thought I might have an internal injury. But there was no way I was going to hospital. It's an
unspoken rule amongst us Fujianese undocumented workers
that unless you're about to lose your life, you don't try to access
the health service. There's no point. You're not entitled to it.
You'll just expose your status to the authorities. And, as a rule,
no one reports robberies or attacks to the police. So the next
day (while I started to recover from my injuries in the flat)
my co-workers just went back to their street sales as normal –
as if nothing had happened. They told me there was almost a
feeling of relief amongst them: they'd been robbed so at least
they'd be immune from these attacks for a while.'

Shortly after this they heard the news that Yu Jian – the Dong
Bi gang leader Ah-Hua had heard being talked about during his
kidnapping – had been arrested and jailed. They knew the news
was good – but had no idea how long he'd be in prison for. The
imprisoning of Yu Jian didn't bring an end to their life under
the control of the gang, which slipped through the police's net
and continued (indeed, continues) its ruthless existence in spite
of the jailing of one of its leaders. As the Fujianese DVD sellers
told me in spring 2006, 'The gang can get away with anything.
And no one seems to be able to do anything about it.' I spoke
to Wai Yin, a leading Chinese community organization in
Manchester. They said they felt powerless about the level of
violence against Chinese asylum seekers who'd failed in their

applications and had to resort to illegal DVD-selling as their only means of survival.

Wai Yin's assistant director Lisa Mok told me, 'About fifteen Chinese asylum seekers come to Wai Yin and ask for help every week. The majority of them sell pirate DVDs and other merchandise on the street, if they're not in low-paid catering jobs.'

These people, like Ah-Hua, are the most visible minority in the city, yet the most detached from mainstream society. The prevalence of gang control in their lives and work means that they're mostly outside the reach of the established Chinese community in Manchester.

After his kidnapping, Ah-Hua managed to keep out of sight for a while, and slipped back into a job in Chinatown as a kitchen porter. He's one of the few lucky ones, who has managed to leave the DVD trade behind him. He tells me it won't be long before he pays off all his debt to the moneylender in Fuqing. He says he's looking forward to the day when he can start to make a better life for his family.

5. Middle of the Kingdom

No idea which direction we're heading in. But I know we're
being sent to a far-away place to work today. Eight pounds,
I can make in a day, when the sun's out. That will pay for
my food for the whole week, and leave a bit to spare.

— a female Chinese worker on a leek farm in Northamptonshire
January 2007

In a bustling avenue of an affluent district in Birmingham, children were pouring out of school on to the pavement, jostling
and chatting with each other as they walked home to tea.
Dragging her suitcase, Ailing (not her real name) wove her way
through the crowd. She was looking for number 57.

Speaking no English, Ailing had recently arrived in England
from the southern province of Zhejiang, the smallest province
in China. Although Zhejiangese people have an established
migrant community in France (over half of the Chinese
migrants in France are from Zhejiang), they're still new in
Britain, numbering not more than a thousand in the whole
country. With no established social network to get in touch
with on her arrival, Ailing had no means to look for work
except to resort to Chinese employment agencies in London,
who charge a fee ranging from £80 to £200, depending on
how new you appear to be.

She'd called twenty agencies to enquire about jobs. Being
well over the age of thirty (a disadvantage if you're applying to
be a waitress), and with no catering experience, she'd decided
to seek domestic work. 'You want family domestic work or

massage-parlour domestic work?' – that was the first question the agencies asked. Ailing had no idea that 'massage parlour' was a euphemism for 'brothel' until her flatmates told her.

Domestic jobs aren't always easy to find in England, the agencies had said to her: more and more women are coming from China to fill domestic vacancies. But she'd struck lucky: one of the agencies found her a job as a nanny in a private household in Birmingham. Gratefully, Ailing agreed to pay a £100 introduction fee and took a coach up the motorway. And now here she was, in front of a cream-painted detached house with large pot plants in the front garden. Number 57. The agency had told her she'd be working for a British-Vietnamese family by the surname of Trung (the name has been changed). She took a deep breath and rang the doorbell.

A pregnant East-Asian-looking woman opened the door. 'Are you Mrs Trung?' Ailing asked. The woman nodded and invited her in. Ailing politely introduced herself and asked her new employer whether she spoke Mandarin. 'A little,' the woman replied with a heavy Vietnamese accent.

Ailing followed Mrs Trung along the shiny marble hallway into the sitting room. It was a large space filled with sunlight from the bright, dustless front window. Ailing had never been inside an English home.

'This is so nice!' she said.

Mrs Trung invited her to sit down while she went to fetch her husband. Ailing sank into the dark-brown leather sofa and looked around in amazement at the built-in shelves, the Chinese porcelain vases, the wide-screen TV on its metallic stand, the hi-fi and the tall loudspeakers. A minute later Mr Trung came into the room. He was a broad-chested, well-built man in his forties. 'Welcome, welcome, Ms Chen,' he said in good Mandarin, shaking Ailing's hand heavily.

The couple showed her around the house and explained her daily duties: looking after their two-year-old daughter, cleaning and dusting the rooms and mopping the kitchen floor daily,

washing and ironing clothes, food shopping at Sainsbury's and
Wing Yip superstore, and cooking for the family. This was
not just a nanny job, Ailing realized: she was to be cook and
housemaid as well.

It was a live-in job, and Ailing was provided with a tiny box
room at the end of the corridor beyond the kitchen. She was
content with this. At least there was a window in her room,
allowing the sunlight in from the garden.

Cheerfully she started her first day's work at six the next
morning, making breakfast for her employers: congee for Mr
Trung, a few slices of toast for Mrs Trung. Then she gave warm
milk to the two-year-old, while Mr Trung got ready for work:
running a Vietnamese-Chinese takeaway in town. Business was
going well, he told Ailing. 'And I have three people working
for me.' Mrs Trung showed her how to prepare a chicken
stew as lunch for her two-year-old. 'The baby needs a lot of
nutrition. You need to make a stew every day.' Ailing thought
it was too heavy for a young child, but she obeyed her hostess's
instructions.

From her first working day, Ailing felt uneasy in Mr Trung's
presence. She was not used to being stared at by men –
certainly not by someone who was her employer. She felt
intimidated by his gaze, and was relieved when, mid-morning,
he went off to work. Only then did she feel able to take a
break. Mrs Trung asked her to sit down and have lunch with
her. Ailing noticed how heavily pregnant she was: due at the
end of the month. She told Ailing she'd been the manageress of
the takeaway before she'd become pregnant, and she'd enjoyed
the busy life, answering the phone, taking orders. Now all that
had stopped, and her life felt empty.

Mrs Trung needed someone to listen to her. She talked
on, but Ailing's thoughts travelled thousands of miles away,
back to China and to her own young son. He was eight years
old – an active and bright boy, as she liked to tell everyone.
As a divorced single parent in China, Ailing had felt unable to

provide a good enough life for him. She'd lived with a sense of regret for years. Eventually, she'd borrowed 140,000 RMB (around £9,300) to procure a six-month business-visitor visa to come to England, in order to try to earn a better life for him. Now he was being looked after by Ailing's retired parents. She felt guilty about asking them to do this, as well as guilty about leaving him.

She was in England with a single mission: to improve the life of her family. She'd use every minute here to earn the money her son and parents so desperately needed. Her wage for this job with the Trungs was £180 a week. Her Chinese flatmate Yuan, with whom she'd shared a room in Oval on her arrival in London, told her this wasn't much for England. But Ailing knew this wage would bring the longed-for rise in standard of living for her son and her parents. As a food-shop worker in China, she'd been earning one-twelfth of that amount.

From her first day she worked hard from dawn till night to justify the wage. Each day she was invited to sit down to lunch with Mrs Trung, who seemed to find it therapeutic to talk to her. She felt fortunate in having such a kind employer, who spoke to her almost as an equal; she'd heard stories of other Chinese domestic workers who were treated as subhumans, paid a pittance and made to live on the family's leftovers. Mrs Trung confided to Ailing that she felt neglected by her husband, who hadn't been attentive to her during her pregnancy. Ailing knew (but didn't say) that Mr Trung was instead giving special flirtatious attention to *her*, which she was trying hard to avoid. She dreaded his return from work at midnight. When she heard his key in the door, she quickly retired to her room.

The harassment increased. At breakfast time, Mr Trung would pat Ailing on the shoulders for no reason, or touch her back. She'd move away and ignore him. But he persisted. This went on for a month. Then one day Mrs Trung went to visit her mother at the other side of town. It happened to be Mr Trung's day off. Ailing was told to prepare his lunch, and to take the clothes out of the dryer and fold them up in her room.

Mr Trung let himself into her room. He stared at her. 'You know, I really like you,' he said, leaning against the door. Ailing ignored him. 'Did you hear me?' he said, more loudly.

'I heard you, Mr Trung,' Ailing replied, without looking up.

'Listen. It's your fortune that I like you. You understand?'

Before Ailing could decide how to respond to this, Mr Trung moved towards her, grabbed her and pushed her on to her bed. She tried to push him away but all his weight was on her, and he started to rape her. She screamed for help. He shut her up with his hand. The more she screamed, the heavier his hand pressed down. She was finding it hard to breathe. The following moments were sheer darkness. Ailing gave up struggling, and simply waited for the nightmare to end.

When he was finished, he rushed out of the room and shut the door behind him. Ailing felt as if she were paralysed. Her arms and legs were covered in bruises. Nausea overwhelmed her so she could hardly move. She just lay there and cried and cried. She'd prepared herself for so many hardships in Britain – hard work, low pay, cramped conditions – but not for this worst of all possible experiences, to be raped by her employer. How would she tell anyone? How, as an illegal worker, could she report this to the police? How was she going to support her son after this?

She heard the front door opening. Mrs Trung was back. She heard her voice, and Mr Trung's. Then there was a knock on the door. 'Ailing, is everything all right?' Mrs Trung asked. 'You haven't done any food shopping for me. Are you going to prepare dinner?'

Ailing dragged herself to the bedroom door. She felt sick. She could still smell Mr Trung's aftershave on her. She let Mrs Trung in.

'What's happening, Ailing?'

'Nothing, Mrs Trung.' What excuse could she come up with

for not fulfilling her tasks? The painful bruises on her body stopped her from thinking. Being pushed for an answer by her attacker's wife, she burst into tears.

'Mrs Trung, please don't hate me. It wasn't my fault. Mr Trung raped me.'

'What nonsense are you talking?' said Mrs Trung. 'Don't you speak to me like this!'

Ailing showed her the bruises on her arms. Mrs Trung, horrified, shook her head in disbelief. She was shivering with shock as she left the room. In the next half-hour Ailing heard Mrs Trung's sobbing and her husband's repeated apologies from the sitting room.

What about me? she thought to herself. I've lost everything.

Ailing took her suitcase out from under the bed and started to pack her clothes, knowing that the news of her dismissal was just outside the bedroom door. She reached for her mobile phone and called her former flatmate Yuan in London, her only friend in England, the one person in whom she could confide.

This was when I heard what had happened – on the very afternoon of the rape, in the spring of 2005. Yuan knew me, and having no idea how to respond to this appalling event, called me for advice. My first thought was that Ailing should call the police. But Ailing could speak no English, Yuan said. Yuan volunteered to make the call, and so did I.

But at that moment, back in the Trung household, the married couple stopped talking and walked towards Ailing's room. Ailing asked Yuan to stay on the line while she opened the door to them. Thus Yuan was able to eavesdrop on the conversation which ensued.

'You can't work here any more, you know,' Mrs Trung said. Her eyes were swollen with tears. 'But please tell us what we can do to help you.'

'I'm going to the police,' Ailing replied. 'I'm going to report the rape.'

'No, you can't do that, Ailing! No one will believe you,' said Mrs Trung. 'Please don't go to the police.'

'They'll deport you back to China,' said Mr Trung. 'You won't be able to work in England again.'

His ruthless remarks made Ailing even more determined to expose him. 'Even if they deport me,' she said, 'I'll still need to report you. I don't know how many women you've done this to. But you can't get away with it this time.' Then Ailing held up the phone in her hand. 'Do you want to speak to my friend about this? He thinks I should go to the police.'

Mr Trung was speechless. The fact that someone outside the house knew about the rape threw him into a state of panic. Mrs Trung was sobbing helplessly again. She went up to Ailing and knelt down in front of her. 'Ailing, my sister, I treated you well, didn't I?'

Ailing nodded.

'I beg you, please, sister, forgive my husband. Forgive us for the pain we brought you. We're willing to pay you, to compensate you. Ailing, please forgive, for the sake of the child soon to be born.'

This emotional display made Ailing feel a mixture of pity for the helpless, heavily pregnant, neglected woman, and contempt for her as she tried to condone and cover up her husband's attack.

'We'll give you £500 for compensation,' Mr Trung said with no emotion.

'Five hundred pounds? Do you think you can get away with it for *that*?' Ailing said. 'I've lost my job because of what you did to me. I'm not prepared to accept this small amount of money.'

Then Mrs Trung started pleading again. 'Please, Ailing, sister, have pity on me! Our baby is going to be born soon. Five hundred is all we can afford. Please, Ailing!' She was on her knees, begging again. Ailing felt an overwhelming disgust. The sight of her remorseless attacker and his wife, completely without dignity, made her feel sick all over again. She couldn't continue this battle any longer. There was no strength left in her. More than anything, she needed to be away from these people and never to see them again. At that moment she decided to accept the compensation. She knew that if she wanted to stay in England she had no choice. Mr Trung's words were horribly true: if she wanted to avoid being exposed as an illegal worker and deported, she'd have to keep the rape a secret.

'Fine. Five hundred pounds. Give me the money. I'm leaving now.'

They handed over the cash. Mrs Trung offered to drive her to the station. Ailing refused. 'Just call a cab for me.'

It was raining. Ailing looked out of the taxi. The city was as damp and misty as it had been on the day she'd arrived, only a month ago. She hadn't had the chance to get to know it. Now she just wanted to put it behind her.

That evening, I asked Yuan to pass Ailing's phone number to me, and I called her myself. Ailing began to speak to me about her ordeal. She asked Yuan and me not to report the rape to the police. This was her choice, and it would have seemed wrong to go against it.

From this moment I was in touch with Ailing, and followed what happened to her next. First, she spent £30 of her compensation money on a train ticket back to London. Yuan assured her he had a place for her to sleep while she looked for new work. She sat on the bench on the platform, in a state of tearful shock. To pull herself back together, she called home and talked to her son. The sound of his innocent, bright voice gave her the strength she desperately needed. 'You'll be good for your grandparents, won't you? I'm sending some money home tomorrow.'

From that moment, Ailing told me, she did not shed another tear. 'I knew I must remain strong for my son and my parents.'

According to the employment agencies that send Chinese

women into domestic jobs, most employers are high-income couples, many of them shop or restaurant owners. I asked the agencies whether they checked or monitored these employers for domestic jobs. Mrs Ouyang runs an agency in south London recruiting mainly northern and north-eastern Chinese women into domestic jobs. She acknowledges that there are risks involved, and says there have been safety concerns among workers. 'A woman was introduced into a housekeeping job by another agency,' she told me, 'and she came to our agency after she had to leave that job as a result of constant sexual harassment from her employer – he made her stay in the room with him while he watched porn videos. We need to watch out for bad employers like that.' She said she would not send female workers into what she called a 'high-risk household' if she received more than one complaint about it.

However, I found out that there's no proper monitoring system in place among these employment agencies. The majority operate like the one Ailing had resorted to: they're unregistered companies that can fold up at any time. I spoke to the man in charge at Annie Agency in London's Chinatown, known as 'the agency by the Chinatown pagoda', which advertises numerous domestic jobs and has hundreds of undocumented workers paying registration fees to be introduced to jobs. He informed me that his company is formally called 'Chinese Community Consultants Ltd' – a typically official-sounding name – which (as expected) turns out not to be a registered company. He insisted there were no physical safety risks involved in domestic work, and that he always makes sure he has knowledge of the backgrounds of employers to whom he sends workers.

'How do you ensure that?' I asked him.

He paused, and said, 'Mostly by phone.'

Indeed, Annie Agency, typical of the majority of the agencies, wouldn't have any idea how to ensure that workers aren't sent to employers like the Trungs.

Back in the flat near Oval in London, Ailing was desperate to find a new job in the days that followed. Yuan advised her not to go back to the same agency – and she didn't think she'd be able to trust an agency again. So – like many other Chinese newcomers – she just began asking around.

She'd heard her flatmates talking about someone known as 'Cong Lao-Da' – a nickname, meaning 'Onion Number One'. This man, they said, recruited Chinese people from all over the country and sent them to pick spring onions and leeks in 'the surrounding areas of Birmingham'. He charged a low rent, they said, and asked no questions about your background.

'Birmingham!' Ailing said to me. 'How can I go back to that place?' But what choice did she have? The rent in London was £35 a week. She'd sent most of her compensation money home. Her remaining cash would run out in two weeks. 'I'll have to take the chance,' she told me. She rang Cong Lao-Da. It was true: he made no fuss, merely told her she'd have to pay a registration fee of £150, and take the coach to Birmingham. She was relieved to find a job so easily.

I made enquiries about Cong Lao-Da, and spoke to people who worked for him. He turns out to be a middle-aged man by the surname of Li, from the rural outskirts of Tienjin. He's known as 'Onion Number One' because he's the major recruiter for all the onion farms in the Midlands.

He started from scratch a few years ago, my sources told me, arriving in England, like so many others with no work permit, little cash and a dire need for work. In his second week in Britain a woman from his hometown introduced him to contacts in Birmingham. He travelled there at once, and spring-onion picking became his first job in England. During that first month, I was told, he lived only on white bread and butter. He worked incredibly hard, and stood out as the fastest and best worker in the fields. Everyone looked up to him as the model worker on the farms, and that was when he first got the nickname 'Onion Number One'. His talents and stamina caught the attention of the Malaysian Chinese recruiter David, who saw the future benefit of having Li working for him. Li had an inkling of the possibilities ahead of him. Working slavishly for David, he was secretly paving the way to taking David's place and becoming the real Onion Number One recruiter. Because David, he knew, had a weakness.

David had arrived in England in 2002 on a tourist visa in search of business opportunities. Initially he, too, had worked on the spring-onion farms, employed by a British-South-Asian gangmaster. Having the advantage of speaking both English and Mandarin, David had worked his way up to recruiting, and it was through him that Chinese labour in the Midlands had started to expand.

His fatal weakness was gambling. The workers told me he used to go to the casino in Birmingham, bringing with him £10,000 each time, which was weeks and weeks of wages he was supposed to pay the workers. He didn't care. 'When he gambled,' they told me, he became so engrossed that '*liu qin bu ren*' – 'he wouldn't recognize family relations of any line'. One day, he played big and lost big. He lost all of the Chinese workers' wages. He couldn't pay up, and he knew it. He told the workers to wait. Then, one night, he ran away from Birmingham, never to return. The workers were devastated at the loss of weeks of hard-earned wages. The British-South-Asian gangmaster was furious: he'd counted on David as a goldmine from whose labour recruitment he'd be raking in profits for years to come. He'd never foreseen that David would disappear overnight. He had to find a replacement, urgently. Of course, he chose the ambitious, efficient Li. This was the golden opportunity Li had been waiting for. Now he could become the recognized Cong Lao-Da, the true Onion Number One.

In the five years since then, Cong Lao-Da has built on David's business and expanded access to numerous workplaces in the Midlands – or 'the Middle of the Kingdom', as Chinese people nickname the Midlands. He's even gone beyond the region and sends workers to mushroom factories on the out-skirts of London. His name has spread far and wide, from the enclave in the Midlands to underground circles in the capital. The Number One he certainly is.

'This time,' Ailing said to me as she got on the coach back to the city she dreaded seeing again, 'I'm going to achieve my aim. In a maximum of four years I intend to return to China and be reunited with my family.'

No one was there to collect her when she arrived at the coach station. 'He's on his way,' Cong Lao-Da's colleague told her when she called. 'Watch out for a blue Treasure Horse [the Chinese term for a BMW].' Half an hour later, he arrived to pick her up. He seemed a calm, reserved man, and he smiled and nodded to Ailing, explaining that he'd come from the outskirts of Tienjin – trying to impress on her that he was a man of modest origins who'd worked hard to earn his way.

He drove her out of the city centre to a run-down part of town called Small Heath: a very different neighbourhood from the Trungs'. The BMW turned into a long street and stopped in front of a small, shabby terraced house. She followed him in, and was overwhelmed by the smell of burning incense. The front room had been converted into a bedroom for three. Cong Lao-Da led her up a narrow staircase to a room on the second floor, which she'd be sharing with two other women for a weekly rent of £25. There was an even narrower staircase in front of her, leading to the loft where some of the men lived.

'It's hard work, and I think you know it,' he said to Ailing as they came back down the stairs. 'But we have more and more tough women from China coming to do this work.'

In the days when Cong Lao-Da had first arrived in England, farm work was seen as a job for men only. Most Chinese work-ers here had been men from Tienjin in the north and Shenyang in the north-east. But economic desperation had brought more and more women to England in the years that followed: the men had brought along their female friends and relatives. In some cases, married couples came to work in England together, in order to earn faster. Now, the ratio of men to women on the farms in the Midlands is about 5 to 1. The women are mostly married and in their thirties or forties, with a child in China to make money for.

'People think of this as a harsh place,' Cong Lao-Da said to Ailing. 'But if you work hard, you'll get what you want.'

As he left, a man came down from the loft and introduced himself to Ailing as Qi Yu. Ailing liked him instantly. He seemed high-spirited, telling her that he'd had his birthday noodles last night, cooked for him by his housemates who were like brothers and sisters to him. They'd played chess all night. Luckily, today was Saturday, their one day off in the week.

I met Qi shortly after this and he told me how he'd come to the Midlands. He'd been working at a food-processing factory in the south, but there'd been an immigration raid and all the Chinese workers had fled. Qi hadn't known where to go. His last resort was to come to the Midlands, known for being the onion-picking territory.

'This place is a *luo jiao di* [a place for resting your feet on the ground – meaning a temporary shelter] for many of us Chinese, you know,' he told me. 'Most of the workers have just arrived from China and have no connections to any Chinese work-seeking networks in England. They take the first available job, because they feel insecure waiting and looking for work in high-cost London. You feel more solid when your feet are on the ground. Make some cash first – then maybe look for better work.'

Some of the workers, Qi told me, have been in England for longer but have been driven away from other jobs, like himself. 'Or there's Xiao Shan,' he said. 'She's a nice woman here, in her thirties, who says she's from Shenyang. She doesn't like to talk about the past. She was doing cockling before, and left

Morecambe Bay a few days before the drowning. Her sister-in-law wasn't so lucky. She stayed on, and died that night at the bay. [She was the girlfriend of Lin, the recruiter I stayed with in Thetford.] Xiao Shan has no relations left in England.'

Qi had been here since David's disappearance and Li's taking over as Cong Lao-Da. There'd been no shortage of work, he told me: he'd worked not only on onion farms but on strawberry fields as well. 'July and August are hectic months here. More people will be arriving in the next few days for the peak season. Our house will have no standing room left!'

He told me about his previous life in China. He was from the suburbs of Tienjin, and used to work in a state-run brick factory for £1,000 RMB (around £66) per month. 'These days you can't live on this wage. My wife worked in the clothing industry. We were finding it tough to cope, even with our joint income. Then we had to pay a penalty of 4,000 RMB [£266] because we had a second child, violating the one-child policy. Some parents are fined more than this, but we got away with paying less because I was able to provide a document to prove that our first child has a disability. The full penalty would have pushed us well below subsistence level.'

The work on the fields here was hard, he told me. He longed to return to China. As he was here on a business-visitor visa, rather than being smuggled, he still had his passport, so it would be fairly easy to get a home-returning certificate [*hui xiang zheng*] from the Chinese Embassy in London. 'But my wife won't let me. She says I should stay here and earn for the family, because choices are scarce back home. The problem is I have no idea when I'll be able to earn enough to go home.'

It was Qi who made Ailing's breakfast for her at 4 a.m. on her first working day: frying some spare spring onions he'd picked the day before, mixing them with cheap noodles he'd bought in Birmingham Chinatown and adding an egg. For Ailing it was too early in the morning to eat. All the men and women in the house crowded into the kitchen for breakfast before putting on their work clothes. Ailing had been told to prepare her own work clothes – boots, coat, gloves and woollen hat. 'It's a huge open space, you know,' Qi warned her. 'Even in the summer you'll get strong winds in the fields.'

At 5 a.m., Cong Lao-Da turned up with a white minibus. Ailing got in, along with fifteen others from the same house. They drove in convoy with another minibus-load of twenty workers picked up from another house in the city. They were on their way to one of the 'little-onion farms' – 'little' referring to the size of the spring onions, not to the farm. (The 'big-onion farms' were the leek farms.)

Sitting at the back of the van, Qi told Ailing that Cong Lao-Da hadn't learned to speak any English in all his years here. 'He's embarrassed about it. So don't keep asking him where we're going. He has no idea how to tell you the name of the place in English.'

During the journey, Qi told Ailing more about Cong Lao-Da, which she later relayed to me. Apparently, Cong Lao-Da never spoke much to anyone. He just got on with his work. He was paid £50 a day for driving the minibus, and also worked in the fields and loaded and unloaded crops, for which he was paid extra money. A ruthless recruiter, he charged a £150–£200 registration fee to workers, unless they happened to come from his hometown, as Qi did – in which case he charged a more lenient £100. His sole preoccupation was working and making money: Qi had heard he'd set up two massage parlours in Birmingham and now recruited Chinese women from all over the country to work as prostitutes.

The British-South-Asian gangmaster is the real boss, Qi told me. He pays Cong Lao-Da, and Cong Lao-Da pays the workers. He also supplies the farms with workers from India and Pakistan. 'The Indians and Pakistanis speak English. They get paid £1 to £2 more per box than us Chinese. We always seem to be the cheapest.' I asked him whether Cong Lao-Da was taking a cut of their wages. Qi didn't think so: 'I've heard that Cong Lao-Da isn't like David. He doesn't take a percentage from our wages as David used to. He makes profits only from our rent and the registration fees he charges us.'

If Ailing had been able to read the road sign, she would have known that the minibus's destination was the town of Evesham in Worcestershire. They arrived at 6 a.m., when the village had not yet woken up. To Ailing, it looked enchanting in the golden early morning light, with its rosy cottages and pubs with climbing flowers and hanging baskets. Just outside the village the minibus turned into a field. Four other minibuses were already parked. Scores of South Asian men and women had already started their day's work.

Each worker was given a few rows of spring onions to work on. Ailing watched how Qi did it: pulling up the spring onions, peeling off the outer skins, cutting off the ends, wrapping nine onions into a bundle and putting the bundle into a cardboard box. 'Each box has to be filled to the top with sixty bundles,' he told Ailing. 'You'll be paid £3 for each box you pick.'

Qi worked fast, as well as helping to teach Ailing. 'Piecemeal work's the hardest,' he told her. 'I think agricultural work in England is all piecemeal work. I'm able to pick ten to twenty boxes a day. So my wages vary from £30 to £60. It takes about an hour to fill a box, so you have to work non-stop to earn a decent wage. When the earth's loose, it's easier to pull up the spring onions and you know you'll earn more that day.' Ailing watched him using his knife to loosen up the tight, dry earth round the onions. 'Bloody hard today.'

Ailing started to pull up the spring onions in her row. Sometimes it took two or three pulls. Feeling the sweat already building on her brow, she worked – and worked. She tried to ignore the ache in her back and the stiffness in her knees. The hours passed till midday, when the workers sat down to have their lunch break. Cong Lao-Da was only a few feet away, Ailing told me, taking a nap with a Chinese newspaper on his head to keep off the sun. A young South-Asian-looking man in jeans and a white T-shirt came up to him and started chatting to him quietly. Ailing was amazed when Qi told her he was the South Asian middleman everyone talked about. He looked young and harmless.

'Never take things at face value here,' Qi told Ailing. 'When he's around, we all keep quiet. People fear him, because he controls a lot of the work here, not only on this farm but all over the region. Cong Lao-Da's much more senior to him in age but listens to him like a puppy. I bet he's talking to Cong Lao-Da about night shifts at the book factory again.'

The book factory: this was the first time Ailing had heard of it. Qi told me about this book factory later. It's a British Asian company in Birmingham called Abstrakt Services, which packages magazines for sales in England. 'We're always sent there to work,' Qi told me. 'It's hell. Our South Asian middle-man has a contract with the factory. He sends workers there every day. When it gets busy, the factory asks for more work-ers. We sometimes have to do night shifts, for five to eight hours depending on demand. For a day shift we get £3.10 an hour, for a night shift it goes up to £3.50. Some of us are allocated just to work in the factory. I do both. Often, after a long day's work on the farm, I go to work in the factory at night.'

Ailing asked Qi if she'd be obliged to go and work there. 'If Cong Lao-Da picks you to go there,' Qi said, 'you've got to do it. Because, if you don't, you're not going to get another chance. Not everyone gets picked for the night work. People count themselves lucky if they do. We all want more work, not less.'

If you were picked for night work, Qi explained to Ailing, it was a sign that Cong Lao-Da appreciated you as a worker. 'You have to be grateful for the extra work in the book factory,' he told her. 'Particularly later, when the winter comes and there's no work on the onion farms – we'll really need the factory job then. Some people leave the region in winter to

find work elsewhere. But Cong Lao-Da prefers it if we stay –
so he keeps our rent!'

Ailing told me that while they were working that afternoon
a Chinese man with long hair walked past, shouting out to
some of the workers. Qi told her that this was another of
the South Asian middleman's recruiters. They were lucky, Qi
said, to be working under Cong Lao-Da rather than this man
from Shenyang whose name was Liu. Liu worked with his
English-speaking Malaysian Chinese partner and lover – Angie
– who acted as his go-between, interpreter and negotiator. She
was ruthless, he said. She took a cut of the workers' wages.
'The northern and north-eastern Chinese don't speak a word
of English, and they're being squeezed for profits and worked
like dogs by those two.'

So things could be worse, Ailing thought, as she toiled
through the rest of the afternoon and into the evening. At
eight o'clock the South Asian boss came up and waved at the
Chinese workers, pointing at his watch. The shift had ended.
The boss counted up everyone's boxes. At the end of the
twelve-hour day, Ailing found she'd only managed to pick five
boxes of spring onions, which earned her £15. This money
was far less than she'd got for the nanny job – and she'd be
paying for food and rent here.

Qi encouraged her, telling her it was only her first day, and
that he'd met women who'd only been able to pick three or
four boxes a day. He'd managed ten, which had earned him
£30. Not that they actually got any money that day. They were
paid every fortnight, Qi explained. 'I don't normally have much
left to send home after paying the weekly rent and buying food,'
he admitted. 'My wife asks why I can't send more. She has no
idea how tough life is in England.'

Exhausted, Ailing climbed back into the minibus for the hour-
long journey back to Birmingham. She'd have to repeat the
whole thing again tomorrow. She longed for rest. Just as they

arrived back outside the house in Small Heath, Cong Lao-Da's mobile phone rang. It was the South Asian boss saying he needed twenty workers to go on the night shift at the book factory, which was beginning in thirty minutes' time.

'I want you all ready in ten minutes, OK?' Cong Lao-Da said to everyone in the minibus. 'You're going to the factory tonight.'

Ailing knew she couldn't say no to Cong Lao-Da after hearing Qi's advice. Bone-weary, she took off her boots in the house, and went into the crowded kitchen to make herself a sandwich to take with her on the night job.

Fifteen minutes later, everyone was back on the minibus for the half-hour journey to the factory. Again, the Chinese had no idea of the name of the place they were going to. (It was actually Aston.) All they knew and cared about was that they were going to earn £3.50 an hour. More Chinese workers were picked up on the way. When they arrived, everyone got off and walked into the factory in single file. It was after 9.30 p.m. The harsh lighting inside an enclosed space reminded Ailing of the sweatshop factories in her province of Zhejiang. Under the white light she saw piles of children's magazines, toys and advertising leaflets stacked up against all four walls. In the middle of the room were two long tables. The workers walked to their positions at the tables, and started to unpack magazines from cardboard boxes.

Ailing chose to stand next to Qi, whom she knew would be patient enough to show her what to do. (There was no official instruction for newcomers.) The South Asian workers across the table were working too fast for Ailing to see exactly what they were doing. Qi showed her how to open the tight plastic covers of the made-in-China toys, insert leaflets into each magazine, put the magazine into the plastic cover, and then put the packaged magazine back into the cardboard box. When a box was filled to the top with packaged magazines you sealed it and started on the next one. All the time, a female South Asian factory boss and a supervisor by the name of Saj were walking up and down, checking the speed of the work. Every now and then Ailing heard Saj bellowing, 'Hurry up!'

'We're supposed to do fifteen boxes in an hour,' Qi told her. 'So you'd better hurry. I'm worried they might sack you.' At the end of the first hour, Ailing was only finishing her eighth box. She was opening the plastic covers and putting the leaflets and magazines in as quickly as she could – how could the others do it so much faster? All the time the factory boss was walking past: 'Hurry up! Hurry up!'

In the second hour she managed to package a further nine boxes. But it didn't seem to be good enough. 'Hurry up! Last chance!' she was told by the supervisor. Qi tried to help her by putting a few of his finished boxes on her stand. She didn't even have time to look at him to say thank you. She was overwhelmed by the fear of losing this job.

At the end of the third hour she counted the number of boxes she'd managed to do in the last hour: still nine. Before she could sense what this might mean, the supervisor Saj came over, pointing his finger at her, and said, 'You! You can go home!'

Ailing wanted to plead with the supervisor that she was doing her best, and to ask for another chance. But she couldn't express this in English. She looked around at her co-workers for help. But Qi couldn't speak English either. '[She is] new! New!' was all he could say. The supervisor ignored him.

'Go home! You are too slow!' Saj gave his order to Ailing again.

'I'm so sorry,' Qi whispered to Ailing. 'This doesn't just happen to you. It happens to lots of other people, all the time. Every week, some people get sent home.'

All the other workers around Ailing took no notice of all this. They carried on working as if nothing had happened, their eyes focused on the comic magazines and toys.

'How do I get home?' Ailing asked in Mandarin. 'I don't know how to get back to the house.'

Saj told her to wait for the next transport home, which would be in three hours' time, when the shift ended at 3 a.m. Ailing was escorted out of the factory building. In the dark, she found a corner near the factory gate, and sat down on the ground. She had no cash on her, having been told not to bring cash on to the site. She couldn't afford a bus ride – even supposing there were any buses around at this time of night.

Obeying her new self-imposed rule, she did not shed a tear. She just thought about the last three hours and felt a burning sense of injustice. What had she done wrong? Surely she couldn't be expected to work as fast as the others on her first shift. She'd tried her best. Or had she? Had she really used up her last reserve of energy? If only they'd give her a second chance! But she knew they wouldn't. Nor would they pay her for the three hours she'd done.

Ailing looked at her watch. It was one in the morning. Later she described to me how lonely she felt during the next two hours, as she sat there waiting for the bus. She missed her son, and home. She thought about those made-in-China toys she'd been packaging. Maybe, sitting outside factory gates all over China, there were people like herself, dismissed for not meeting factory demands. Maybe they, too, were the sole breadwinners for their families.

Her housemates were sympathetic the next day. They told her stories about other Chinese workers getting dismissed as she'd been. Discipline was always harsh, and no one dared to challenge it.

Yet workers kept coming. They came to the Midlands to look for safe and secluded employment. From the Vale of Evesham to the backstreet factory in Birmingham, Chinese workers took refuge in a haven away from public eyes, where the use of their 'black labour' had not yet drawn official attention. Qi said to me, 'This is a completely sealed-off place. Events pass us by. Whatever's happening in the outside world doesn't seem to touch us. And whatever goes on here isn't known to the outside world. It's a safe haven, and you don't need to move on too soon.'

The idea of a 'safe haven' was a bitter irony in Ailing's case. She'd come to the Midlands because she'd been forced out of her last job and was desperate and without resources. As the months went by, she realized that the longer she stayed, the more trapped she became. Workers like her become more cut off, with fewer and fewer means to look for work elsewhere to improve their income or prospects. This world of work in the 'Middle of the Kingdom' might start as a shelter but it turns into a place of entrapment.

When the spring-onion farm work came to an end in October, some Chinese workers, including Ailing, were to leave the area to look for other work to last them through the winter. Others decided to stay put. To find out how the stayers make a living in deep winter, and to confirm how the system works and who's in control of it, I went undercover in January 2007, as an undocumented Chinese worker from Zhoushan in Zhejiang province, where Ailing comes from. Through a contact, I'd heard that Cong Lao-Da was eagerly looking for workers to fill the labour shortage during the winter. Via the contact, he asked for me to go to Birmingham as soon as I could.

Cong Lao-Da was there to meet me in his blue 'Treasure Horse' when I arrived at Birmingham coach station. He was wearing a shiny leather jacket over a black polo-neck jumper. He's now the major Chinese recruiter in the region: rivalry with the other recruiter, Liu, has been a motivator, and he's found more and more farms to send workers to. 'Business is growing,' he told me as he drove. 'You'll have a lot of work to do here.' He's now in charge of three houses, each crammed with workers. During the temporary break in spring-onion farming, there's more than enough work in the book factory, he told me. Work never stops there, and becomes hectic over the peak Christmas season.

I was relieved to find Cong Lao-Da, as people had described to me, 'not too difficult to deal with'. He never pressed for answers when I couldn't instantly respond to his questions. He drove me to a house in Oldknow Road, where eleven people stay. Before we got out of the car, he asked me for the deposit of £50 which his contact in London had told me about before I set out. 'This is to make sure you stay here for a minimum of two months. Once you've worked for two months, the deposit will be returned to you,' he explained. He didn't charge me the heavy registration fee he used to charge to workers like Ailing. I was told by my co-workers that this change was due to labour shortage during winter. He wanted to attract more workers to the area.

He showed me into the bedroom where a woman called Ah-Fang introduced herself to me. She was a short-haired Malaysian Chinese woman in her early fifties. 'You two are going to share a bed,' Cong Lao-Da told us. He said my rent would be £25 a week. 'No problem,' I replied, trying to contain my surprise at the prospect of sharing a bed with a stranger. This was the only double bed in the house, I later found out, and it always had to be shared. Cong Lao-Da made money out of each usable space. I could see that Ah-Fang wasn't happy. But she put on a smile and gave me a hug when we were told about the arrangement.

As soon as Cong Lao-Da left, Ah-Fang started telling me about how to live cheaply here. 'If you get lost and can't find the house, remember we're near Asda. If you go to Asda after 8 p.m. you'll be able to get a roast chicken for 80p. A good deal! And you can get some bargains at the Asian shops in Coventry Street.'

Ah-Fang told me she'd been here for over a year. 'There's a book factory near here where most of the workers get sent,' she said (and I feigned ignorance). 'I worked there but they sent me home because I was too slow. So now Cong Lao-Da only sends me to work in the fields.' She resented the paucity of work she was getting, but saw no choice but to stay. 'I have no one in a big city like London. And I have little chance of finding other work because I'm older.'

I recognized all the symptoms of entrapment in the 'safe haven' that I'd heard about from Ailing. An increasing number of Chinese-speaking female workers like Ah-Fang have come to the Midlands since 2006, and have found it a 'haven' away from the expensive and exposed metropolis. Those from northern China are mainly on business-visitor visas. Some of the women from China and Malaysia are on student visas. Others like Ah-Fang are on tourist visas, which they've outstayed. 'I'm a dragon,' she said (her sign of the zodiac). 'I'm not likely to spend my life stuck in a small place back in Malaysia.' Her working life before she arrived in Britain had been marked by low pay and a low living standard. She'd worked as a bus conductor and a kitchen porter, before moving to Singapore, where she got a job assembling electronic aeronautical parts in a factory. Here she'd worked for twelve long years before moving to a car-assembly plant that had paid slightly more.

In Singapore she read an advertisement put out by a local snakehead about travelling on an arranged package to the United Kingdom. She resolved to go, and paid £7,000 to the female snakehead to arrange her visa. This woman coordinated with a Malaysian snakehead man by the name of Khor in London, who promised Ah-Fang three jobs for a registration fee of £360. In fact, only two jobs were realized. The first was as a *you bao* in a Chinese restaurant for £120 a week. But the restaurant didn't pay her. So she asked Khor to get her a second job. He contacted the well-known Chengxin agency, who got in touch with one of the onion-farm recruiters, Angie, asking her to get an onion-picking job in the Midlands for Ah-Fang. 'But Angie was such a harsh recruiter,' Ah-Fang told me. 'I had to turn to Cong Lao-Da.'

My other room-mate, a Malaysian Chinese woman called Xiao Ling, had been here since the summer. She was here on a student visa, but had done no studying: she'd been working herself to the bone on the farms to support her family in Malaysia. She was in her early thirties, but looked tiny and much younger. I couldn't believe she was capable of toiling in the fields for twelve hours a day throughout the peak season.

I discovered that since Ailing and Qi had left in the winter of 2005, this little world had remained a dark and harsh shelter for those pushed out of work in the capital.

I spoke to a Fujianese housemate who'd left London two months ago when he couldn't find any more work as an electrician. He was one of the latest newcomers who spent 300,000 RMB (£20,000) for his journey – a higher fee charged by the snakeheads these days as it has become harder to be smuggled across Europe and to enter Britain. What's worse, work has become harder to find.

'It's becoming more and more competitive there,' he told me. 'These days, English people prefer to employ Eastern Europeans, who do the same good-quality work for the same money, and the employer doesn't need to worry about using illegal workers.' Here in the Midlands he was earning a third less than he'd earned as an electrician. But he wasn't sure if he'd be able to find any work in London after the winter.

My first evening was spent with Ah-Fang, looking through the Chinese free papers for dating adverts. 'I'm looking for a Chinese husband,' she said. 'Someone in his fifties, with legal status, who can give me a secure retirement. An agency set me up for a date with a chef in his fifties from Hong Kong, but that was a disaster. He didn't even buy me a cup of coffee! Said he was in a rush. The rule about dating is that the woman at least gets taken out for coffee as a basic gesture of goodwill. But this guy was the frugal type. I must have frightened him away!'

She tried to make light of this, and her housemates teased her about her campaign to try to find a partner. But beneath the self-mockery I could sense loneliness and desperation. For Ah-Fang, to find such a man is perhaps the only hope she can cling to if she wants to change her life for the better. She admitted to me that working in England for a year had changed her into a more temperamental and melancholic person. Sometimes, she said, she fell into deep depressions that no one could lift her out of. Often I heard her speaking to herself, and she would repeat things she'd already told me. The next minute she'd be engrossed in the dating-advert newspaper, not responding to anyone.

It was not easy to share a bed, for either of us. I slept close to the wall to give Ah-Fang more space. I felt like an intruder. To get out of bed to use the toilet (downstairs, beyond the kitchen), I had to clamber over her carefully and feel my way in the dark, trying not to wake the house up.

The South Asian gangmaster, whom Ailing and Qi had told me about, was still a daily topic of conversation. It felt as if the whole house was living under the shadow of this man who was the supreme controller of their housing and their livelihood. (He owns the house and rents it to Cong Lao-Da, who acts as a second landlord.) On the following day I did meet him, and I think I must have been the first Chinese worker ever to ask him his name. He looked taken aback, and took a few seconds to answer. His name is Amin (he later let on that his surname is Mohmed), and he's a young British Bangladeshi man. Despite the fact that he's feared by all the Chinese workers, he appeared to me to be nothing but an opportunistic profiteer. His manners are casual and boastful – he puts his hands in his jeans pockets, and shrugs when he can't answer your question. He knows how much he's feared, and thinks the Chinese have no idea how cheap they are as his army of workers.

He told me he runs a labour-recruitment company called Speedline Solutions Ltd, based in Birmingham, and another called Stonehouse Recruitment Ltd based in Smethwick in the West Midlands. Later I researched these companies, and found that Speedline Solutions Ltd is in the process of being closed down, voluntarily – although Amin told me, in November

2007, that it was still operating. Despite the fact that it supplies labour in agriculture, it's not licensed by the Gangmasters Licensing Authority (GLA), a regulatory body set up by the government to put the Gangmasters (Licensing) Act (enacted in summer 2004 following and in response to the Morecambe Bay tragedy that February) into practice, i.e., to regulate those who supply labour or use workers to provide services in the food-processing and packaging, shellfish-gathering, agriculture, forestry and horticulture industries.

The stated aims of the GLA are to 'safeguard the welfare and interests of workers whilst ensuring labour providers operate within the law'. Since October 2006 when the Act came into full effect, it has become illegal to provide labour in the above industries without a licence from the GLA. Under the Act, gangmasters found guilty could face a prison sentence of up to ten years or a £10,000 fine, or both. It is also a criminal offence for a business (in the above industries) to use an unlicensed labour provider: those who run the business could face a prison sentence of up to six months, a £5,000 fine or both.

Stonehouse Recruitment Ltd, as found, has been granted a licence by the GLA. I put in a Freedom of Information request to the GLA, asking for its records of inspection of Stonehouse Recruitment Ltd, to find out how the company had managed to fulfil the required criteria for a licence. But the GLA refused to disclose the information to me, saying that 'disclosure of such information could prejudice the ability of the Authority to carry out its duties effectively. . .' and was 'likely to prejudice the licence-holder's commercial interests by revealing information of potential usefulness to their competitors to the detriment of the licence holder.'

Amin has been operating as a gangmaster in the Midlands under both Speedline Solutions Ltd and Stonehouse Recruitment Ltd, and has been making use of undocumented Chinese labour for almost a decade. He has contracts with about a dozen farms and pack-houses in Worcestershire and Northamptonshire, and is also the main labour provider for the notorious 'book factory', Abstrakt Services Ltd.

On Friday morning at 7 a.m. I was sent to work at Abstrakt Services along with ten other Chinese men and women. I found that the work regime there had not changed at all since Ailing and Qi had left.

Xiao Ling made me a lunchbox before we got on the minibus. 'I have some extra food to spare, so I thought I'd make you some lunch to take to work.' She told me we'd only have one half-hour break in the eight-hour day. She said that on the previous day she'd earned £26 for more than eight hours' work – which worked out at £3.25 an hour, to be paid in cash by the supervisor Saj a week later. 'That was at a speed of twenty-six boxes an hour at the busiest time,' she said. 'People get dismissed all the time if they can't reach the day's target. On my first day in the job, I was shocked to see the workplace – people working like machines, with supervisors walking about and shouting abuse all the time. I thought to myself – God, is there such a place in this world? But the sad thing is that in the winter this is considered a *good* job. People would prefer to work in the book factory than outside in the cold fields.'

My 'work station' was between two Chinese men who kindly showed me what to do. (As with Ailing, there was no official instruction.) It took five minutes to learn, then a further five minutes to unload magazines from a box. This left only fifty minutes in the hour in which to meet the target of fifteen boxes of packaged magazines. I knew this was beyond my capacity as a beginner, but I resolved to work as fast as I could.

It took me forty minutes to do three boxes. Just as I was starting on the fourth, the supervisor Saj stopped me. 'You have to go home,' he told me.

I was furious. 'You didn't show me how to start the job, and you didn't even give me time to get used to the place!'

He was taken aback by my reaction. Chinese workers weren't supposed to have the courage to argue, nor were they supposed to be able to speak English. He paused, then said, in a softer voice than before, 'Sorry. The manager said you must go home.'

'Are you going to pay me for the hour?' I asked, knowing they never paid anyone they dismissed.

'No,' he replied.

'You dismissed me without notice, and you're not paying me. Do you really think I'm going to accept this?' I became angrier still.

'Listen,' said Saj, 'your attitude is wrong. Let's leave the site. I'm driving you back home.' He started to escort me out of the building.

My co-workers later told me that the supervisor had never driven anyone home. As a rule, they simply dismiss you and leave you to return home on your own or wait for the next minibus at the end of the shift. My room-mate Ah-Fang, for instance, told me that when she'd been dismissed, she'd had to wait and sleep in the canteen until the minibus came.

During the drive, I asked Saj who it was who'd actually made the decision to dismiss me without notice. 'It's the factory boss,' he said. 'It's nothing against you. It happens to people who are slow.'

I reminded him that he hadn't shown me how to do the job, or given me a chance to get used to it, or given me any notice for dismissal.

'You're right,' he said – but he couldn't give an explanation for the discipline meted out. As I'd heard from other workers before I myself experienced it, instant dismissal without pay is the norm among new workers.

A minute later he said, 'You know, this is not a British company. It's not the same as other companies in this country. It's an Asian company.' He was implying that Abstrakt Services doesn't feel a need to abide by the rules.

Then he told me that there was other work around, if I needed it. He said that he and his colleagues run a labour-recruitment agency, and send people to work on spring-onion farms. He wouldn't tell me the name of the agency, but I gleaned from this that Saj works for the South Asian gang-master Amin, and is closely involved with Cong Lao-Da and Liu.

A few days after this, I called Abstrakt Services Ltd. and asked to speak to the factory's managing director Gulan Qazi. I told him I was writing about migrant workers and asked for his comment on the malpractices at his workplace. Gulan Qazi refused to talk. His assistant told me, 'You can go and print what you like about us. It will only be fiction.'

On my second evening at the house in Oldknow Road, Cong Lao-Da's assistant knocked on our bedroom door. 'It's time to pay the rent for next week,' he said. I told him I'd just paid my weekly rent when I'd arrived two days ago.

'No, no, that's not how it works,' the assistant explained. 'Our rule here is that you pay your weekly rent every Saturday. It doesn't matter how many days you've stayed here.'

Again – a clever little way of making money out of the already impoverished workers. I told him I didn't have any cash on me. He said that, as a favour, he'd let me pay tomorrow.

Having heard that I'd lost my job at the book factory, my room-mates reassured me that I'd be able to get work on the spring-onion farm soon.

The farm they were talking about, I found out, was E. V. G. Europe Ltd (Evesham Vale Growers Europe Ltd), in Evesham, Worcestershire. This was not the same farm where Ailing and Qi had worked, which was White House Farm. White House Farm rents 120 acres of land to Simms & Woods, a year-round supplier to British supermarkets, caterers, wholesalers and restaurants. The farm grows 1,000 acres of spring onions, 200 acres of leeks and 150 acres of swedes at its eighteen sites in Worcestershire, from March to October.

'It's no good there any more,' Amin told me. 'The farm has

attracted too much attention recently. (The farm came into the spotlight in 2003, when three Iraqi Kurdish farm workers were killed in a minibus on a railway crossing near the farm when their gangmaster had failed to call the signalman to check that the line was clear.) And on top of that, I haven't been paid well there – they only paid me £4.80 per box [of spring onions]. And they're always late!'

This rate of pay from the grower does not leave labour providers like Amin enough to pay workers anything like the minimum wage. (The current agricultural minimum wage is £5.70 per hour for a standard worker aged twenty-two and over.) However, when I talked to Amin again in August 2007, he told me he was sending Chinese workers back to White House farm in six weeks' time to harvest leeks. 'I get the Chinese to do the outdoor work, and the legal workers to do the indoor packaging work,' he told me.

During the past decade, and particularly in the summer seasons of 2005 and 2006, hundreds of workers have been sent to White House Farm, not only by Amin but by other (mainly South Asian) gangmasters. Amin believes he's actually running the business more fairly and kindly than other agencies, who sometimes don't pay their workers at all. The huge demand for work at White House Farm has been met by the supply of labour from at least five major gangmasters in this time.

One of them, whose company Newtex Ltd in Oldbury is GLA-licensed, told me he supplied South Asian labour to the farm's pack-house. Newtex Ltd is a member of Ethical First, a body set up in 2003 to help gangmasters to abide by the Temporary Labour Working Group Code of Practice, and later the Gangmasters Licensing Act. (Theoretically, this means that Newtex Ltd is on the side of the 'good, law-abiding gang-masters'.)

The managing director of Newtex told me his duties consist mainly of managing and supervising the gang labour supplied by other gangmasters, at the farm's request. He's known

Chinese workers for years. 'They're the best people we've had on the farm,' he told me. 'They never bargain or argue with you for anything. They just work hard.'

Five minutes away from White House Farm is E. V. G. (Europe) Ltd, where the Chinese are also sent to harvest spring onions for seven to eight months each year. The farm has a reputation for good produce: in 2002 it won the top award in the Fresh Produce category of the Quality Food and Drink Award for its Sungold tomatoes developed for Sainsbury's. The farm grows cereal, fruit and vegetables on its two sites at Lower Moor and Blackminster. It employs an average of 250 seasonal workers. Amin has an annual contract with E. V. G. and has been working with them for six years. 'That farm's much better,' he told me in August 2007. 'They pay me £4 for a much smaller box of spring onions, and they're always on time. And the good thing is I'm the only one sending them workers.' At that point he was in the process of transporting more than 200 migrant workers to this farm from Birmingham – Chinese, Indians, Pakistanis and Romanians – all to pick spring onions in the coming weeks and months.

Regarding the below-agricultural-minimum wage paid to Chinese workers by Stonehouse Recruitment Ltd, Roger Bloom, Technical Manager of E. V. G. (Europe) Ltd, said in February 2008: 'We are concerned with your statement, and if true we were not aware of this happening. We do not support this kind of practice in any way, and ensure that any labour provider we use is paid in accordance to be able [to] pay their workers the minimum wage. We currently do not use Stonehouse Recruitment, and have not done so for the last five months; should we use them in the future, we will reinvestigate their practices. As you may be aware, all labour providers in the UK are governed by English law and are required to be licensed by the GLA (Gangmasters Licensing Authority) in order to operate. Without a licence it is illegal to provide labour, it is also illegal for companies such as ourselves to enlist the services of an

unlicensed labour provider. In order to obtain a licence, the
labour provider is audited by the GLA, against set standards
which include worker welfare, remuneration etc. Stonehouse
Recruitment had been audited and been granted a licence by
the GLA. As a large employer of people, we go to great lengths
to ensure that our employees and those employed by third parties are paid in accordance with UK law and treated fairly (after
all we want people to continue to work for us as we need them).
We always pay above the national minimum wage. Where
piece-work is paid, which is common in horticulture, we pay
the rate which equates to the equivalent of the hourly minimum
wage. We always pay a premium to the labour provider, so
that they should be able to pay the minimum wage, after their
deductions for their costs. As a result of such stories, we no
longer work to the minimum standards set down by the GLA,
but do have our own procedures, which try to ensure that this
sort of thing does not happen.'

On the farms in Worcestershire, however, the number of
Chinese workers has not decreased since the enlargement of
the EU and the arrival of new EU workers. For the farms, the
Chinese have remained the 'best people' to use, for their lack of
knowledge of working conditions in agriculture in Britain and
their lack of language, making them relatively easy to manage
and exploit.

Back at the base in Birmingham the question I was asking
was would I be offered another job, after proving myself so
unproductive at the book factory? Cong Lao-Da told me he
wasn't sure if I'd be able to work at the leek farm where everyone was going the next day. 'It's very tough,' he kept telling
me.

'Give me a chance,' I begged him. 'I'll only know if I can or
can't do it once I've tried.'

So I joined the team of ten from our house to travel to the
leek farm the next morning. We got up at 4 a.m. There was a
queue for the toilet. Some people were wrapping Sellotape

round their feet to keep the wind off in the fields. (This was mid-January.) I'd borrowed a big, chunky pair of walking boots from a co-worker, and I put on my thickest jumper. Ah-Fang wore an extra jumper upside down so it could act as a scarf round her neck. Then we put our lunches and personal belongings into a black plastic rubbish sack, so we could put it down on the muddy ground.

After breakfast we waited outside to be picked up. An Afghan worker walked past, on his way to work. Ah-Fang stopped him for a chat. 'Have you got a new job for me?' she asked him. Our housemates teased her. 'Ah-Fang's always looking for any opportunity to jump team!'

At 5 a.m. we heard the noise of an engine, amplified by the silence of the street. It was the minibus, driven by Amin. Most of my housemates went back to sleep as soon as they got in. Amin drove around the city for ten minutes, picking up more people. Then we headed out of town in an unknown direction. I tried to keep track of the road signs. We went on the motorway through Coventry and then towards Northampton. There was nothing in the bleak East Midlands landscape to keep me awake. I dozed off.

When I opened my eyes it was 8 a.m. and the minibus was bumping along a track surrounded by farmland. We got off and walked into the leek fields against the cold wind. The leek plants looked full and rich in the morning light. They welcomed us from a distance with their fresh, strong smell. We were given four rows to work on each. Everyone started working straight away. Cong Lao-Da's assistant ('the rent man', as he was known) showed me how to do the job. (This, at least, was an improvement on the book factory.) He handed me a knife. 'Pull it up,' he instructed, pointing at the fat, heavy-looking leek in front of me. I did so, with some difficulty. 'Now shake it around. Get rid of the dirt. And then cut off the very end bit, carefully, without cutting off too much.'

I cut off the end bit. 'No, no, I told you not to cut off too much. Or the whole leek will disintegrate. Now cut off the other end, so it fits into the basket. All the leeks have to be cut to the same size.'

The job didn't look too difficult. It was just a matter of getting used to it. Picking a dozen baskets of leeks in a day should be no problem, I thought.

I set to work in earnest, trying to loosen the earth with my knife and pull up the leeks. They seemed reluctant to be pulled: tied to the land, happy in the warm, tight earth. I had to pull once, twice, three times with each one of them.

'Leeks are harder than spring onions,' one of my co-workers told me. 'If they're too small and thin, don't bother. The supermarkets won't take them.' I looked at his basket. It was already half-full. I tried to speed up. Most people were kneeling down to work, but I found that if I knelt, the leeks were even harder to pull up. I had to stand to give myself space and strength.

'Ah!' I shouted. 'It hurts!' I never knew you could be cut by a leek. In all the hurry to get warm at 4 a.m., no one had told me to wear proper thick gloves. Instead the 'rent man' had given me a pair of thin transparent gloves, which were inadequate for these strong plants. My co-worker in the next row looked at me sympathetically but helplessly each time I let out an 'Ah!' of pain.

'Getting bitten again?' he teased.

Selecting the large-sized leeks took time. I was told to go through all the leeks, chop off the tiny ones and flatten them into the earth. The mass of flattened leeks created a strong smell so powerful that I had to turn my head away and wipe my eyes. The land looked nicely worked on. But I'd only completed one basket.

One more hour into the job, I managed to complete the second basket. ('Make sure you fill each one right to the top,' my co-workers had warned me. 'If it's not full, you won't be paid.') My back was aching. I looked around, and saw Ah-Fang sitting on the top of an upside-down empty basket having her sandwich. I decided to do the same. This is piecemeal work, and you are solely responsible for your pickings and earnings. But no one else was taking a break. (Except, that is, for Amin. I looked into the minibus, and saw him in there with his feet up, reading a newspaper.)

After a five-minute break I got up and continued picking. I couldn't have managed without that break. I didn't understand how my co-workers could continue working at such a pace without a break. Their physical strength was amazing. I worked for two more hours and managed to fill two more baskets, making four in all. At twelve thirty Amin finished his long rest and sauntered towards us. As he approached, a co-worker of mine quickly took a few leeks out of one of his baskets and put them into mine. 'There – now it's filled up,' he whispered. I remembered I wouldn't get a penny for an unfilled basket. I thanked my co-worker for this act of comradely generosity.

Amin came to count up our baskets. He seemed to be using body language to communicate with the 'rent man', who didn't speak much English. There was a lot of pointing and nodding, but few words were spoken. The two men seemed to understand each other well. The rent man noted down the number of baskets we'd each filled.

We'd be paid 80p per basket, in cash, next week. Working for the entire morning, from eight to twelve thirty, I'd picked four baskets of leeks, which had earned me £3.20 altogether. Never had I been at the receiving end of such a demoralizing wage.

Amin signalled to us to walk back to the minibus. We were like a herd of cattle, now being taken to the next leek farm, ten minutes' drive away. I saw the sign 'Bridge Farm' as we drove through its gates. Amin parked once again, and let the workers out into the huge cold fields.

I decided to stay in the van and have a conversation with Amin. (As in all my undercover work, the luxury of being able to stand back gave me a pang of guilt.)

'Why aren't you going out to work?' Amin asked.

I told him my hands were in agony from the leeks, which was true. The deep cut in my right hand, painful in the cold wind, would be exacerbated by more picking. Amin couldn't order me to work, as the work was piecemeal. He was surprised I could speak some English. He started to boast about the scale of his business, and told me about Cong Lao-Da. 'Lao-Da's been working for me for a long time. I pay him £1,000 a week for driving, recruiting and working on the farms. He's very good – better than other recruiters I've had. Whatever I pay him, he gives directly to the Chinese, without taking a cut.' (That means the 80p for each basket of leeks is money directly from Amin. There's not much a recruiter could take from 80p.)

Amin talked on, unaware of my enthusiasm for the subject. 'Your people like this kind of work. We've had so many of them working at White House and many other farms. I've been sending them everywhere.' Then he reminded me that work on the spring-onion farms would be starting again soon. 'There'll be loads of work for you at E. V. G.,' he said. 'You'll love it!'

While we were talking, my co-workers toiled from 12.45 to 3 p.m., without stopping. At the end of the shift, Amin went out again to count up the baskets, and brought the workers back to the minibus. Ah-Fang was the first to climb back in. She looked tired out from the work and the wind. Her boots were heavy with mud. But she announced cheerfully, 'I made £16 today! That's enough to last me through the week.' She kept repeating this on the three-hour journey back to Birmingham, until the Fujianese ex-electrician (who hadn't managed to make so much) told her, with a grin, to stop boasting.

Speedline Solutions Ltd, Stonehouse Recruitment Ltd, Abstrakt Services Ltd and Simms & Woods Ltd did not respond to the allegations.

★

The day after I left the house in Birmingham, Ah-Fang called me to ask how I was. 'You're so lucky going to London,' she said. 'I'll never have the confidence to work there.'

'Well,' I said, 'you can rest assured I'm not coming back to Birmingham to invade your sleeping space!' She offered to look after my leek-picking wage for me till we saw each other again.

From that day we were in regular contact by phone, and very soon I told her my real purpose for working in the Midlands. The relief that someone was listening to her, wanting to hear and tell her story, made her voice crack with tears. 'So many things have happened in England . . .' she said.

In the following weeks and months after our short spell of sharing a house and working together, Ah-Fang led me into another underground world: a world where thousands of undocumented Chinese women endure dangerous and exploited working lives behind closed doors.

She was soon to go to a very different kind of house.

6. The Zone Six Women

If you don't want to do the whole session, you can just buy
parts. Three pounds for touching her face and hair, £10 for
touching the upper part of her body, £20 for fondling the lower
part of her body. Would you like a cup of tea first?

— a Chinese female housekeeper at a brothel in Cheam, Surrey
February 2007

'I've got a temporary job for a week as a housekeeper at a
massage parlour in Cardiff,' Ah-Fang told me on the phone,
a few days after I'd left her in the house in Birmingham.

'Massage parlour? Cardiff?' I was surprised. That was where
I studied during my first year in Britain. Never had I associated
the Welsh capital with the sex trade.

'We're still waiting for the spring-onion farms to start their
picking season in March,' she said. 'I really need another job for
a while.'

From Cardiff she called me again. The job was quite scary,
she said — and later she'd tell me exactly why it was scary.
'But I'm getting £180 for a seven-day week, with board and
lodging. My tasks aren't hard — just cooking meals for the girls
and showing customers the way.'

When the job ended a week later, Ah-Fang took a late-
evening coach back to Birmingham. In the dark she felt her
way upstairs and across her room to her bed, trying not to wake
Xiao Ling. She felt for her torch under the pillow, switched it
on, counted her week's earnings — £180 in cash — and hid the
money amongst her clothes in the bottom drawer.

She couldn't sleep. She was thinking about Cong Lao-Da. He hadn't been pleased that she'd gone to work in Cardiff for a week. He'd made her pay the week's rent to keep this bed. He'd told her he was going to charge her a new deposit of £50 to secure her work on the farms. There were still weeks to go before spring-onion picking began, and her cash might not last her that long.

That night, she told me, she sat up studying the job advertisements, box by box, in the *Chinese Business Gazette*, one of the free weekly papers she regularly picked up from Birmingham's Chinatown. 'Oriental Massage', 'China Red', 'One Night Passion'. Ah-Fang circled these with a pen.

'Massage parlour', as every Chinese worker knows, is a euphemism for 'brothel'. There are more than 600 Chinese 'massage parlours' in London alone – half the number of Chinese takeaways in the capital, as Chinese like to joke. Most of these parlours advertise vacancies in the Chinese newspapers.

After the week in Cardiff, Ah-Fang had some experience of working as a massage-parlour housekeeper, and she felt she could continue with this kind of work.

'Are you sure you can handle it?' I asked her, when she told me what she was planning.

'It isn't for everyone,' she said. 'Some women think they'll be able to do it, but they run away after the first hour. It's one of the toughest and most dangerous jobs for Chinese women in England. But I'm helped by my age: fifty-two. Usually being old is a disadvantage in job-seeking, but in this job it's an advantage. My age is what protects me.'

The next day she started to call the parlours. 'Sorry, the job's gone,' she was told each time. It surprised her how quickly the vacancies had been filled. She turned to the page where agencies advertised, and dialled the number of an agency called Xianglong ('Fortunes and Prosperity').

The Chinese woman who answered the phone told her she'd have to pay the agency a fee of £50 to be given a job as a housekeeper in one of the parlours. But Ah-Fang wasn't going to fall for that ruse. 'I insist,' she said boldly to the woman, 'that the £50 is paid to you via my employer, once you've found me a job.' To her surprise, the woman accepted this.

'So where do you want to be based?' the woman asked. 'We can find you a job in London sooner than anywhere else. No need to worry about accommodation: they're all sleep-in jobs. Remember: £50 is for one job only. If you lose the job, you'll need to pay a new fee of £50 to be placed elsewhere.'

Ah-Fang couldn't argue. With everything agreed, the woman passed Ah-Fang's mobile number to the owner of a massage parlour in London.

He called her straight away. He was Malaysian Chinese, and liked the fact that Ah-Fang was from Malaysia as well. He told her she'd be paid £180 a week. (This was riches compared with the £50 a week she'd been earning picking leeks for Cong Lao-Da.) But he didn't tell her the name or address of the massage parlour. 'We're in a residential area, in Zone Six of London. It's not easy to find. Come to Victoria coach station tomorrow and we'll pick you up.'

'At last,' Ah-Fang said to me on her mobile phone as she took the coach to London, 'I've achieved my dream of leaving the world of work in the Midlands. But I'm not sure,' she said with a giggle, 'whether I'm moving up or down on the career ladder.' She admitted to being nervous about going to a capital city, never having lived or worked in one. 'Everyone in Birmingham thinks I won't last. They told me it's a jungle in London. You get dismissed as often as you get employed. Cong Lao-Da thought I'd never leave Birmingham. He thinks I'm too old and useless. If things turn out badly, I think he'd allow me to go back to Birmingham – as long as I paid him.'

I tried to reassure her that there was a world without Cong Lao-Da, but she didn't seem to be listening. She carried on telling me about her 'city phobia', as she called it with a self-deprecating laugh. To me, she seemed a brave woman, willing to go alone into an unknown world – through the back door of a city, into a desperate job. I sensed she knew this, especially when she tried to laugh her fears away.

She told me exactly what happened next. The Malaysian Chinese boss, whose surname was Lee, picked her up at Victoria as planned and drove her all the way to so-called 'Zone Six'. Ah-Fang had no idea which direction they were going in. The journey took more than forty minutes. 'Are we still in London?' she kept asking. Eventually they arrived at a comfortable-looking suburban town. 'Zone Six,' said Mr Lee. 'This place has a railway station.' Ah-Fang was later to find out that she was in Cheam, which is actually in Zone Five on the Transport for London system, near the border with Zone Six. All she could see were rows of detached and semi-detached houses with front gardens. Hardly anyone was about. 'A massage parlour – in this quiet place?' was Ah-Fang's initial reaction.

They turned into a narrow lane that looked so quiet and residential that she thought they must have made a wrong turn. But the boss parked outside a small block of flats. He showed her up the stairs. When he put the key in the door of the second-floor flat, Ah-Fang asked him whether he owned the place. She regretted the question: the man scowled and shook his head without saying a word. She was later to learn that all Chinese massage parlours rent their premises: impermanence is of the essence.

As they entered the flat, the first thing that confronted Ah-Fang was the airless humidity of the place, and a strong smell of cheap perfume. She avoided breathing through her nose for the first few minutes, as she tried to adjust to the over-powering smell.

A middle-aged Chinese woman came out into the reception area. 'So you're Ah-Fang. You've done *baomu* [massage-parlour housekeeping work] before, I hear.' Ah-Fang could tell from her accent that she came from north China. She had sharp, thin eyes, which Ah-Fang described to me as 'penetratingly mean-looking'. Smartly dressed in her *qipao* (the formal long tight dress which became traditional costume during the Qing Dynasty), she stuck out her chest in a self-assured way as she walked around. Ah-Fang soon understood that she was the manageress, and that she was much more in charge of the place than the Malaysian Chinese man. (This, I was to discover, is a common set-up for massage parlours. A Chinese woman without documents looks for a British-Chinese man to be her partner, ideally someone with language skills, ID and a bank account. He uses his status to rent premises and she uses her trade knowledge for the day-to-day running of the parlour.)

The manageress began to tell Ah-Fang about the job. 'You're in charge of this place every day. You make sure you're at the counter at 9 a.m. You open the door to customers, sit them down and ask them if they want tea or coffee. Then you take them up to the Misses [*xiao jie*, literally 'ladies', the term commonly used to refer to female sex workers]. When the customer takes his pick, you come back to the counter. In the evening, you clean the place and cook supper for the Misses. The agency told me you know how to cook.'

'Yes, I do,' said Ah-Fang. 'I cook good Malaysian Chinese dishes.'

'Well we [meaning she and her Malaysian Chinese partner] don't normally come in here and we don't eat with you. So you sort it out with the Misses, OK? They may not like anything too spicy. If it's not too busy, you can finish work at around midnight. When it's busy you finish when the last customer leaves.'

'Which is my day off?' Ah-Fang asked.

'Day off? You must be joking, madam. Have you got any clue about this line of work? You work seven days a week. You live here, OK? I thought you understood.'

'Where do I sleep?'

'That's your bedroom,' the manageress said, pointing to the

other side of the sitting area, where a partition made of thin wood created a small sleeping area with no window. No room for anything but a folding bed in there, thought Ah-Fang. ('But at least I've got it to myself,' she said to me later on the phone. 'Could be worse, could be a lot worse.')

The two Misses had slightly bigger rooms, with windows. Ah-Fang didn't begrudge them that. 'Their work isn't easy,' she said to me. 'They should be allowed some real privacy after they've finished work.'

A week or so after Ah-Fang started the job, I asked her if it would be possible for me to have a quick look at the workplace and a chat with the Misses. She was hesitant. Visits by anyone except customers were strictly forbidden. Risking her job, she said I could visit for a few minutes.

The next day I made my way to Cheam. I was half expecting frilly pink lace curtains, but the flat was not at all like that. It was bare, lifeless and beige – like an empty flat an estate agent might show you around. There were no pictures on the walls, just a television and sofa for the waiting customers. Only the smell hinted at the flat's current occupancy.

The two Misses were very reluctant to talk, as expected. I reassured them that they and their workplace would not be identified. The older of the two (I'll refer to her as Xiao Fen) broke the ice. She told me she was from 'the countryside', refusing to give specifics. She never reveals her real origin or her real age to anyone in the parlours, and certainly not to me. Her accent suggested a southern province, perhaps Hunan. I guessed she was in her early forties. Her eyes, puffy from lack of sleep, were lined heavily with black eyeliner.

She'd been in England for three years, and had spent two and a quarter years of that time working in the kitchen of a Chinese restaurant in London for ten hours a day, to support her ten-year-old son in China. She'd felt enslaved by the low wage but hadn't dared give up the job. She'd been constantly numb with exhaustion. 'It was so slow making that money,' she told me, 'slaving away in that dark place, day in, day out. When was I ever going to send enough money home?'

Then one day, seven months ago, she saw an advertisement for a massage-parlour job in the Chinese newspaper. She felt tempted to dial the number. She didn't tell anyone about her secret thoughts of working in such a place. No one would understand. Back home in China, prostitution was frowned upon, to say the least. People said it took a certain kind of mean, low woman to do such work. But Xiao Fen knew she was no different from other women, wanting to earn a living not only for herself, but more importantly for her son.

The idea of making a living from sex work preoccupied Xiao Fen in the following days. She knew that in two years of such work she'd be able to make as much money as it would take her eight years to make in a full-time kitchen job. An undocumented Chinese sex worker can earn up to 1 million RMB (£66,700) within two years if she works for ten to twelve hours a day. As she walked into the kitchen the next day, she wondered what it would be like to strip naked in front of strangers. Would it be so very bad? As a divorcee, did she feel a moral duty towards anyone? No one at home would ever need to know.

While she was weighing the pros and cons of a possible new job in the sex trade, fate stepped in and made the decision for her: her employer at the restaurant decided to lay her off and replace her with someone introduced by the chef. She was left with no income. A few days later, she dialled the number of the massage parlour. She got the job at once.

She didn't tell the boss she'd never worked in the trade before. She thought that would make her more vulnerable. On her first day, fortunately a weekday, she was given only three customers – two middle-aged men and a man in his twenties, all locals. Luckily the men were all quite straightforward and undemanding. Xiao Fen's inability to speak English acted as a protection, helping her to detach herself mentally from what she was doing.

After surviving that first day she thought, Well, it's not so bad after all. It's just a matter of pleasing men, and women have been doing that since time began.

But the workload grew rapidly. By the end of the week she was being given thirteen or fourteen hours of work a day. It was hard to cope. Showers after each session didn't seem to help her get back her strength. She had to carry on doing the job through her periods, with a dull pain lasting through the sessions. A customer could pick her at any time of day or night. And she was constantly moved from parlour to parlour, to ensure variety for the customers.

'The hours are a little longer than in the restaurant,' she said to me, 'and we always have to share our earnings fifty-fifty with the boss. The price is £60 per half-hour, but I get paid half that amount, in spite of the fact that I do all the work! But on the whole I'm making much better money than in the restaurant. Even on a quiet day, I'm earning about £100.'

The other worker at the parlour is nicknamed Yan-Erh, meaning 'Swallow'. No one knows her real name. She's heavily made up, and perhaps in her mid-thirties. She came to England from Shenyang on a six-month business-visitor visa, and was working as a greeter for a Chinese restaurant for a year, earning just under £4 an hour. One day her flatmates introduced her to a friend of theirs who owned a massage parlour. She was strongly tempted to take on a better-paid job. She still had a third of the borrowed fee to pay off in China (the money she'd paid for getting to Britain). She desperately wanted to start sending more money home to support her daughter and her parents who were depending on a tiny pension to live on and to look after their granddaughter.

'The job's hard,' she said to me, 'but it's live-in and your food's cooked for you by the housekeepers. If you work your hardest, for thirteen or fourteen hours a day, you can make

£500, just in a day. That would take you three weeks to make in any restaurant job. I'm sending a lot more cash home. My daughter thinks I'm now working in a better-paid restaurant! She hasn't the faintest idea! But I'm so happy to know she's able to buy things she needs. Things are definitely improving at home. My plan is to send her to some after-school English lessons.'

There are an estimated 3,000 undocumented Chinese women working in the sex trade in Britain. (The secrecy of the job makes an exact count impossible, but that is the number estimated by various massage-parlour owners I spoke to.) The majority are in their thirties and forties, with a child or children in China. They are working in city centres and in suburban areas all over the country. Most have come to Britain from central and north-east China on business-visitor visas, which have run out. A small minority of them, from southern China, are failed asylum seekers. They've never worked in the sex trade before, and did not plan to. Before joining it, they worked in other industries such as catering, food-processing and domestic service, all of which paid low wages and enforced long working hours with no employment rights and no job security. The women are motivated by the need to earn fast to pay off their borrowings and to improve the living standards of their families at home. Most of them stay in the job for two to three years to make enough money, and then return to China.

A large part of Ah-Fang's job at the parlour in Cheam is to look after the Misses. She manages the parlour completely on her own, on behalf of the bosses, who run two other parlours, one in Sutton, only a few stops away. 'They run more than one parlour,' Ah-Fang told me, 'so that if one gets closed down for any reason, the customers can quickly be transferred to another.'

Clearly security is a big worry. It's for that reason that Ah-Fang's bosses rarely come into the parlours. The manageress uses her mobile phone as the contact number advertised in the local papers. Customers call her to find out the addresses. They are all local men, many of them regulars. Once they've called the manageress to inform her of their visit, she rings Ah-Fang and tells her to listen for the doorbell. 'It's a clever way of working,' Ah-Fang told me. 'The bosses control the contacts and keep the premises a secret, while the Misses and I hold the fort. If the police raid the place, we're the ones who get arrested and deported. The bosses can just move their businesses elsewhere. The manageress never comes into the parlour to pick up the earnings. She calls us from the car park outside. She comes to collect the cash each day. I have to go down and hand it over. Same with the food shopping, but that's once a week. She buys the food and we pick it up from outside.'

I visited their other parlour in Sutton. It was a five-minute walk from Sutton station, in a ground-floor flat of a quiet block of private flats on a peaceful road. A man was unloading furniture from a van and the door of the building was open, so I walked in. I rang the bell of Flat 1, and a Chinese woman opened the door a crack. 'Who is it?' she asked. As she wasn't wearing make-up, I guessed she must be the housekeeper like Ah-Fang. She saw me and quickly closed the door. Clearly I was no customer. This sort of visit from a stranger was a warning sign. I rang again and again, but she didn't answer. I found out that the owner of the flat was M. J. Gleeson Group plc, a construction and property development firm. The odd thing is that this Sutton parlour was raided twice – once in winter 2006 and again in early 2007. However, the bosses were able to reopen it only a week after the raids. Presumably there must be some sort of agreement between M. J. Gleeson Group plc and the bosses.

I approached M. J. Gleeson Group plc for comment and Steve Peters, managing director of Gleeson Regeneration and Home South, said: 'M. J. Gleeson Group plc can confirm that it owns the freehold to the property at the Sutton address. The leasehold of the property was sold to a third party some twenty-four years ago. We would like to assure you that M. J. Gleeson Group plc takes such allegations as made by yourself in your letter extremely seriously and we will be asking the property management company to investigate your claims. Should this investigation uncover anything untoward, the relevant authorities will be notified.'

I talked to Ah-Fang every two days during her work in Cheam, and was given a glimpse into the working day and night of such a place. It seemed to be a relief for Ah-Fang to have someone from outside to chat to, as she was not allowed to leave the premises (except to go down to the car park when the bosses came). Our conversations were often interrupted by the sound of customers ringing the doorbell.

'Can't talk now,' she said, one afternoon. 'Call me after 2 a.m.'

I did, and she told me they'd had twelve men that day. 'All locals. All sorts. White, black, Asian. Young as eighteen, old as seventy. Local men seem to have a special liking for foreign girls. They always ask what kind we've got. The more exotic, the better. For some reason, Korean women are in high demand at the moment. When customers ring the manageress, she lies to them and tells them we have Koreans in our parlour. So Xiao Fen has to say she's Korean. She's dyed her hair light-brown to look Korean. Anyway, the *guilao* can't tell the difference.'

'A long day for you and the Misses,' I said sympathetically.

'Yes,' she said with a yawn. 'First we get the early bird types. They drop in on their way to work, some of them in their smart suits. You wonder where they're going. Could be estate agents working in a busy office in central London. At the other end of the day we get the ones looking for fun after a night out. Maybe they just didn't manage to pick anyone up in the bars. It doesn't matter what sort of men ring the bell: we have to welcome them all. For the Misses, it's easier with the well-dressed middle-class ones. At least they're clean and tidy.

But even with the smelly drunks they still have to put on a smile. Those who pay have the say. The Misses just have to close their eyes and put up with it.'

Part of Ah-Fang's job is to explain the prices to the customers in English. 'You need to be thick-skinned – I've learned that,' Ah-Fang told me. She's got used to repeating phrases like '£60 for a half-hour' and '£100 for an hour' again and again during the day.

'Why don't you give customers a price list?' I asked her.

'You must be joking! A price list would be the best evidence for the police if they came in.'

To me, she didn't conceal her contempt for the customers. 'Some of them are not only sexually demanding in their session, they then bargain relentlessly when the session's over. Some pay for an hour's session, but finish halfway through and demand half the money back! They want the best and want it cheap. Out of £60 per half-hour, the Misses are only getting £30. Imagine getting £30 for letting these men walk all over you! Occasionally you get customers who don't want the full service – either because they're first-timers or because they don't have enough cash. Then I have to tell them about our *mai lingjian* [selling parts] service.'

I was astonished and asked her what she meant.

'Yes, *mai lingjian*! We sell body parts here, just like most brothels do. It's called "making the best use of goods". I say to customers, "If you don't want to do the whole session, you can just pay for parts. Three pounds for touching the Miss's face and hair, £10 for touching the upper part of her body, £20 for fondling the lower part of her body. And you can only do these in the waiting area, not in the rooms."'

As I was digesting this information Ah-Fang told me more. 'For those who want a full session in the room, then I tell them they have to wear a condom. Some bastards don't want to wear one. One of the Misses told me that a customer took off his condom halfway through the session without asking for her consent. That's just disgusting and unacceptable. I also have to tell them that they must wear a condom for oral sex. These men could be carrying all kinds of disease, for God's sake! But there's a rule that if a man doesn't want to use a condom for oral sex, and if the Miss agrees to it, he has to pay £10 extra, directly to her. And in this case she can keep the cash to herself, without having to share it with the bosses. It's a way for the Misses to earn a bit of extra cash if they decide it's worth taking the risk.'

During her chats with me on the phone, I noticed that Ah-Fang spoke in quite a nonchalant way about the job, as if she was completely used to it. But I detected beneath the surface that she was far from comfortable with the clientele and with the whole idea of commercial sex.

One day she told me about her background. She'd grown up quite lonely and neglected, although she was the fourth child of a large Hakka family of seven siblings. (Hakka is an ethnic group in southern China.) Throughout her teenage years, her father was working all his waking hours as a delivery man, earning a meagre living for the family. She'd never had a conversation with her mother about the opposite sex. The only person she could talk to was her younger sister, who needed advice herself. Ah-Fang found consolation in Buddhism. She often visited a temple and asked the deities for advice on her future. Religion was her only emotional support when she left home to work in an electronics assembly factory in Singapore. 'My beliefs sustained me through those dark days. I saw my colleagues getting hurt at work, losing their fingers in terrible accidents. I was lucky to survive intact.' Her religion was still sustaining her now in England, and whenever she could she visited the True Buddha Temple in Willesden Green, though she couldn't visit it these days, as she had no day off.

As a Buddhist, she told me, she found it almost unbelievable to hear herself talking about prices for sex services with customers. 'I never thought I'd come to this!'

As usual, she disguised her disgust with a giggle. But I knew she loathed the moral and the physical aspects of the job. 'I can't help worrying that I might catch something from this place. I even get worried when the Misses wash their underwear in our kitchen basin! I can't help feeling a bit nauseous. I have to tell them to wash their pants in the bathroom!'

As well as dreading having too much work, the Misses and Ah-Fang live in fear of having too little. One day in Ah-Fang's first week, two men came in to look the Misses up and down and select one each. But they didn't want either of them. 'You're not good enough,' they said, and left.

'What am I supposed to do when they decide to leave?' Ah-Fang said. 'It's their choice, isn't it? The only thing I could do was tell them to come back next week when we'll have some new ladies in. Then the manageress calls me and asks in that piercing voice of hers how many customers we've had that day. When I tell her we've only had five, and it's a Friday, supposed to be the busiest day of the week, she gets hysterical. "We invest a lot in this business, spending £100 a week on advertising, and you can't even keep our customers." Then she pointed at me and said, "Look at you, in that old jumper! You're frightening our customers with your old age. And you never smile, do you? You look more like a mad old auntie than a proper housekeeper! If you want to keep your job, you'd better fix your appearance."'

Her words hurt Ah-Fang, but not enough to make her leave. 'I've seen so many bosses like her in my life. They can't break me any more.'

The Misses told Ah-Fang not to allow the manageress's words to get to her. They told her that the manageress was actually pleased to have her because she could at least speak a few words and phrases of English. They told her she'd already lasted longer than many other housekeepers they'd met. 'Most of them get sacked within a week, because they can't keep the customers! You're doing fine! You're still here!'

In order to prevent customers taking one look and leaving, Chinese massage parlours have an elaborate system of 'swapping'. Ah-Fang explained it to me.

'These men come to the parlours because they're bored with their wives and girlfriends. You know what men are like! They like a change – and it's the same at the parlours. They don't want to see the same Misses every time, never mind how pretty they are. So the Misses get rotated each week, sent to different parlours. They have to perform well in their week's slot at each parlour, to make sure they'll be invited back again. At the moment, our two Misses have got themselves completely booked up for months at different parlours. Their diaries are full till July!'

Swapping, I discovered, is standard practice in the sex trade – and the amount of swapping a parlour does is a sign of how well or badly it's doing. I met Mr Lo, a Chinese owner of another massage parlour in London, who admitted that not much swapping was going on in his parlour. 'I've only recently opened and I haven't built up the social networks yet. I don't have very many Misses to circulate. It'll take a few months to build up the business. I'm only making a profit of £200 a day, when other parlours are making £500. Besides, as our customers are locals, economically average and not very fussy, we don't worry too much about the ages of our Misses – mostly over forty. We don't feel the need to do too much swapping.'

Mr Lo contrasted his own modest business with other much more profitable parlours – the ones with Chinese-only clientele. (These number just one in fifty Chinese-owned parlours.) 'The Chinese clients are much more picky. They pay more for the service, and they definitely demand variety. Those parlours employ younger ladies, and they do swapping all the time. They can make profits of £1,000 a day.' Lo looked envious as he spoke. He told me he wanted to expand his business, and was thinking of buying an old Methodist church he'd seen for sale and converting it into a two-storey parlour.

The pressure to compete with other brothels is also immense for Ah-Fang's manageress. That's what makes her so furious when clients go elsewhere: she feels she's losing out to rivals. Ah-Fang and the Misses decided to spare her the pain of this information – and to spare themselves the hysterical telling-off – by simply not informing her of the number of customers that had walked out.

But the manageress was not so easy to fool. She keeps a record of every customer who calls her to ask for the address of the premises. If the number of callers differs from the number who pay, Ah-Fang is questioned. The manageress complains about how little money the business is making (an average of £750 a day, of which half goes to her and half is divided between the Misses). 'And then,' said Ah-Fang, 'she goes and cuts costs by providing us with cheap and insufficient food. Our weekly diet is a bag of chicken wings and three long slices of pork, to share between us. Now and then she comes in to check how much rice I put in the cooker. If she thinks it's too much she gets angry.'

Ah-Fang was finding it a strain living under this woman's constant mistrust and suspicion. The manageress didn't even trust Ah-Fang with the money, often accusing her of not letting on how many customers they'd had and sharing the takings directly with the Misses.

But the hardest thing of all for Ah-Fang was the absolute restriction of movement. With no breaks or day off, she could hardly ever leave the flat. The only time she could sneak out for ten minutes of fresh air in the car park was before 9 a.m. if no one was around. When her working day was finished, long past midnight, she finally felt free to make a few calls to friends before going to bed.

She confided to me that she was finding this deprivation of freedom increasingly suffocating and intolerable. But she couldn't see a way out. 'The bosses want to avoid any exposure of our work and our status. They think that if we go out we'll run the risk of being arrested. If that happens, they'll have to close down. So they're being doubly careful about keeping us in here. Even when we need to send money home – especially the Misses, who have children to support in China – the manageress won't allow us to go out. She says she'll send the money for us via a Chinese bank when she goes up to Chinatown. So we have to entrust all our cash to her – and she charges us a £20 service fee!'

Ah-Fang was gradually losing all sense of what was happening in the world outside the dreary flat. She couldn't even tell me what day of the week it was when I called her. She didn't know anyone in the area, and had not the slightest idea about the kind of neighbourhood she was living in – apart from knowing that it was quiet, very quiet. 'The Misses are the only human beings I talk to here,' she said. 'At least they give me variety! When there are no customers, and if the Misses aren't trying to have a nap in their rooms, we chat for hours, about everything under the sun!'

Ah-Fang asked Xiao Fen some searching questions, such as how she coped with the men, physically and emotionally. Xiao Fen tried to smile the questions away, but she did admit to Ah-Fang that the work could put a huge strain on you. 'We get these sickos, the kind who are fixated on Oriental women. They make you do all kinds of crazy things. You have to pose and tease before he gets into action. The whole session leaves you completely exhausted before it finishes.'

Ah-Fang told her about a Chinese girl she'd met during her week at the parlour in Cardiff, who'd had to do escort service. 'At least you don't have to do that,' Ah-Fang said. 'This girl – she got driven by this client, a respectable-looking man, all the way to the beach. There, he made her strip off and wear nothing but a pair of black stockings. He made her walk up and down the beach for a whole hour. She said she was tired, and freezing cold, but he wouldn't let her stop walking. "Carry on, just carry on," he said. She was nothing but a piece of

'Oriental flesh for him. She strolled back and forth in the cold. When he finally felt satisfied he drove her back to his house. There he did his full session. What a joy that must have been!'

The Misses laughed at Ah-Fang's story. 'Crazy *guilao*!'

'Don't laugh – the woman got a big tip that evening. *Guilaos* don't usually give tips.'

'I know,' said Yan-Erh, who was listening to the conversation. 'We make good money, but it's not easy. I don't feel my body can cope much longer. I'm going to have to take a break for a few months after the summer. My working life has to continue in England for some years yet. I can't afford to ruin my health doing a job like this.'

As she spoke, a customer walked in. Yan-Erh recognized him: a white man in his forties, a regular for her when she's at this parlour. He knew she was being swapped to another parlour next week. As she went into her room with him, Xiao Fen said to Ah-Fang, 'Yan-Erh's age is her advantage. That's why she has regular customers. Who doesn't like younger women? But I've got to look on the bright side, haven't I? This is, after all, the only job in England where we can earn a bit more than the locals. I've heard that the locals only get something like £40 per half-hour (also to be shared fifty-fifty with their employers). It's the only job where we benefit from being foreign.'

'Have you been sending money to your son?' Ah-Fang asked her.

'Yes, of course. I've been sending £900 a month. I've paid off all the money I borrowed to come here. If I keep going like this for a few more years, I'll be able to set up a small shop of my own back home.'

'I'm sure you will,' said Ah-Fang cheerfully. 'You'll have such a good life. Then you'll know that this has all been worthwhile.'

For Xiao Fen, despite the earnings and the prospect of improving her living standard in China, her self-sacrifice in the massage parlours all over 'Zone Six' of London will remain a permanent record, never to be erased from her memory.

After that chat with Ah-Fang I was flicking through the ads in a Chinese newspaper, and spotted an agency advertising massage-parlour jobs. The name was familiar – Good Luck. Then I remembered I'd come across this agency before when the woman who ran it had rung me to tell me about her life in England and why she'd set up an agency. She'd told me how busy she was leading Chinese workers into all kinds of jobs, from restaurants and takeaways to factories and building sites. But she'd omitted to tell me that she also led women into jobs in the sex trade. I couldn't resist picking up the telephone and asking her about this.

'I worked as a housekeeper in a brothel once,' she said to me. 'Believe me, I know what a hard life it is in there. But some women are desperate. They need the money you can earn in these jobs.'

I told her I'd like to get a job as a housekeeper in a brothel to try to see for myself what the work was like. At that suggestion she revealed to me her true feelings about these workplaces. 'No, no. I wouldn't recommend it. It's dangerous to work in those places.'

I wondered: if it's so dangerous for me, why is it not danger-ous for the undocumented Chinese women from whom she demands a fee of £70 to £100 for placing them in a brothel?

The element of danger was revealed to me during further talks with massage-parlour owners. They acknowledge that the job comes with high safety risks. But they shrug their shoulders at the question of responsibility. 'It's the women's free choice to work here,' one owner said to me.

'But do you inform them about the risks before they accept the job offer?'

He refused to answer the question directly.

A parlour owner named Mr Lo said to me, 'Women get

quick cash in this job. But they pay the price of safety. I'd say that massage parlours are the most dangerous places to work in England. Ninety-nine per cent of Chinese women who've worked for me have experienced physical violence at work. And when that happens there's nothing much the parlour can do.'

It's not the physical violence during sessions with customers that's the real danger – although that happens on occasions – but robbery by local gangs, and the bodily harm that goes with it. 'If you're a Chinese-run massage parlour,' Ah-Fang said to me, 'your business will be known to the locals in the area, no matter how secretive and secluded you try to be. For the local gangs, Chinese brothels are an excellent target because we always have cash around and we never report any attack to the police. What would we say to them? That we're working illegally and selling sex? In the eyes of the authorities, we're illegals doing an illegal job, and we have no right to ask for any protection.'

Ah-Fang found out that in the week before she'd arrived at the Cheam parlour it had been robbed. The Misses told her that two customers had come in and had their sessions. Afterwards, instead of paying, they'd taken out knives and told them to hand over all the cash they had. The Misses hadn't dared to refuse – not after hearing so many stories about Chinese women getting stabbed when they say no to robbers. Ah-Fang told me that at the Cardiff parlour she'd met a Miss who told her that robbers had not only taken her money but kicked her down the stairs as well. 'These people are brutal,' Ah-Fang said. 'They don't care that you're a woman. Every day we live in a state of fear that something bad's going to happen to us: not only minor bodily harm and robbery, but even rape. I know a woman who got caught in this unfortunate situation. She was a housekeeper, like me. The men had guns. They took all her cash and one of them raped her.'

It's an ironic fact that if a woman works in one of the

brothels that are protected by a criminal gang, it will be a safer place for her to work. It's the ordinary little underground ones in places like Cheam that are the most vulnerable. The owner of a small massage parlour told me about this. He said (with some envy), 'You get these large-scale businesses in the city. They're run by 14K [the Hong Kong-originated mafia]. If you use Chinatown as the starting-point and drive for twenty minutes in any direction, you'll find these places if you look for them. They do all kinds of profitable business, such as people smuggling, cigarette smuggling, money laundering, cannabis dealing and catering; prostitution's just a part of it. They're discreet about their sex business. They restrict their clientele to Chinese only, and only advertise in the Chinese newspapers. They recruit their Misses via a number of select agencies who specialize in particular ethnic groups, such as Chinese, Korean or Thai. They're also highly protective of their business territory. Take the parlours in Wood Green and Seven Sisters, for example. Red Tower's a well-known one. The 14K man in charge of that territory not only enjoys an affluent lifestyle, driving around in expensive cars, he also ensures that any new sex business will be subjected to 14K attacks when it opens. Only recently, they smashed the windows and destroyed the furniture of a newly opened parlour up there.'

It seems incredible that a little massage parlour in Cheam can seem innocuous, but a comparison to the big sharks in the city centre render it so.

Ah-Fang, meanwhile, carried on working in the parlour, waiting for pay-day. She'd been there for a month and a half and still the manageress hadn't paid her. She was getting worried, because she knew housekeepers were supposed to be paid on a weekly basis. She'd also heard that manageresses could under-pay housekeepers if they decided they didn't like you. 'There's no real set wage,' she said to me. 'It doesn't matter how much the boss has verbally agreed to pay you. The whole thing's a *hei dian* [black shop], after all.'

'Are you thinking of leaving?' I asked her.

'No way! If I stay, she might pay me soon. If I leave, I get nothing from her.'

It was a busy week. The new Misses were popular. One was from Singapore and one was Malaysian Chinese. Ah-Fang admitted to them that she envied their money-earning power. 'I wish I could make a few hundred pounds a day like you do. The bosses depend on your bodies for profit, so they must pay you. It's a different story for a dispensable housekeeper like me.'

The Misses told her she was right in a way: the bosses need to keep up a good reputation among the sex workers, otherwise no one would want to go and work for them. 'If you want quick cash,' one of the Misses said to Ah-Fang, 'you're in the wrong job. Housekeepers never make much money. Why did you come here?'

'Well, I'm old,' said Ah-Fang, 'with no real skills. I can't see myself getting any other work, except a domestic job like this.'

In the following days, with these new Misses, the number of customers increased dramatically. This was good news for Ah-Fang's job security, but bad news in another way: the stream of customers attracted the attention of neighbours, who complained to the landlord. Ah-Fang told me on the phone that the landlord had decided to evict them, and they'd have to move to other premises the next day. The next day, however, the relocation plan was cancelled. No one at the parlour knew how it had happened and what kind of deal the boss had made with the landlord. The whole thing unsettled Ah-Fang. 'What worries me is that if any of these frustrated neighbours calls the police, the parlour will be shut down. The bosses will just cancel their mobile phones and vanish without paying me.'

As it turned out, the bad news was of a different sort. The manageress informed Ah-Fang that she was going to be replaced by a new housekeeper, 'someone who can keep the customers'. Ah-Fang was paid £20 less per week than agreed as a result of her 'poor performance'.

'I can finally have my day off now!' Ah-Fang was almost singing to me on the phone as she left the parlour.

The first place she went to was the True Buddha Temple at Willesden Green. I went with her to this tranquil place, and thought how beautiful it must have been to her after her long incarceration in Cheam. She prayed on her knees for an hour. Then she picked out a fortune stick (*qiu qian*, asking the deities for guidance by choosing a stick at random with a message folded up on it). She read the words aloud to me. 'When you try to reach the lilies in the pond, you will fall in each time.' She paid the monk £5 for interpreting the message for her. ('The monks here don't have a wage,' she explained to me, 'and they rely on believers' donations to live.') I asked if she believed in the monks' interpretations of her problems and her future. 'Definitely, yes,' she said.

It wouldn't, perhaps, have taken a monk's wisdom to interpret the depressing message on Ah-Fang's stick: her job-seeking could only mean ongoing anguish and misery. The foretelling turned out to be right. Ah-Fang tried to stave off what the message had predicted by studying the Buddhist text *The Power of Unveiling the Divine State*. She recited every sixty words a thousand times each, then put a circle on the worksheet attached to the text. I asked her why she was doing this exercise. 'To improve my chance of getting good work,' she said.

Two weeks later, desperate for money, she got a new job as the housekeeper of a brothel in Archway, north London.

A few nights later she called me at midnight in tears. 'There were ten of them, all kinds of nationalities,' she sobbed. 'I let them in because I thought they were customers. Two came in, then three, then ... It was too late when I realized they had weapons. They pointed a knife at me, pulled my hair and pushed me on to the floor. They said, "Take out all your cash now!" I couldn't even see what was happening to the Misses.

Then one of them started shaking my head so violently that I lost consciousness.'

The robbers had even taken her mobile phone, and she'd managed to find my number from her friend Xiao Ling in Birmingham. I asked if she wanted me to call the police. 'No! No!' She wouldn't even tell me the exact location of the brothel.

It was only after this horrific incident that Ah-Fang found out that such robberies happened three or four times a month at this brothel. The south-London branch had been robbed three times in a week, and its housekeeper brutally attacked because she only had £10 on her. The boss refused to install a CCTV camera inside the parlours to enable the staff to see the customers outside, because he was afraid it would attract the attention of the police. The way he dealt with the problem was simply to keep up a high turnover of housekeepers.

A second robbery occurred two weeks after the first one, and this was Ah-Fang's cue for dismissal. The brothel owners knew that once a housekeeper has experienced a series of robberies, she becomes reluctant to open the door to customers. 'You're in shock,' the manageress said to her. 'You should take a rest for a while.' Ah-Fang knew what she meant by 'a rest'. It was time to visit the True Buddha Temple again.

She did so with me. As we walked in, people were reciting their prayers. All I could hear was what sounded like a rhyming song repeated again and again. Ah-Fang was reluctant to join in. 'These people are at a much higher level than me. I'm just a beginner.' Not wanting to disturb the praying people, she led me into the temple's library, where she carefully looked through Buddhist textbooks, trying to find some elementary ones for me. It seemed to me that she had no alternative but to believe that her working experiences in Britain had some kind of spiritual meaning.

She waved goodbye to me at the temple gate as I walked away down the wide stone steps. 'I have to stay and wait to speak to the Master today,' she said. 'I have so many problems to ask him for help with!'

As I left I felt glad that Ah-Fang was finding consolation in her religion. I thought of the thousands of other Chinese women who were continuing, without a ray of hope, to work in the underground trade in which Ah-Fang had become entangled. I decided to go undercover for a few days as a receptionist and housekeeper in a massage parlour. I wanted to be able to describe from first-hand experience what such a job was like.

Finding a job was easy. Through a London contact, I heard about a vacancy for a brothel housekeeping job in Burnley, Lancashire. I associated Burnley with economic decline, racial segregation and the riots of 2001, but I did not think of it as a place with its own sex trade employing undocumented Chinese. As I travelled through rainy Lancashire towns on a slow train, I could only imagine the homesickness of those Chinese women struggling to make a living in this northern landscape.

The massage-parlour owner, named Mr Li, picked me up at Blackburn station. He was smartly dressed, from north-east China and he seemed a little unconvinced when he saw me. 'Are you Li Yun?' That was the name I was using for this job. 'You're younger than I expected.' (I'm thirty-eight, and it's an unspoken rule that applicants for housekeeping jobs in massage parlours are over forty.)

Mr Li bought me a can of Coke as a gesture of goodwill, and we got on a train from Blackburn to Burnley. On the way there he told me a bit about himself. He'd been in Britain for eight years. 'My first job was in a kitchen – that was hard,' he said, looking at me intensely as if he was seeking common ground with me. He'd been working in the sex trade for four years, starting off in Mile End in London. 'It's difficult to keep a business going there. It's rough. Too many risks. Too much robbery. It's different in Burnley. It's a small community and the customers are mostly regulars.'

He made it sound a cosy and attractive world. 'Blackpool is the nicest seaside place around. Good fish and chips! And you can visit Manchester, not far away. Nice Chinatown there.' I nodded, and he turned to business.

'You'll be paid £180 for working seven days a week,' Mr Li told me. 'You're not supposed to leave the premises during work time. You have one day off per month. Don't worry. If you become more experienced, your pay will go up.'

We arrived at a two-storey terraced house in Briercliffe Road in Burnley. He introduced me to his sister, a woman in her mid-twenties. 'She's the manageress of this parlour,' he told me, 'and she'll be training you for the job.'

I looked at her and saw that in spite of her young age she had the manner of a harsh boss, an oppressor of women. I recognized the type. She started lecturing me at once. Not only did I have to do all the household and receptionist duties such as cooking, cleaning, washing sheets and keeping accounting records, I must also keep an eye on the Misses. 'You must make sure they work a full session, not cutting short. If it's a one-hour session, you can't allow the Misses to come out before the hour ends. Understand?'

Unlike in Cheam, the manageress of this parlour visited daily and sometimes stayed overnight. This meant we were under her constant mistrusting gaze. She didn't approve of conversation between the Misses and me. She didn't even like the two Misses talking to each other. 'The bosses don't want us to know too much about the workplace,' Mei whispered to me – she was here for a week. The Misses were treated as commodities to be exchanged among the parlours, and their needs were irrelevant to the manageress. 'No need to ask them about their preference for food,' she said to me. 'They're only staying for a week. They need to adapt to the way we do things here.'

While I was at the parlour there was, as it happened, only one Miss on duty. She was joined by a Thai woman in her forties just before I left. Mei was the one whose working life I witnessed.

The doorbell rang. It was a customer, an overweight man in his twenties. He gave off a strong smell of sweat. The manageress shouted out to Mei, 'Customer here! Are you ready?' I heard Mei run across to her room. 'Yes!' she called back, once she'd presumably put on her work clothes. Then the manageress told me to lead the customer along the narrow corridor to Mei. When we were in front of her room, scented with strong perfume, she opened the door gently. She was wearing a bra and lacy pants. She looked tiny and thin. In the dim orange light she displayed herself like an ornament, with a tired smile under her high cheekbones. I was so overwhelmed by the emptiness of her watery eyes that I forgot what to say to the customer.

'Hurry up,' the manageress called to me.

'Er – how long would you like to do it for?' I asked the customer. 'It's £50 for half an hour, £90 for one hour.'

The manageress butted in: 'But if you have two orgasms in the half-hour session, you'll have to pay £70.'

'That's right,' I said (although this fact was news to me).

The man, clearly hardly able to afford one orgasm, let alone two, asked me, 'Anything less than half an hour?' The manageress replied for me: 'Yes, it will be £40 for twenty minutes, but no preliminary massage.' He took three seconds to weigh up his budget against Mei's charms. He chose the twenty minutes. When his time was up, two other men were queuing in the reception area. As I was explaining the prices, one of them turned to the manageress and asked if he could also have a session with me. 'No, no, the receptionist doesn't do sex,' she replied, hustling him into the room. (Now I understood why bosses preferred their housekeepers to be in their forties or fifties.) Towards the end of the session, another man rang the bell. 'Quick, quick, into the kitchen!' The manageress asked the man waiting in the reception area to hide himself. (This was getting to be like a bedroom farce.) The rule is that customers shouldn't be allowed to meet one another, as Burnley is a small town and word will spread.

Two hours later, after the men had left, Mei finally had time to breathe. She didn't want to stay in her workroom – which was also her bedroom. She came into my room to have a rest, and offered me a glass of wine. John Lennon's 'Imagine' was playing on the radio. I noticed that Mei wasn't really having a break – she was already starting to powder her face again, ready for the next customer. 'I don't know when I'll finish work tonight,' she said to me. 'Could be 1 a.m., could be later. These men don't respect me. The sight of them makes me sick. But I've no choice. I have a sixteen-year-old son at home, and I need to earn fast to pay for his education.' She told me her husband had died in a car accident a few years ago. 'I suppose I could try to earn some cash doing other work, but I don't have time to waste in those low-paid jobs.' She told me she was earning £200 to £250 a day here, with about ten customers each day.

When it got dark, the manageress told me to close the curtains and turn on a small lamp in the reception area. 'We don't want to attract attention from outside. OK? Don't turn on the main light!' So we sat in semi-darkness for the next seven hours. Mei's entire evening was spent serving customers, while the manageress relaxed on the sofa downstairs enjoying Hong Kong soap operas, whose piercing sounds came up the stairwell. I crept downstairs and watched her devouring a large tub of vanilla ice cream while Mei was serving a bald fifty-something in her bed. On the television the song 'Small Town Story' by the Taiwanese singer Deng Lijun was playing in between the soap operas. '*This small town is filled with stories of joy and sorrow.*'

Peering through the curtains, I saw locals walking home with their Somerfield shopping bags, oblivious to what was going on behind these walls.

It was 2 a.m. by the time the last customer left. When I went to say goodnight to Mei, she looked exhausted. She'd removed her make-up, and now she looked like herself – a mother, who has crossed continents to work in order to support her son.

'I'm leaving tomorrow,' she told me. 'I'm being sent to a parlour in Blackburn.' In the next month, Mei would be toured around four parlours in different northern towns. 'For me,' she said, 'all these places are the same.' She started to pack her clothes into her suitcase, ready to leave the next day. It would be, for her, just one of countless bleak journeys.

7. At the Back of Gerrard Street

Ken Livingstone, the mayor of London, came to Chinatown
that day. He met business representatives and had lunch at the
China City Restaurant. He made a speech saying the 70,000
Chinese in London are contributing a great deal to the capital's
economic and cultural life.

*– Mrs Huang, an undocumented kitchen worker in
Chinatown, remembering an event that happened during
one of her twelve-hour shifts
Summer 2007*

In the summer of 2007 I was wandering through London's
Chinatown, from Lisle Street to Wardour Street and then
through to Gerrard Street. It was nearly lunchtime and couples
were sauntering along arm in arm, deciding which restaurant
to go into. The spacious, airy one with white tablecloths?
The smaller, cosier one with glazed ducks hanging in the
window? I was hungry too. My mouth watered at the fragrances
wafting through the open front doors. But my main reason
for being here was to ask restaurant employees questions. It was
the week when the Transport and General Workers' Union
(TGWU, now part of UNITE) was launching a campaign to
make the rules governing restaurant tips and service charges
more fair to workers.

A small group of tourists decided on the attractive, elegantly
decorated Gerrard's Corner, famous in London dining guides
for its 'good-quality, authentic Chinese cuisine'. I followed
them in. A Chinese waiter swiftly came to sit me down at a

table in the corner, and politely asked me what I'd like to drink. I asked for tea. He darted off, and I watched his movements. He never stopped. Customers came in, he smiled, sat them down, took orders, brought drinks, brought food, smiled again, took more orders. For a brief moment, when no one was demanding his attention, he stood still; but the manager nudged him to go to the door to welcome more customers in. So he darted off, wearing his smile again.

When he came to pour tea into my cup, I asked him in Mandarin, 'Excuse me, could you tell me if your restaurant charges a service fee?' He looked at me and I saw the exhaustion behind his smile. He replied, 'The restaurant does have a service charge. We will have nothing to eat if you customers don't pay the service charge and a tip on top of that.' I asked him how much he was paid. Holding the teapot in his hand to justify talking to me for longer than he should, he said in a low voice, 'We're paid £5 a day as a base rate of pay. That's all we get if we don't get any tips from you.'

As I discovered during discreet chats with many waiters in the following days and weeks, the term 'base rate' (*di xin*) is cleverly and euphemistically used by employers to deflect attention from the fact that it is the only wage coming out of their own pocket. For the waiter at Gerrard's Corner, that daily £5 is the sole reward his employer gives him for working eleven to twelve hours a day, six days a week. This wage structure, I found, is in place in ninety-nine per cent of the restaurants in Chinatown, the heart of the economy of the Chinese community in London. While the businesses here pride themselves on being a tourist attraction with their high standard of cuisine in a restaurant capital of Europe, they are leaving it to the customers (with their little rewards in coins or digits keyed into the chip-and-pin machine) to compensate for the pittance they pay their staff.

The 'base rate', I found, can vary among different restaurants and different waiters. At the Imperial China Restaurant, waiters are paid £50 to £60 a week as the 'base rate'; at New Loon Fung it's £50, at Crispy Duck Restaurant it's £30 to £35. At Y Ming Restaurant on Greek Street it's £50 to £80, depending on experience and length of service (as the owner told me – although one of the waiters told me there was no base rate at all). And there are places with worse practices: in Furama Restaurant waiters reveal that, apart from the £30-a-week base rate (which stays the same no matter how long you've worked there), they're only paid nine per cent of the service charge, and are not allowed to keep the tips, which go into the owner's pocket. A waitress who has been working here for a month tells me she doesn't get any of the service charge distributed to her at all.

It's not as if these restaurants are little upstart businesses owned by shady villains who don't know any better. Imperial China Restaurant is owned by Chu Ting Tang, a respectable community leader whose name is associated with the growth and success of Chinatown. He's the president of the London Chinatown Chinese Association (LCCA, formed in 1978), which works with the council, the police and the Greater London Authority, and organizes the spectacular annual Chinese New Year celebrations in Trafalgar Square. He's also a successful businessman, owning numerous Tang family concerns such as Jialihua Restaurant on Gerrard Street, New Harbour Grocery, Euro Travel and Jade Travel. Y Ming Restaurant is owned by Christine Yau, Chair of the London Chinese Community Centre (established in Chinatown in 1980). Ms Yau is known to be an 'outward-thinking' community leader who mingles with council officials and local politicians. She is seen as a leader who promotes the idea of the modernization of Chinese catering. But does this 'modernization' involve paying workers a decent wage?

I walked up Gerrard Street towards Newport Place and decided to go into New China Restaurant, a relatively new business, known for its authentic central Chinese cuisine. I wondered whether they'd have different practices. When I approached a waiter, the manager came up to me and asked what I wanted. Unlike many restaurant owners who belong to an older generation that arrived from Hong Kong in the 1950s, this manager is one of the new generation of entrepreneurs who have come from China to set up businesses in the past decade. He speaks Mandarin and uses an up-to-date vocabulary to demonstrate that he's with the times. I asked him about the wage structure in his restaurant. He shrugged, smiled a smooth smile and tried to charm his way out of my inconvenient questioning. 'There's nothing to dig here,' he said.

But I persisted. In the end he sat me down at a table and said, 'In Chinatown the relationship between employers and employees is a harmonious one. When the business isn't doing so well, because there are fewer tourists around, both employers and employees suffer. When the business is doing well, we all benefit from it. Then it's mutual prosperity. We're all in the same boat.' I pressed on about the wage structure, and encouraged the waiter standing next to him to say something. The manager finally frowned and said, 'That is our business secret.'

Later one of the waiters at this restaurant told me that their wages come mostly from the twelve and a half per cent service charge. But, although he has worked here for more than a year, this worker has no idea what percentage of the service charge goes towards paying wages. 'It's completely up to the boss.'

My conclusion, at the end of these preliminary meanderings among the restaurants in Chinatown, was that most waiters here, under a variety of pay systems, are being paid well below the national minimum wage, working up to seventy-two hours a week. One of the waiters summed up the situation when I asked him how he'd describe his work in Chinatown. 'There is only one word,' he said: 'Harsh.'

That is not the full story, however. All of the above is only the surface of what really goes on behind the scenes in London's Chinatown. Most of these waiters, many from Hong Kong and Malaysia and a few from China, may not be earning the national minimum wage, let alone Ken Livingstone's London living wage of £7.20 an hour, but, in the eyes of their less fortunate peers, they are seen as enviably lucky. Waiters, as the 'front face' of restaurants, tend at least to have legal status to live and work in Britain.

Yes: legal status, or *shen-fen*. That, as every worker without it would say, is the difference between heaven and hell. Those with *shen-fen* can renew their visas if they want to earn more. They can have bank accounts, and go to a GP. They can use their real names. They don't have to live in dread of the next workplace raid.

Behind the underpaid staff with legal status is the concealed foundation of the Chinese catering trade: in the airless kitchens behind these restaurants, or standing with placards in the street as 'greeters' in the pouring rain, or doing deliveries on bikes in London traffic, or unloading from lorries, or silently pushing trolleys of dimsum, we meet our old friends the undocumented workers, without whose toil most of the 5,000 Chinese restaurants and the 10,000 Chinese takeaways in Britain would go out of business.

Despite their dependence on this status-less army of labour, few restaurateurs in London's Chinatown are willing to talk about employing them. It's an issue they prefer to keep quiet about, hoping that if they do, no one will find out. I tried to make enquiries, but didn't get very far. So I decided the only way to get a true picture of the working life of an un-documented worker here was to pretend to be one myself. In July 2007 I went around Chinatown in search of a job as a worker from China without *shen-fen*.

I was told that Chuen Cheng Ku Restaurant had job vacancies. It's in Wardour Street, facing Gerrard Street, and is popular locally for having food trolleys, which many diners prefer to ordering from a menu. I walked in at 10.30 a.m. and asked for a job – any job.

'Do you know how to push a trolley?' the manager at the door asked me.

Eagerly, I said yes. He led me into the restaurant and asked the manageress of the dimsum-trolley waitressing team to come and speak to me. A severe-looking woman in her forties, she introduced herself as Hao Jie, 'the Good Older Sister'. 'You want to work full-time or part-time?' she asked in a heavy Cantonese accent that told me she was either from Hong Kong or the Cantonese-speaking Guangdong province of China. I told her I was on a student visa (which officially permits you to work for a maximum of twenty hours a week), but was willing to work any hours.

'From Monday to Friday your hours are 11 a.m. to 4 p.m.,' she said. 'At weekends, it's 11 a.m. to 5.30 p.m.' I nodded enthusiastically. She handed me two sheets of dimsum menu and told me to memorize all the items before I started work the next day. King prawn dumplings, pork dumplings, bean-curd rolls, phoenix feet (chicken feet), sea snail, beef tripe, spare ribs, lotus seed buns . . . there were about thirty items on the list.

'You'll be paid £3.20 per hour,' she said. 'If you work at night, you'll get £3.50. You'll need to pay a deposit of £20 for your uniform, and another deposit of £30 to ensure you won't leave the job without giving two weeks' notice.' (We have to give two weeks' notice if we want to leave; but the employers don't have to give us any notice if they want to dismiss us.)

I had to buy my own black skirt to go with the restaurant's uniform, a traditional Chinese bright-red top. My job title, I was told, was '*tui che*' (trolley pusher), but when I arrived at work I found I'd be called by the name of the food on my trolley. I would be known as 'Roast Duck'. That was my only identity here.

As instructed, the six other dimsum-trolley-pushers also arrived at 10.30. As a new worker, I waited for a possible health-and-safety tour around the workplace, but it never came. Hao Jie did not even explain to me where things were in the kitchen, let alone tell me about potential safety hazards. She simply told us all to load food on to our trolleys. I looked at all the items on 'Phoenix Feet's' and 'Prawn Dumpling's' trolley, to refresh my memory of the dishes I'd memorized, just in case there was some kind of test. Xiao Ying, a new worker from Fujian who'd started here yesterday (I've changed her name), was opening the lid of each steamer, one by one, trying to remember the names of the dishes. She spoke no English, so this required a great effort.

My Roast Duck trolley was the heaviest of all, carrying not only roast ducks but also roast pork, roast chicken and a large pot of congee with fermented eggs and pork threads. With all this weight, it was hard to manoeuvre it round the corners of the room across two sections of the restaurant. I grimaced as I passed Xiao Ying, and she whispered to me that her feet were in agony after standing all day yesterday. 'Today I've put a bit of toilet paper between my foot and my shoe. But I'm still limping.'

From noon onwards, customers started to arrive in large numbers. Some were tourists, some were men in suits out for a business lunch. The waiters ushered them in and showed them to their tables. As soon as they sat down, all seven of us trolley-pushers rushed towards them one after the other, touting our wares. Eagerly I pushed my trolley up the aisle, at the end of the trolley queue. By the time I reached the table, people's plates were overloaded with food from the trolleys in front of me. But I was here to sell food. That was my job. So I said, in my politest voice, 'Would you like some roast duck?'

We trolley workers, I realized, are like street sellers in a glamorous market. We display our delicately presented products and call out the names of each item. Customers enjoy the exotic sight and sound of Oriental girls offering them things; their senses are titillated by the colours and fragrance of the little dimsum dishes passed under their noses, but they don't like the pressure of having to accept one of the more expensive items and have the box ticked on the bill. I watched my co-workers. Some were enviably pushy. One of them kept prompting and coaxing an unsure customer – 'Yes? Prawn dumplings?' and tutted audibly when the customer said, 'Can we eat these first before we order more, please?'

My trolley was not the most popular as the roast dishes cost around £6 a plate, much more than the small dimsum dishes on other trolleys. On that first shift I only managed to sell twelve plates. The team leader kept telling me that when I only had three ducks left I should come into the kitchen to heat some more in the microwave. Workers were pressurized to work as fast as they could, at times compromising food hygiene. Dishes of all kinds were piled next to each other in the kitchen, without anything to separate them. We rushed into the kitchen to take new dishes when we'd run out. We heated food in the greasy microwave, but were told not to cover it. There was no time, apparently. I was told to spread oil on the roast ducks so the microwaved birds would look fresh and sizzling, as if they'd just come out of the oven. This technique worked well: customers always looked impressed, saying 'Wonderful!' when I came back to them with the glistening ducks.

After the first three hours of standing and walking around this large restaurant that stretches from one street to another in Chinatown, I was feeling very tired. My feet were sore and I desperately needed to sit down. But there's no break here. You must push the trolley around without stopping, even when there are hardly any customers. The only place where you can sit down is on the toilet, and I noticed that all the other workers made the most of their quick trips to the staff toilet. They always drank tap water here, as there was no time to drink water in the kitchen. It was during these momentary breaks that I managed to have quick chats with some of the workers. Xiao Ying told me this was her first job in England. She had no idea that £3.20 an hour was an extremely poor wage, well below the minimum. Another worker told me she came from Guangdong province and took up this job because, without papers or resources, she didn't know any better. Another told me that although she'd been here for a year she'd never had a pay rise.

At 3.50 p.m., ten minutes before the end of my shift, the team leader came up to me and said, 'Are you OK with this job?' I thought she was being kind and caring for my well-being. I told her I was fine and thanked her. 'Well,' she said, 'you'll start your job tomorrow.'

Tomorrow? I thought I'd started today. My feet certainly told me so. I asked Xiao Ying what the team leader had meant. 'It means you're not going to get paid for today's work,' she told me. 'I'm not sure if I'll get paid for my first day yesterday.' I was indignant. Xiao Ying didn't want to annoy the team manager by asking questions, as she'd only just started this job. I, on the other hand, had nothing to lose. I went up to the Good Older Sister and asked her, 'Hao Jie, am I going to get paid for today's work?'

'No,' she answered with a frown. 'This is your learning day. Pin your hair tightly, or the shop manager won't let you work here.'

Before leaving work I was told to clean the trolley in the kitchen. I took all the plastic doors off the trolley and washed them one by one in the sink. Everyone seemed to use the same sink to wash dishes and trolley doors. Some dirty dishes were still being soaked in the water I was using. I saw other workers carrying and fixing gas bottles to their trolleys – a skilled task that no one was trained to do on an unpaid 'learning day'. I asked Xiao Ying how she'd learned to do it. She replied, 'Just by watching other people.'

When I arrived at 10.30 the next day, I signed in like everyone else – but noticed that the other workers stated their time of arrival as 11 a.m., even though they'd arrived at 10.30. This, I found, was another small way workers were paid less. Hao Jie said that 11 a.m. is the time we actually start serving customers, so that's the time from which we'll get paid. No one seems to question this half-hour docking of pay. In fact, no one questions the restaurant about wages at all. We're paid £16 for a day shift, and that's that. Xiao Ying was finding out how little this was when you're trying to live in London. She said to me, 'I spent almost £3 on transport getting here and back. It's hardly worth the while!' She told me that after spending £10 on a skirt and shoes for the job, and paying the £50 deposit to the restaurant, she was almost penniless. I thought to myself, Now I understand why restaurant staff don't smile in Chinatown. (One of the reviews in the London eating guide describes the Chuen Cheng Ku restaurant staff as 'grumpy'.)

She confided to me (and the thought saddened me deeply) that she has a huge debt to pay a moneylender in China – the 300,000 RMB (at the current rate, about £20,000) she borrowed to come to work in this imagined 'first-rate country' (without first-rate pay). She is in her early twenties, and I can foresee that she'll be spending the next decade labouring in workplaces like this – if she avoids being rounded up in a police raid and deported.

That day, the assistant manager gave us receipts for the £50 deposits we'd paid to the restaurant. She announced, 'Keep your receipt! Otherwise you won't be able to get your money back.' On each receipt it said, 'In case of damage or loss, we will not reissue this.' That worried everyone. I saw Xiao Ying and all the trolley-pushers rushing to the lockers to put the receipts in their bags. They were too precious to lose.

The restaurant's much-feared owner rarely visits the restaurant, and I didn't see him. But two shop managers were constantly walking around to supervise the workers. I noticed that they never spoke to us trolley workers, not even to nod or say hello. It was as if we didn't exist. The waiters are better treated and better paid – although the restaurant adopts a base-rate wage structure just like the majority of restaurants in Chinatown, and the waiters' £250 a week came mostly from tips. At least they're spoken to like human beings. We trolley workers are in a different category. Our job is thought of as non-verbal, physical: pushing trolleys, cleaning. Our team is formed of undocumented workers eager to get on any shift for any reward. The employers don't even ask for our details or our phone numbers. They know we'll come back, because we're desperate. And there's no shortage of us. For a full week, six days of shifts, we'll be paid £96, all in cash. Overtime pay is out of the question. Everything is clear and simple: £3.20 an hour. We can take it or leave it.

Nor are we given any respect. In the eyes of the management, we're nothing but cheap, status-less labourers whose work is taken for granted. The way we are given our food is an example of this basic contempt. All Chinese restaurants and takeaways provide workers with food: that's part of the package. The waiters in this restaurant are allowed to eat from plates. We trolley workers, however, are fed in a different way. In the morning, just before the shift begins, meat and vegetables are poured into one deep metal container for all of us to eat out of with our own chopsticks. I found that after the food had been flipped over by six other trolley workers searching for the better morsels, I lost my appetite. No one complains about this cattle-trough feeding technique. Xiao Ying, I noticed, never said a word during these meals. She wolfed the food down, chewing hard and loud, trying to amass the energy she needed to get through the next shift. Eat and work, eat and work again: that's the rhythm of life for trolley workers.

By the end of that day I had blisters on my feet and had to drag myself to the tube station. The next morning, I felt asthmatic and knew I'd be unable to push trolleys that day. So I called Hao Jie to tell her I was off sick.

'Don't you realize it's Friday? We need you to come in today!' she barked at me down the phone.

'But I'm asthmatic. I can't work.'

'Why didn't you tell me that yesterday?'

'Because I didn't know yesterday I was going to be asthmatic today.'

She put the phone down on me. On Sunday evening I called her to confirm my shift for Monday.

'I was about to cross your name off for good,' she said. 'You're not going to take a day off again this week.'

That episode showed me how irrelevant workers' health was to the managers of the restaurant. A worker taking a sick day means less productivity for the bosses – that's all. To prevent an asthma attack on Monday, I felt I should have my inhaler with me during my shift, otherwise I'd have to leave it in a locker which wouldn't be opened until the shift ended. So I tucked the inhaler discreetly into my trolley as I pushed it along. When I came back from reheating some ducks in the kitchen, I found my inhaler had been thrown into the deep metal container in front of the trolley where the trays were kept. 'Don't carry your inhaler in the trolley,' Hao Jie said to me.

She had definitely taken against me – a troublemaker who asked too many questions and took days off. I noticed she tried to humiliate me in front of my colleagues. She changed rules and blamed me for not remembering them. In the morning she told me to heat the roast duck in the microwave for six minutes. In the afternoon it changed to three minutes. 'Didn't I tell you?' she shouted out.

'But this morning you told me it was six minutes,' I pleaded.

'No! I meant six minutes if it was two ducks!'

There was no point in arguing. I gave up and accepted the scolding. This kind of bullying is common here. No one talks back. No one even dares support a co-worker in an argument. There's too much fear: fear of losing the means of livelihood, fear of not being able to repay debts – and this fear guarantees the permanent upper hand of the management over the workers. Xiao Ying, I noticed, spoke less and less as she became more familiar with the workplace.

At the end of the shift, I was paid my wages from last week: £16, sealed inside a pocket-size plastic bag. The precious, pitiful £16! My assumed name, Li Yun, was written on it. At the bottom of the bag were the words 'Reusable: please return'.

The job sickened me, both literally and metaphorically. I could leave. This stark difference between my situation and my co-workers' was heartbreaking. I changed into my own clothes in the staff toilet. As I walked towards the front door, the waitress didn't recognize me and took me for a customer. She smiled warmly and opened the door for me, saying, 'Goodbye. Come again!' The waitress standing next to her recognized me. 'She's one of the trolley-pushers,' she told her colleague. The smile on the waitress's face vanished and she let go of the door. That was my last depressing moment as an employee at Chuen Cheng Ku Restaurant.

The Chinatown Hygiene Partnership (CHIP), which works closely with the London Chinatown Chinese Association, told me that it has recently targeted thirty-three high-risk catering businesses in London's Chinatown, following major hygiene inspections in 2005 and 2006. CHIP has been set up by Westminster Council to improve hygiene standards and awareness among food businesses in Chinatown. Richard Block, the operations manager of the Community Protection department of the council, told me, 'This is because the food team has found that catering businesses in Chinatown were struggling to get to grips with food-hygiene regulations. It seems that inspection alone can't make them comply.'

I made a Freedom of Information request on 26 November 2007 to find out whether Chuen Cheng Ku Restaurant is one of the thirty-three targeted high-risk catering businesses. And, sure enough, it is. CHIP says that it has been giving training to food handlers as well as head chefs and managers at targeted businesses such as Chuen Cheng Ku to lower the risks in the areas of cleaning, pest control and cross-contamination of food.

*

After experiencing Chinese-restaurant work from its bottom end, it was time to go to the top to try to see things from the managers' point of view. I discovered that the casual exploitation of workers has been a gradual trend. It was not always like that.

Chinese catering had its birth in Britain after the Second World War, when British soldiers returned from the Far East with a liking for Chinese food. In the 1950s many from the rural New Territories of Hong Kong migrated to England for a new life; and these people were to become the majority of the Chinese caterers in the 1960s and 1970s.

It was in the 1960s that Mr Chen Jun, now a seventy-five-year-old well-known Chinatown restaurateur, decided to come to Britain. When you look at his sumptuous Luxuriance Restaurant in Gerrard Street and his hectic social life as the Chair of Yangzhou Association (Yangzhou is his hometown) and the Deputy Chair of the Chinese Federation of Commerce and Industry in the UK, you wonder how he (and many restaurateurs like him) got to this position.

Chen is one of the few Chinatown restaurateurs who's willing to talk about the past and the present, and how Chinatown catering businesses came about and continue to thrive. He sat me down in his Gerrard Street restaurant and told me his story.

'I was a rice farmer in Yangzhou, Jiangsu province. The regular floods there meant I was unable to make a secure living in my hometown. In the late 1940s I decided to go to Shanghai to look for work, and there I got a job as a hairdresser. At that time a lot of people were moving to Hong Kong, as a step up to a better life. As an ambitious, single twenty-year-old I followed suit in 1952. But wages in Hong Kong were not high and competition was fierce. I found myself working for others as a hairdresser and trying to support a new-formed family. Then one day a customer came in to have his hair cut, and he told me all about England. He said his friend was running a hairdressing salon in London and asked if I was interested in going to work there. I was excited at the prospect. That customer became the guarantor of my work permit into the UK.'

Chen worked for a Chinese hairdresser in Covent Garden, earning £100 a month. He liked England, and extended his work permit, year after year. Eventually he decided to make a life in London and his family came to join him.

'In 1970 I opened my first shop, a hairdresser's, at eight Gerrard Street. Just up there!' He pointed to the first floor of the building across the road. 'It's still a hairdresser's today! Ten years later, when catering was booming, I bought my first restaurant from a Pakistani businessman, and named it Luxuriance. I found catering was much more profitable than hairdressing, so I devoted most of my time to my new business.'

For the little Chinese business community gathered around Gerrard Street at this time, life was looking good. Britain began to recognize the People's Republic of China in 1972, which proved a positive thing for the new Chinese entrepreneurs here. Gerrard Street was becoming associated in people's minds with all things Chinese. It was starting to be known as 'China Street'. I could see the pride on Mr Chen's face as he went on, 'Chinese food was called "chop suey" [which literally means "mixed bits"] at the time, and it was beginning to attract a much bigger audience. Things were getting better and better for us. And the rent was only £9,000 a year. The number of Chinese restaurants continued to increase, and then in 1985 the authorities came to the decision that this place would be called Chinatown.'

At that moment a large group of Chinese tourists came into the restaurant. Mr Chen stood up to greet them warmly, and recognized from their accents that they were from his home-town. I saw what a fluent and persuasive speaker he must be at his conferences: to this captive audience of hungry tourists he launched into a lecture on the importance of being united as a Chinese nation.

Five minutes later he returned to my table to continue the

story. But his tone changed. After that pinnacle in the mid-1980s, the prosperity of Chinese catering businesses gradually began to stagnate. Three decades after the catering boom, the first-generation Chinese restaurant owners experienced a new thing: a shortage of labour. The steady supply of kitchen workers (mainly chefs recruited from Hong Kong) was no longer sufficient to fill the demand. And it was not as easy as they'd expected to find a new workforce to take on the jobs. Catering was then, and still is, notorious for its long, anti-social working hours and its low pay. (Today, the average annual income for a catering worker is £9,000 or less, according to the Low Pay Unit.) Catering as an occupation had little appeal, either for local workers or for the existing ethnic-minority communities, including the British-born Chinese.

I spoke to Jabez Lam, a leading Chinese community activist. 'The children of the first-generation restaurant owners,' he told me, 'have grown up and been educated in Britain. In the past, these younger family members would have helped out in the restaurants and takeaways. Now they have better employment opportunities and don't wish to follow their fathers into the catering trade.' For the young British-Chinese, Jabez Lam said, leaving the catering trade meant leaving the 'ghetto' and finding a place in mainstream British society. Mr Chen told me it came as no surprise to him that none of his own four daughters wanted to take on his catering business. 'They have their own careers to think about,' he said.

Faced with a continuing shortage of labour, the restaurants and takeaways have to find a new and reliable workforce: ideally, one that speaks the same language and is familiar with Chinese cuisine. Thomas Chan, the chairman of the Chinese Takeaway Association, estimates that between 30,000 and 50,000 workers (from chefs to kitchen porters) per year are needed in the Chinese catering trade in Britain.

Why don't they recruit directly from China? Theoretically they could, and it should be easy, but in fact only a few large restaurants (ones with over a hundred seats) are likely to employ a small number of kitchen workers from China on work permits. The system of applying and recruiting from China is fraught with complications. To get a renewable work permit, an applicant from China needs to prove a minimum of three years' substantial catering experience equivalent to National Vocational Qualification (NVQ) Level 3 or above. 'This is difficult as most applicants could only reach Level 2,' Thomas Chan told me. Applicants over the age of twenty-five are also at a disadvantage. Information in China about applying for a work permit with Chinese employers in Britain is not easily accessible. Lacking language skills and knowledge about Britain, applicants have to resort to intermediaries to apply for permits for them. For this they have to pay a high fee – up to £10,000 – to an agency that works with Chinese employers in Britain and that shares the profits with the employers. This fee will pay for the worker's visa application, passport and an invitation letter from the British–Chinese employer. (The worker will have to pay for his own plane ticket.) The work permit he eventually gets will tie him to his British–Chinese employer in the UK, who will pay him a low wage (starting at £150 a week) and make it difficult for him to change jobs.

In order to be allowed to recruit a worker from China, a restaurant owner in Britain will need to prove that he can't find anyone from the local workforce suitable to do the job. Wu Siqiang, who owns Rong Cheng Restaurant in Shaftesbury Avenue, told me, 'If you own a restaurant with a hundred-plus seats, you're allowed to apply for about five employees directly from China to work in your kitchen. But if you own a smaller restaurant, it's harder. My restaurant seats eighty-six, and I'm allowed to apply for three to four workers from China out of my nine kitchen workers. The rest of the workforce has to be recruited from among the Chinese workers already here.'

Among the Chinese workers already here are asylum seekers waiting for a decision from the Home Office (with no support from the government, and no permission to work), failed asylum seekers and undocumented workers who have never registered themselves with the immigration system. They're readily available, desperate for work and willing to do it for small reward. Thus the line is crossed: employers don't ask too many questions and take these workers on. Chen Jun at Luxuriance was honest about the restaurateurs' reasons for avoiding recruiting directly from China: 'It costs employers to apply for overseas workers. Those work permits from China require the employers to provide the whole package, i.e. food and accommodation, so it turns out to be a more expensive way of recruiting than simply getting workers from the existing pool of Chinese workers in Britain – the Fujianese workers, students and overstayers from all over China. They're already here! Rent and rates are high in Chinatown, and employers of course prefer to be economical about their workforce.' Chen also recruits in this way. His kitchen workers are mainly from Fujian and north-east China, living in England, introduced to him by friends and contacts.

'Internal immigration controls,' Jabez Lam explained to me, 'forbid those waiting for asylum decisions and those who have been refused refugee status to work or to claim housing benefits or other welfare provision. The Chinese catering employers see these people as the ideal option, not only because they fill the labour shortage but because, by being so cheap, they help maintain a competitive advantage for the businesses.' Thus, he said, the state's policies create a situation in which labour-hungry employers help themselves from a pool of exploitable workers. An enclave of exploitation is created, defended and endorsed by all those benefiting and profiting from it. Within this enclave, the undocumented workers are earning thirty-three per cent less than the most lowly of the legally employed staff.

I went to speak to more undocumented workers in London's Chinatown, to find out whether their daily working life bore out what I'd discovered during my short sojourn in their world. I found that the average wage for a kitchen worker is £200 to £250 a week for an eleven to twelve-hour day, six days a week – that is £3 to £3.70 an hour.

Lee Ho Fook in Gerrard Street is nicknamed '*hei dian*' (black shop) by Chinese workers. Many have suffered in its kitchen, but workers are reluctant to speak about their experiences, for fear of reprisal. Qiu worked in its kitchen cutting vegetables, sixty hours a week, for £120 a week (£2 an hour). 'The nine in our kitchen had no overtime pay, no sick pay and no holiday pay,' he told me. 'The only three days we were allowed to take off in the whole year was during Christmas, but that was not paid holiday. Our accommodation was provided by the restaurant [this is unusual in Chinatown]. It was upstairs at the back of the building and was so overcrowded! Ten people lived in two rooms on the third floor.'

I met Xiao Fan, aged thirty-eight, from Tienjin, who arrived in England six years ago with the sole aim of making enough money to support his then seven-year-old son. He spent the first three years in the kitchens of Chinese takeaways, keeping his head down, working all his waking hours in order to send money home. He managed to make enough money to get a mortgage for a one-bedroom flat in Tienjin which was for sale for £20,000. His wages did not go up a penny during those three years. His colleague Yu Hui, from Fujian, couldn't endure the work any longer and decided to go to Morecambe Bay to pick cockles. Xiao Fan couldn't persuade him to stay: Yu Hui had two children to support as well as a debt to pay off. Xiao Fan waved goodbye to him at the bus station. Two weeks later his chef informed him that Yu Hui had drowned at Morecambe Bay.

'I talked to my wife that evening about the loss of lives and the terrible hardships of Chinese workers in Britain,' he said to me. 'But I don't think she could feel it the way I do. She thinks of Britain purely in financial terms – a place to work and make money – and doesn't seem to understand that we experience far, far more than that when we come here.'

After Yu Hui's death, his wife had to work as a labourer on a building site in Fujian, while their elder son, aged twelve, had to discontinue his schooling and work as a rubbish collector to help his mother support the family. Xiao Fan, meanwhile, decided to leave his low-paid takeaway job. A friend from Tienjin had introduced him to a well-known restaurant in London's Chinatown: Furama Restaurant in Macclesfield Street.

'Those working days in Chinatown,' Xiao Fan told me, 'turned out to be my unhappiest in England. Six of us were stuck in Furama's tiny basement kitchen day after day. We worked such long hours that we rarely saw daylight. The ventilation was poor. We relied on one small fan. The workload was almost unbearable. The pressure was immense. The restaurant simply loaded the maximum amount of work on us in order to save costs.

'The chef in charge of us was in a different class. He was earning about £500 a week. Our assistant chef had worked there for a long time and was earning £360 a week [£5 an hour]. I was below him – my job title was '*zhen ban*' [vegetable chopper]. I was earning £310 a week [for twelve hours a day, six days a week, i.e. £4.30 an hour]. Below me were two kitchen porters, who were treated really badly. One of them, in his forties, was responsible for chopping meat and helping with all duties in the kitchen, and he was on £280 a week [£3.80 an hour]. They paid him so poorly because they believed he had nowhere else to go because he's an older worker and spoke Mandarin rather than their language, Cantonese. Below him was another kitchen porter doing the dishwashing. He worked the same hours as the others, with the heaviest workload and the lowest pay of all: £230 a week [£3.20 an hour]. Everything's in cash, so there's no trace of these wages if the tax office ever comes to check up.'

Xiao Fan looked wistful as he sat across from me in a café on the edge of Chinatown, describing those days. 'During our daily break we were exhausted but had nowhere to go. We just stood at the rear exit having a cigarette, or wandered around Gerrard Street. Occasionally I'd go into the casino on the corner to watch people in there. Not to gamble! I certainly wouldn't gamble with this hard-earned cash. It was really just for a change of scene, to take my mind off that hot, humid kitchen.

'We weren't given any annual holidays. There's no such thing as "paid holiday" in Chinatown. It just doesn't exist. Here in Furama Restaurant, when you've worked for four months and the boss decides to keep you on, he pays you a week's wages for the holiday. But he doesn't actually let you take a holiday. We were made to work non-stop throughout the year, with only two days' break over Christmas but no pay. And if you're sick you won't get paid at all.'

I could hear the anger rising in his throat as he spoke to me. 'The outrageous thing is that they treat you as if they're doing you a favour by giving you a job! They impress on you that lots of other people are outside the door, waiting for a job in the kitchen, so you'd better work your hardest or you'll have to go. Normally I choose to stay in a job, however hard it is, because I want to earn a stable income for my family. But the hard work in London's Chinatown made me snap. After ten months in those subhuman conditions I decided enough was enough. It was better to starve than sacrifice all my dignity. I resigned.'

It was clear he was deeply saddened by the working conditions in London's Chinatown. 'Just like in China,' he said, 'what's lacking here is a conscience. These restaurateurs make profits by whatever means they can. They were migrants once! They managed to find a place for themselves in this country, slaving away from scratch with their bare hands. I know they worked incredibly hard in those days. They were probably exploited and trodden on by the bosses and the host country when they started. Decades on, these old migrants have grown rich. When they look at us new workers coming in, they think, These people must go through what we went through. They must struggle and endure the same harsh conditions, the same pain.

'That's the sadistic mentality which seems to reign here. The difference is that when those migrants started here, they had legal status. They know we don't have it, and that gives them a way of inflicting pain: they heartlessly squeeze cheap labour out of us. As the saying goes, when the former slaves exploit the new slaves, then you get the harshest slavery.'

After talking to Xiao Fan I spoke to a typical worker 'waiting at the door' in Chinatown, desperate for any work. His name is Xiao Chen. I'd known him two years ago as a builder, and I heard he was now (in August 2007) working in the kitchen of Young Cheng Restaurant on Shaftesbury Avenue. Young Cheng is a popular chain of Chinese restaurants – there are three Young Cheng restaurants in London's Chinatown alone. They're almost always full at lunchtime and in the evening. The Young Cheng restaurant on Shaftesbury Avenue gets an overall 8.8 out of 10 from its customers this year: food quality gets 9.0, service 9.0 and value for money 10.0.

The London Eating Guide gives it a rave review: 'This cheap and chaotic café is a hidden gem in the money-sucking black hole that is the West End ... Very quick, so good for pre-theatre or cinema, and open from six-ish till pretty late, which is convenient. Two thumbs up.'

But do any customers ask what life is like for those who work from midday to 'pretty late' to produce the efficiently served, good-quality food at Young Cheng?

I went to the restaurant and asked for Xiao Chen. A waiter pointed to the staircase leading to the kitchen downstairs.

There he was, having a quick lunch with the other kitchen workers just before the eleven-hour shift that would end near midnight. He was surprised to see me. 'Let's talk over there,' he said, and led me to another table.

'How are you doing here?' I asked him.

Looking around to make sure the landlord (who'd intro-duced him to the job) wasn't listening, he said, 'It's £250 a week. D'you think that's doing OK? [He works eleven hours a day, six days a week – which makes his wage £3.70 an hour.] My blood pressure's going up and up. The job's exhausting, and they allow nothing but a half-hour break a day – that's when we have our lunch. We finish at 11.30 p.m. By the time I get home on the bus it's 12.30, and I normally don't get to sleep till two or three.'

The harshness of working conditions came as no surprise to Xiao Chen after experiencing life in the construction trade in Britain, where wages were delayed or not paid at all. Three years ago, he borrowed 60,000 RMB (£4,000) from an agency in Shanghai to apply for a six-month business-visitor visa to come to England. A year of hard manual labour in the building trade earned him the money to pay off the debt, and since then he's been trying to send money home. But the construction company he worked for in the second year, Zheng He, failed to pay six months of wages to him and eighteen of his colleagues. Xiao Chen and his colleagues told me that the owner of the company was Liu Zeyang, the son of the head of the foreign trade department in Sichuan province. (Corruption, they felt, had followed them from China to Britain.) They'd waited, and made demands, but eventually they'd had to leave the job with-out a penny. Since then Xiao Chen had been going from job to job, mostly working as a temporary labourer on building sites in London, and now he'd wound up in Chinatown.

'I was planning to return home after two to three years of working in England,' he told me, 'but it hasn't worked out that way. Money's harder to earn than I'd expected, and I'm having to stay longer. I find waiting unbearably frustrating. The hardest thing for me is to be away from my family.'

When I visited him again at Young Cheng the following week he was chopping large chunks of spare ribs. I noticed his hands were red and swollen. The long hours, hard work and lack of sleep were taking their toll on his blood pressure. 'I just don't know how long my health can hold out,' he confided to me.

As well as the stress caused by overwork, workers like Xiao Chen live with the constant fear of having their status exposed in a surprise immigration raid. The largest raid of 2007 happened across Chinatown on 11 October, when a hundred immigration staff and police stormed into five restaurants, arresting forty-nine workers as part of the government's BIA (Border & Immigration Agency) operation to intensify the crackdown on illegal working.

The Golden Dragon restaurant on Gerrard Street was one of the restaurants to be raided. Thirty officers stormed in and arrested three waiters and seven kitchen workers. The manager, Robert Lee, spoke to me about it afterwards. 'The workers were treated like terrorists, pushed around, handcuffed, interrogated.' His staff spoke little English and were so frightened by the presence of so many officers that some of them couldn't answer questions. Another witness, Bobby Chan, a community activist at Central London Law Centre, said, 'The officers behaved unreasonably aggressively, and some of them, I believe, were racially motivated in their behaviour.'

Chen Jun's Luxuriance was another of the raided restaurants. He told me what had happened. 'This was the first-ever raid in my restaurant. I was shocked and appalled by the aggressive manners of the police and the immigration staff. Two of my kitchen staff – one from Fujian, one from Hunan – were arrested and bundled into a police van in front of my customers' eyes.' He told me he had no idea about the two workers' immigration status. As it turned out, the arrest of the Hunan worker was a mistake: he did have proper documents. (Rolf Toolin, the BIA's Deputy Director of London and SE Region, personally apologized for this mistake, but insisted that 'I cannot apologize for my department. We will not have the permission to publicize our apology.') For the other (undocumented) worker, that arrest meant an abrupt end to his dream of making a better life for his family. He faced certain deportation back to China and a fine or imprisonment on arrival.

The human rights of the arrested workers were believed to have been violated. After the raids, a meeting behind closed doors was held between Chinatown employers and the BIA's Rolf Toolin, who forbade the presence of any journalists (but I stayed in the meeting with my head down). At this meeting it was alleged by Central London Law Centre that seventeen of the arrested workers (being held in Dover at the time of writing) had requested legal representation but had been refused. It was also alleged that a detained worker was refused food and water during his detainment. The BIA responded, 'We will look into these.'

The British Immigration Minister Liam Byrne announced in 2007 a new system of a possible two-year prison sentence and fines of up to £10,000 for employers who knowingly employ undocumented workers, which has come into effect in February 2008. The BIA promises to hold consultations with Chinatown employers, when they will be 'trained on immigration matters, such as how to check workers' status'.

I asked Chen Aiguo, the Deputy Chair of the Fujianese Chinese Association in Britain, about the impact of the increasing number of workplace raids on his community. 'Some of the Fujianese workers call us [the Association] from the detention centres, asking for help,' he told me. 'They have nowhere to turn to. It's not fair on them. As they're already in the country, surely they should be allowed to make a living and survive. They should at least be given that chance.'

The work is terrible, but being dismissed is worse, and in this climate of fear among employers, dismissals of undocumented kitchen workers are commonplace. Employers have been dismissing undocumented workers ever since May 2004, when the then Home Office Minister Des Browne wrote them a letter warning them to abide by Article 8 of the Asylum and Immigration Act, 1996. ('The employer shall be guilty of an offence if the employee has not been granted leave to enter or remain in the United Kingdom.') An estimated 500 workers in and around Chinatown were sacked immediately. The employers then voiced their concern about the crackdown on employing illegal workers, saying that their businesses were suffering as a result. (Some Chinatown restaurants told me their business had declined by twenty per cent.) But they didn't feel remotely guilty about getting rid of their undocumented workers without paying them redundancy fees.

The Fujianese bore (and still bear) the brunt of all this, as they make up seventy to eighty per cent of the catering workforce in London's Chinatown. They suffer the most discrimination of any Chinese group, because they're seen as the least likely to have proper status. One restaurant in Chinatown dismissed every Fujianese worker in that summer of 2004, with or without documents. 'They did that just in case we're illegal,' a Fujianese worker told me.

Sackings like that are now happening again in Chinese catering businesses all over the country as the stricter regime of immigration controls started operating in full scale in 2008. And so we see, again, the kind of situation that reduces people like Ah-Hua in Chapter 4 to selling DVDs on the streets and descending into the sinister enslavement of brutal gangs. Having no work and little cash, they'll do anything to survive. If they are arrested, they can be detained for indefinite periods of time. I set out to discover what might happen to a worker after he or she has been bundled into one of those police vans.

First I spoke on the phone to two people who had experienced immigration arrests close at hand. One was a mother, Mrs Huang, herself an experienced kitchen worker in London's

Chinatown. Her son, aged twenty-five, had been working in a Chinese restaurant in Bayswater, west London, for three years without papers. He was arrested in a raid in autumn 2007 and detained. Mrs Huang was beside herself with worry, terrified at the thought of what might happen to him when he returned to China – would he face a prison sentence? She looked everywhere for help, imploring Chinese community associations to come to her aid. But it was all in vain: he was deported. To her immense relief, he avoided a prison sentence, but faced a fine of 4,000 RMB (£267).

Then I spoke to Ting, a twenty-five-year-old woman from Fuzhou city in Fujian province, who was speaking to me from Yarls Wood Immigration Removal Centre in Bedfordshire. She told me that after being smuggled to Britain she'd got her first job as a so-called 'dumb waitress' (one who doesn't speak English) in London's Chinatown. 'They asked me for my papers. I told them I didn't have any. So they employed me on a part-time basis and paid me a third less than the waiters. They've always employed Fujianese workers at that restaurant. My Hong Kong boss had always sorted out my National Insurance for me and there was never a problem. But one day we got caught up in a raid, and I was arrested.

'I don't know what my destiny will be. The Chinese Embassy won't let me return to China because I have no ID.' (The snakehead had kept hold of the passport she'd used for getting here, and she had no passport of her own.) 'In their eyes, I'm not a citizen of China. And, of course, Britain doesn't intend to let me stay. It will only be a matter of time before they deport me. But, truly, where are they going to send me? I don't know where to go, what to do.'

She told me about her thirty-two-year-old friend Ah-Jie, who had been through even worse than this. I went to find him at Dungavel Removal Centre in South Lanarkshire, Scotland, and discovered the macabre series of events that had led up to his detention.

He sounded surprised that I wanted to visit him. 'No one's visited me since I've been here,' he said on the phone. 'It's a difficult journey to get here.'

It *was* a difficult journey. From Glasgow it's a half-hour train journey to Hamilton, and here there are three buses a day (run by Dungavel) to take visitors to and from the removal centre a further fifteen miles away. I missed the bus and resorted to a taxi. 'Is it a friend of yours you're visiting at Dungavel? That's a terrible place to be,' said the driver with a shake of his head.

We passed the pretty conservation village of Strathaven. That was the last glimpse of affluence. As we turned a corner, a huge barbed-wire complex came into view. Dungavel was a prison before it became a detention centre, and it still looks and feels like a prison. The place is notorious for breaching the human rights of its detainees, including the children of asylum seekers. I showed my ID at the metallic entrance, was searched, and was told I wasn't allowed to bring anything into the visiting room apart from a few coins for the coffee machine. I was told to leave the things I'd brought for Ah-Jie (a cup and a T-shirt) with the officers. (I later heard that Ah-Jie never received the T-shirt.)

A visitor is only allowed to see one detainee a day, and the meeting is watched by security guards. As I wasn't allowed to take in a pen and paper, I had to borrow some from a nearby guard. 'I just need to jot down a few items to bring to Ah-Jie next time,' I explained.

The first thing Ah-Jie said to me was, 'I wish this could come to an end. I can't live this isolated prison life any longer.' He told me the Chinese were in a minority, among the 200 detainees. 'We're treated in a racist way because we don't speak English. Our needs are ignored, even basic things like interpreting, which is so badly needed.'

His original intention, when leaving Fuqing in 2005, had been to be smuggled not to England but to Canada. He'd been told work was easy to find in Canada's well-established Chinese community. He'd borrowed 420,000 RMB (around £28,000) to pay the snakeheads for arranging his journey. 'But the journey was badly planned,' he told me, 'and I ended up staying in France for a year, waiting for the next transport. The waiting kills your spirit. In the end I decided to cut the journey short, and so they smuggled me to England for a lower fee — 280,000 RMB (£18,700). I arrived in Dover in May 2006.'

Totally naive about working in England, and with no friends or contacts to give him advice, Ah-Jie did exactly what so many other newcomers do: pay a registration fee of £150 to an unregistered Chinese agency in London in order to get a job. The job he got was as a kitchen porter at a Chinese restaurant in Cambridge. After a year of not working in France, the only thing he wanted to do was start working straight away. His employer didn't ask questions about Ah-Jie's lack of papers. He was told to work twelve hours a day, six days a week, for £155 a week (£2 an hour).

He was content. But a month later the restaurant owner dismissed him, giving the reason that the restaurant was feeling the threat of tightened immigration controls and didn't want to risk a penalty. Ah-Jie had to leave within a week, with no redundancy fee. What he didn't understand was why the restaurant hadn't worried about his status when they'd taken him on. 'The restaurants all know about our status,' he told me, 'because we're the only people who go through these agencies. No one else would.'

He went back to the same agency, who got him a second job, this time at a Chinese restaurant in Bristol. The hours were the same, the wages £150 per week. Again, his new employer didn't question his status: it was an open secret. And, again, he was dismissed within a month. He knew this wasn't a coincidence.

'The chef told me on my first day in the job that I wouldn't last, because no one else had. All the previous workers, without papers like me, had been sacked after two or three weeks after they'd paid the agency fees. New workers were sent to replace them and were sacked after the same length of time. It's clear to me that the restaurants work with the agency to profit from us. But there's nothing we can do about it. The employer's excuse is always that "we don't have papers" and that he's "extremely worried about workplace raids".'

Having lost his second job, Ah-Jie went back to London and searched desperately for work. He called another unregistered Chinese employment agency he'd spotted in a job advertisement in the *Chinese Business Gazette*. The agency boss told him he had a good job for him as a driver in Newcastle, an easy job, which would earn him £150 a week. Ever-optimistic, Ah-Jie accepted the job gratefully, agreeing to pay the agency £200 in a fortnight's time.

On arrival in Newcastle he was told his job was to drive a Chinese 'technician' each day from his home in central Newcastle to an office on the outskirts and back. The work was easy and painless. He felt fortunate to be doing this restful, pleasant job instead of kitchen work. He told his parents on the phone about it, calling it 'a daily trip out' (instead of a job).

But it turned out that the 'office' on the outskirts of town was nothing but a large cannabis plantation in a top-floor flat. And the 'technician' was the man employed to water the cannabis plants every day.

Coming from a rural farming family in the farm-filled suburbs of Fuqing, Ah-Jie didn't have the faintest idea about drugs. 'I didn't even know what cannabis looked like. When I first saw the plants I thought they looked like the tomato plants we have in China. It never occurred to me they were drugs!'

At the end of his second week, when he was due to pay the agency fee, his employer (a Vietnamese man whom he never met) transferred his wages directly to the agency. 'The only thing I knew about the boss,' Ah-Jie said, 'was that he owns a restaurant in London.' The cannabis plants must have brought this restaurant owner extra profits on the side.

Three weeks later, the 'office' was raided. The 'technician' and Ah-Jie were both there at the time and were arrested for producing cannabis. Ah-Jie pleaded ignorance, to no avail. He was turned into a criminal. His boss got away.

Deportation is inevitable. But where will he be deported to? 'I have no ID,' he said to me. 'I can't get a home-returning certificate from the Chinese Embassy. They don't regard me as a citizen. Britain will have to force China to take me back. That will mean I'll have to pay a higher penalty than the normal penalty of 4,000 RMB [£266] when I arrive back. It may be as much as 8,000 RMB.' (That's £533 – a hefty sum when wages for a manual worker in China are £38 a month.) And he may face a prison sentence. 'I can't tell my parents. It will break their hearts. I'm telling them I'm still working. But they've started asking why I haven't been sending any money home recently.'

I asked him whether he'd ever contacted any of the Chinese community associations for help and advice. He shook his head. 'We came to England only to work. We didn't have the time or the opportunity to set up contacts with those kinds of people. Even if we did get in touch with them, I don't know what they could offer us apart from a courtesy chat.'

Ah-Jie's journey to Britain has ended in despair. Back in London, meanwhile, the increase in immigration raids has not brought an end to 'illegal working'. It has simply driven it further underground, and covered up the issue of exploitation. (Some restaurants have taken the simple measure of hiring 'look-outs' to stand outside their premises watching out for any sign of a raid.) London's Chinatown continues to employ undocumented workers, but it has become harder than ever to get people to talk about their existence and their rights.

What about the Chinese community leaders in London? When you think of community leaders, you imagine them leading and supporting the new arrivals, the lost, the exploited. Sadly, it seems the community leaders in London's Chinatown are not the solution but part of the problem. They tend to be people who arrived in London between the 1950s and 1970s, and set up businesses that are now thriving. Their own wealth accumulated on the backs of waves of Chinese migrant workers. The expression 'Chinese community' is always on their lips as an abstract concept. But for many of them it seems to exclude all those whose labour forms the basis of what they like to call 'community life'.

I approached Chinese for Labour, as some of its members come from an activist background, and I was curious to hear what they had to say about the suffering of Chinese workers under the New Labour policies, which are in many ways responsible for the deepening of this suffering. I spoke to Mee Ling Ng, Chinese for Labour's Chair, who was the first Chinese councillor ever to be elected in Britain (in Lewisham). These were her words: 'The government should develop a workable, honest and transparent managed migration policy to address the UK's shortage of skilled and semi-skilled labour ... The government should recognize that the Chinese catering trade also requires skilled chefs and bilingual hospitality staff such as waiters and managers.'

But doesn't the catering trade also require non-bilingual kitchen workers and porters at the bottom to keep the whole thing going? Ms Ng drew the line here. 'There is a need to distinguish between legal and illegal workers. The government should tackle employers who illegally employ illegal migrants (and exploit them) by tightening the system, resourcing it better and giving more powers to take employers to court and making fines heavier. The onus should be on employers and employment agencies to check the status of potential employees.'

I also approached Katy Tse Blair for her views. She's a leading member of Chinese for Labour, co-founder of the Islington Chinese Association and a member of the 48 Group Club, which promotes business links with China – and she's the former Prime Minister's sister-in-law, married to Tony Blair's brother Bill. I asked her about the support offered by the existing Chinese community to the new migrants from China. She simply said, 'The support is limited due to a lack of resources.' I also asked her for her views on the impact of Labour policies on the undocumented Chinese people in Britain. She declined to comment.

As a rule, silence is what maintains the status quo. The community leaders in Chinatown not only own and run the businesses that are the core of its economy, they also have control over the Chinese newspapers, who rely on their advertising for survival. This makes it extremely hard to challenge their practices in the Chinese press.

There's a Chinese expression '*jia-chou bu ke wai yang*', meaning 'ugly affairs in the family should not be announced outside'. It certainly seems to apply in this case of Chinatown's 'family'. Anyone who dares to speak out or rock the boat will be resented and punished. For those who need to keep their place in the community, the easiest thing is to keep quiet, not kick up a fuss, not look too deeply into what lies beneath the prosperity. To the outside world, Chinatown presents a convincing picture of an impressively 'self-sufficient' Chinese community. And mainstream Britain is happy to go along with the fiction that any exploitation that does take place is the Chinese community's own affair.

So the lid is kept on the whole seething mass of exploitation and misery. But once or twice in the past, the Chinese workers have risen up in revolt. In 1984 Jabez Lam and other activists formed the Chinese Workers Association, which aimed to unionize Chinese workers. When, in 1986, four Chinese workers (who had legal status, or *shen-fen*) were sacked by the restaurant chain Wheelers in Brighton after demanding an adjustment of their wage level, they went on strike for three months. Their courage was backed by the TGWU and by the

Chinese Advice & Information Centre, whose volunteers helped on the picket line. In the end, the Chinese workers won compensation.

Then, in 2001, when four Chinese workers (again, with legal status) at the New Diamond Restaurant in Lisle Street were dismissed for joining the TGWU, they fought back and formed the Justice for Restaurant Workers Campaign. Chinatown was leafleted and pickets were organized to discourage customers from dining at the New Diamond. It was uplifting to see hundreds of workers marching through Chinatown with red banners saying, 'We want our basic right to be paid the national minimum wage', and 'We have the right to join a trade union'. I'd never seen Chinese workers with their heads held so high. It went against all the stereotypical images of 'docile' Chinese workers who meekly put up with whatever life throws at them. Lots of Chinese workers and staff – including workers without *shen-fen* – came out of their restaurants in support. The four workers won the dispute, and were offered compensation by their employer.

Today, workers in London's Chinatown live in daily terror of further raids. But in the midst of this fear you can detect a new militancy coming into being. Six days after the raids of 11 October 2007, a three-hour-long anti-raid strike was held in Chinatown. Blending into the crowd of workers out on the streets, a few members of Britain's hidden army of labour – the undocumented workers – dared to join them. They walked along in the fresh air, waving placards and chanting the simple message in Chinese: 'It's no crime to work.'

Imperial China Restaurant denied all allegations and said: 'In most restaurants, waiting staff are paid a basic wage and additional income are [sic] based on service charge and tips, although the figures mentioned are incorrect.'

Mr Tsao, managing director of Young Cheng Restaurant, said he doesn't have time to respond to the allegations in writing nor speak on the phone. Instead his assistant called on his behalf and said: 'We employ people to do different jobs on different pay, but we've never employed anyone to work in the alleged conditions.'

Michael King Sun Lam, managing director of Lambro Investment Ltd T/A Lee Ho Fook Restaurant, said: 'Waiters were indeed paid a basic salary of £60 net. On top of this sum they would share ten per cent of the turnover and also share any further tips given by the customers. This is a standard industry norm. In 2005–2006, kitchen porters were paid £120 net plus food and lodging. This equated to an average of £180 net per week and so was above the statutory minimum wage. Hours of work were 5 p.m. to 12 p.m. for six days a week. That is 42 hours they were working for and not 60 as suggested. There was no overtime as hours were detailed and given to employees and they were adhered to. Any workers were paid in full during absence for sickness. Your suggestion [regarding entitlement to holidays] is denied totally. Workers have the equivalent of four weeks' holiday now and back in 2005–2006. In 2005–2006, we gave beds to workers as part of their employment package. We only employed eight workers and they shared six bedrooms with two bunk beds in each room. The rooms are more than adequate for three to share. The only reason any further people stayed was if the workers themselves invited their friends to stay. Once management were notified of this, then the workers' guests were asked to leave.' [Note: The £180 net per week stated by Lee Ho Fook Restaurant was, in fact, still below the National Minimum Wage of £4.85 an hour between October 2004 and October 2005, £5.05 between October 2005 and October 2006, and £5.35 between October 2006 and October 2007.]

Chuen Cheng Ku Restaurant, Gerrard's Corner Restaurant, New World Restaurant, New Loon Fung Restaurant, Crispy Duck Restaurant, Furama Restaurant and New China Restaurant did not respond to the allegations.

8. Moving On

Like many of my hometown folks who have waved China
goodbye, I came to England to see the misty legend in real life.
Looking for a place to live, looking for a job to last, getting
helped, getting duped, getting by. Among all this I've learned
the local ways and how to survive. I've learned that, no matter
where you come from, you'll gain if you strive. Now, years have
passed me by, and strangely, I've fallen in love with this
changeable weather, the rain, and the cloudy days.

– Li Fulin, from Tienjin in China
January 2007

They lack a National Insurance number, a National Health
number, a fixed house number, many even lack a passport
number: but what many of the undocumented workers we've
met in this book do have – their treasured possession – is a
mobile phone number. Think back to Ah-Hua calling his wife
in Fuqing after being unloaded from the lorry on his arrival
in London ('I got us into this trouble, and I'll get us out'); to
Ailing, in shock after being raped, calling her son in Zhejiang
from the platform of Birmingham station; to Ah-Fang stuck
in the brothel in Cheam, calling me as her only channel to the
outside world . . . such moments bring brief shafts of light and
fresh air into the lives of these exiled characters, whose time in
Britain is a kind of imprisonment. It seems that any money left
after paying for food and lodging and sending money home is
spent on phone top-ups.

To me, the phone numbers themselves are a treasured

possession. The people I met researching this book are often on the move, their lives in constant flux as they search for new jobs, or get transported from farm to factory, or move from city to city in fear of immigration raids. But thanks to the numbers in the back of my notebook, I can find them – and they can find me.

Over the past five years, many of the people who started as interviewees have become friends. They live in my thoughts, as friends do. I've learned so much from them. They are fathers, mothers, sons and daughters with all the feelings of love, worry and aspirations for the family that everyone has, although their families happen to be thousands of miles away. They are just like you and me, except that they happen to be victims of the ruthless economic upheavals in their home country, which have driven them to travel across the globe in search of a sustainable life for their family. They didn't set out to be particularly heroic and selfless – or illegal and hidden: they've just followed the only path available to them, and the consequences have followed.

A feeling of mutual trust has developed between us over the years of interviews, visits and revisits. The characters have generously shared their life stories with me, and taken me with them to see what they've been through. Some of them have provided me with access to workplaces that would have been extremely difficult to get into without their help. During long conversations, they've given me insights into their exploitation and how it affects their lives in a deeper psychological sense.

I've longed to help them in return. I've felt helpless, often, witnessing their plight and knowing I can't give them the one thing they need more than anything in this country, namely status. To have that as my protective armour in the working world of Britain, and to know how defenceless these people are without it, has been a constant source of anguish. But I've been able to help them in small ways. I've given them advice about the health service and how to get help as an undocumented person. I've advised them on how to get help if they're arrested. I've helped them try to extract owed wages from employers: I successfully demanded wages from an employer of Lao Zhou (he was one of my housemates in Thetford), and from an employer of Gao Jun (whose story I followed in Selsey). These things were not difficult to do, but for the Chinese maintaining good health or being able to send a bit of money home had become difficult.

If the stories in this book have made you feel affection for the characters whose true stories they are, you may be asking yourself – as I often do – 'I wonder what became of such-and-such a person.' Have they 'accomplished the mission' (in Gao Jun's words) of improving living standards at home? How do they assess their working lives in Britain? In this chapter, we'll catch up with some old friends.

Three years after Zhang Guo-Hua died in Hartlepool, I went to visit his widow, Mrs Zhang, in King's Lynn. This was in late 2004. When she'd come to Britain straight after her husband's death in 2001, it had been on a six-month business visa. She'd outstayed it and stayed on in England: with no husband to provide for the family, she now felt the duty to be the breadwinner, sending money home each month to support her two children in north-east China. (They were being looked after – as is so often the case in these situations – by her parents.) She'd got a job in a flower factory, planting seeds in a greenhouse.

I visited her on her only day off. I sat on a stool in the kitchen of her crowded flat on London Road in King's Lynn, watching her making dumplings. She was good at it. While chatting away to me, she made hundreds of dumplings to last her and her flatmates through the coming week.

She told me she'd hidden herself away since her husband's death three years ago. 'I didn't allow myself to sink into depression: I knew I had to pluck up courage, move forward, get a job. I found a full-time job processing flowers on the outskirts of King's Lynn.' (At this time there were around 2,000 undocumented Chinese workers in King's Lynn and the surrounding area working in flower- and food-processing factories as well as on the farms.)

For Mrs Zhang, King's Lynn was just another town, indistinguishable from the rest. And to the workers in the factory, she was just another worker on the line. No one knew of her tragic loss. She kept it to herself. She was earning just over £4 an hour, which left enough to send money home regularly.

'I felt that life was slowly improving,' she said. But then one day in early 2004, as she was speeding up her work at the factory towards the end of the shift, her arm got trapped in the conveyor belt and she was badly injured. 'I was off work for over a month. But the flower factory refused to pay compensation for the injury. I was told I wasn't to be compensated because I was working illegally. This brought back such painful memories of my husband's death.'

Mrs Zhang was treated in A&E when the injury occurred, and was allowed to stay in hospital for a short time. But she was entitled to no further medical care. (The government is proposing to close off even this avenue: it intends to limit the use of health care by undocumented migrants and failed asylum seekers. This will mean that in future even at A&E departments staff may be asked to check documents.)

As soon as she recovered from the injury, Mrs Zhang went back to the flower factory to work. 'Work isn't easy to keep, and I do need this job,' she told me. 'Dignity doesn't buy food and provide for the children. Therefore, dignity is something I've learned to compromise in my time in England.'

She and the other Chinese migrant workers who shared the flat tried to keep their heads down: earning money to send home was their only reason for being there. But keeping their heads down did not guarantee an undisturbed working life.

'The Chinese workers in King's Lynn have been experiencing increasing racism and racist attacks,' Mrs Zhang told me.

'Every week I hear of Chinese people being targeted by local youths. The flat I used to live in with other Chinese workers was always getting bottles thrown in through the windows. Sometimes we were just preparing dinner and a bottle would be thrown in, smashing the glass. We felt so unsafe we had to move out. Now we always stay indoors in the evenings, and we never walk home alone after work.'

There's one body the Chinese can turn to for help: the West Norfolk and District Chinese Association. I talked to its chairman, Kwai Li, and he explained the context. 'The locals aren't used to the Chinese newcomers with their visibility and their different cultural habits. Since the migrants started coming in larger numbers from 2003, the attacks have become more frequent – not only in King's Lynn but in other towns like Thetford and Norwich. We receive calls every day about verbal and physical harassment. The number of attacks is on the rise.' This was happening at the time when politicians, such as Henry Bellingham, the Conservative MP for North West Norfolk, talked of migrants taking local jobs.

The local police, Mr Li said, were reluctant to recognize the racial motivation for the attacks when they were reported via his Chinese Association. 'Recently a Chinese man was attacked in the town centre of King's Lynn. I helped him with translation at the police station, but I saw that the police weren't taking any notice of the racial intent of the attacker. I often feel that the police don't take the attacks seriously. The police officer didn't even ask that Chinese man to sign his statement. They just don't seem to bother. I got the impression they want to sweep it under the carpet.'

There was a shared feeling of powerlessness among the new Chinese migrants. 'King's Lynn is no longer suitable for us to live and work in,' a man from Tienjin who was working at the Heiploeg & Lynn Shrimpers factory said to me. 'How can we defend ourselves against racist attacks?'

The workers were even finding it impossible to integrate

themselves with the established Chinese population in the area. When they tried to seek help from the local Chinese Association, it seemed their only contact with the local Chinese community. But a single, insufficiently funded organization like that can only offer language assistance and basic support. It's not capable of putting pressure on the authorities, such as the police, to take action to protect the migrants from constant threats and attacks.

So, one by one, the new migrants were leaving the area to seek work elsewhere. Mrs Zhang managed to stay on until late 2006, when she returned to China to be reunited with her children. I've heard that she's now working in a shop in her hometown of Yuhong.

Lao Zhou was the first person to call me after my undercover work in Thetford ended. I explained to him my true reasons for working there, hoping he'd still be my friend after discovering my true identity. There was a brief silence, then he said in his usual relaxed yet wry voice, 'I thought it was odd that you couldn't cook any northern food!'

In the two weeks since I'd left Thetford, the employment agency Pertemps had told the Chinese recruiters to 'go quiet for a while' to avoid inspection. 'That means there won't be any work for us for the time being,' Lao Zhou said. 'I'm going to have to look elsewhere.'

A few weeks later he called me again. 'I'm moving to a village in Lincolnshire. Away from all the attention.'

'I'll come and visit you soon,' I said. I did visit him, in late October 2004 – a week before Bonfire Night. His job was packing fireworks for the firework-distribution company Bright Star. It was in a place called Hemswell Cliff – a chillingly lonely place, I discovered. The minicab drove me for miles along a country lane. In the dark I saw a torch flashing. It was Lao Zhou, in his raincoat, signalling to me from the side of the road.

We were delighted to meet again. 'I couldn't tell you my

address,' he said, 'because the caravan I'm living in hasn't got a door number.'

With Lao Zhou leading the way by torchlight, we walked into a deserted industrial estate. I could hear our footsteps echoing around us.

'It's here.' Lao Zhou pointed to an ageing caravan. 'Bright Star puts me here because part of my job is to keep an eye on the fireworks warehouses next door. I'm a fireworks security guard, living next to a mountain of explosives! Fun, isn't it?'

He sat me down at the table in the caravan and lit the gas stove. 'I'll cook you some of my northern dumplings,' he said, remembering how much I'd enjoyed them in Thetford. We didn't stop firing questions at each other all evening. 'On weekdays,' he told me, 'I share the caravan with four fellow workers – three locals and one Albanian man. There are two tiny bedrooms and one of us sleeps on the couch. I get along well with them and we sometimes have dinner together. We've managed to build up a common language, just using basic words and body language! They love my Chinese tongue twisters. They don't understand the meanings, but the tones and rhymes make them laugh.'

His friends weren't here now: it was Friday evening. At weekends, the locals returned to their families and the Albanian went to work on another job. This gave Lao Zhou more space in the caravan. But he found the solitude intimidating at night. 'I keep the TV on when I'm alone. The sound of human voices can help to keep away any unwanted visitors.'

His phone rang. It was Bright Star fireworks calling him to say there'd be overtime work at the weekend, with Bonfire Night approaching. That sounded like good news, I said. 'But we Chinese workers don't get overtime pay,' Lao Zhou told me. 'Unlike the locals, we receive a fixed weekly wage of £200 regardless of hours worked. We work up to seventy-two hours a week, sorting and loading fireworks for distribution all over Britain, and maintaining the warehouses. But I'm happy enough with the wages. In Thetford we didn't even get that – remember?'

I slept on the bed in the smallest of the two bedrooms, snuggling down into my sleeping-bag to banish the smell of sweat that pervaded the cramped space. I woke up to the sound of sizzling: Lao Zhou was making me his northern pancakes with eggs and spring onions for breakfast. I walked into the kitchen area and we laughed at the strangeness: in Thetford, we'd always had to queue to use the kitchen. I sat at the table again and admired the way he'd tried to make a home in this desolate place. There was a little lamp with a dim bulb, and he'd hung a Chinese calendar on the wall.

After breakfast we walked to the firework-sorting house, about a mile away from the caravan. 'I like to watch the sun rise across the landscape,' Lao Zhou said cheerfully. This landscape was an array of run-down warehouses and muddy fields. Soon another semi-derelict caravan came into view.

'My colleague Ming lives in here,' Lao Zhou explained. 'He shares the caravan with five other Chinese workers – some of them have arrived from Morecambe Bay. They've been dispersed by raids.'

We knocked and went in. There were no curtains on the windows of this caravan. The wall boards were peeling off. There was a rusty cooker and a threadbare couch.

Ming started talking as soon as we walked in. He gave me his potted life story straight away. 'Coming from a rural back-ground in Fujian, I've never had anything going for me in China. I spent my twenties seeking employment, failing, trying to set up my own business, failing again, being smuggled to Singapore for work and getting deported.' None of this seemed to have embittered him. His life had been an endless optimistic quest for betterment. 'I paid £20,000 to be smuggled to Britain: that's £20,000 for a new life!'

Lao Zhou and I were both fascinated by Ming's story and kept him talking as we walked to the work site. 'I was burdened with debt,' Ming continued, 'and foolishly got involved in smuggling, for which I was imprisoned in a British jail for four months. Prison was like death. It pushed me to break clean from the smugglers after my release. Now I've got this job here, I'm regularly sending money home to my wife and my two children in China. I manage to send about 10,000 RMB [about £666] a month, all from my own hard work.'

At the work site, the workers began their day's shift of sorting and loading thousands of fireworks – made in China, they told me, by Panda. (Panda supplies Bright Star's 25 million fireworks each year, as well as supplying to other retailers all over Britain. It employs more than 300,000 workers from the deprived provinces of Hunan and Jiangxi. It was in a Panda factory in Wanzai, in Jiangxi province, that nine workers were killed in 2001 as a result of an explosion.) I stayed and watched Lao Zhou and his colleagues at work until I was asked to leave by the supervisor.

I found out that the British Health and Safety Executive (HSE) had brought two improvement notices against Bright Star in 2004 for failing to make sufficient assessment of employees' health-and-safety risks and for not monitoring or reviewing safety measures. I asked Bright Star about this and they confirmed it. They said, 'The HSE notices only require that we rewrite our health-and-safety manual to apply to our current site at Hemswell. All our workers are given training and guidelines.'

But Lao Zhou, Ming and the other workers I spoke to said they hadn't received any training or safety guidance in handling explosives. They also told me they'd asked for a pay rise during the busy period, but the request had been turned down.

Having met Lao Zhou and his colleagues, stayed with them for two days and listened to their stories, I was surprised by Bright Star's response when I put the working conditions to them. 'We did employ some casual workers but that ended in April 2004.' The company denied all my allegations, and said,

'It is incorrect that we pay workers £200 fixed pay in cash. All our employees are on the books, paid monthly on an hourly wage. It is incorrect that our workers live in caravans with poor facilities. We do have a few mobile homes, but no workers live there.'

Lao Zhou didn't have the faintest idea about Guy Fawkes and the gunpowder plot. But he did know his work would dry up after the fifth of November. 'After that date,' he said to me, 'we won't have a roof over our heads.' He was right. In the week after Bonfire Night he was dismissed without notice.

A few weeks later I heard from him again: he'd moved to Didcot in Oxfordshire to work in an Asda warehouse, having found a job through the agency Totaljobs. Here he earned £179 a week for a 37.5-hour week (a wage of £4.70 an hour), an improvement on all his previous jobs. He worked there for almost two years.

In the winter of 2006 he called me to say he was in London. He told me he was planning to return to China in two years. Meanwhile, he'd found a way to make quicker cash: he'd responded to an advertisement in a Chinese paper asking for volunteers to be on a private experimental medical programme at Hammersmith Medicines Research (HMR). 'They want to find out if a medicine called Prasugrel will have different effects on people of different ethnic groups.'

There were side-effects such as nausea, headaches, sleeping problems and high blood pressure. But Lao Zhou told me he was determined to go through with it for the reward of £1,500 on completion of the programme at the end of the eighth week. 'It'll be my highest earning in Britain!' he said.

'Like ants on a hot wok.' That was Ren's expression, describing the way he and his Chinese friends were frantically darting about in search of new work in London after being forced to leave the Selsey salad factory in 2004. Indeed, they were desperate, and felt as vulnerable and insignificant as insects.

After two weeks of frantic searching, Ren found (through an agency) a job as a warehouse labourer in Exeter. 'I'm reluctant to set out into the unknown again,' he told me. 'But the phone calls from home keep coming: my family needs the cash. That made the decision for me.' So he took the four-and-a-half-hour coach trip to the south-west of England.

He told me just before he left that Xiao Yun (his temporary partner in Selsey) had gone to work in a Chinese clinic in Manchester. 'I actually got her the job, via a contact of mine. My friends say I'm stupid to send her away to another city. But I feel the duty, as her best friend and an older person (even if I'm no longer her lover), to help her plan her life. Friendship and love are so precious when you're struggling alone in this country. But, at the end of the day, we're all on our separate paths, trying to find betterment in England. I wouldn't dream of getting in the way of her path to happiness.'

Ren knew nothing about Exeter, except that many Chinese people without papers were working for low wages in chicken factories and flower farms in the area. His employer sent a man to pick him up from the coach station, from where he was driven straight to a huge warehouse at a Chinese supermarket a few minutes away. He was told to start the job at once, unloading goods from vans and taking them into the supermarket.

As the company he was working for was Chinese, not English, he hoped working conditions would be better than in his previous job in the salad factory. He'd be working for his fellow countrymen, after all. He was told he'd be working a seven-day week, which came as a surprise; but he was content. He was glad to have a job at all.

The next day he found out a less welcome fact: he had not one job to do here, but two. First, starting at 9 a.m., came the nine-hour shift in the supermarket warehouse: a long day of physical work with only one half-hour break. Then at 6 p.m. they were picked up and sent to work in the employer's restaurant in town. Here they had to work as kitchen porters, doing dishwashing and cleaning, until 12.30 a.m.

Ren's hourly wage for this was £1.80 an hour. When he received his first weekly wage of £190 in cash after a 105-hour week, his employer told him it was the 'mainland rate'. By this, the employer meant it was the 'mainland China rate'. Ren realized that the 'mainland rate' is the underground rate of pay given to people of his status by many first- and second-generation Chinese caterers in Britain. He came to understand that these wealthy entrepreneurs are the overseas supporters of the ruling power in China. They welcome the changes taking place there since the economic reform, which forced people like Ren to leave home. It meant that cheap labour was easier than ever for them to get.

'I'd always been brought up to believe that "blood is thicker than water",' he told me. 'China, *zu-guo* [motherland], we were told, embraces all those who belong to it, whether you're living in the country or overseas. I thought that our ethnic origin would unite us, especially if we were abroad as migrants. But at this Chinese-owned supermarket and restaurant, the "brotherhood" of the Chinese folks is not thick blood but thin air.' Ren was depressed at this new-found division.

Nonetheless, he needed the money. He carried on working for fifteen hours a day. But he began to develop backache from lifting heavy boxes and stomach pains from the long hours of working with only one meal-break. He felt his physical health deteriorating. The working years in England had worn him out. He knew he had to stop. He became one of the few who quit the job: nothing but an unfit and unproductive 'mainlander', in the eyes of the employer.

On the coach back to London, he called Xiao Yun to ask how she was getting on in Manchester. She was fine, she said: she was going to train as a massage therapist and acupuncturist. She was also learning some English.

Ren's search for work started again. In London he met a few men from his hometown who were also out of work. They all had building skills, so they decided to form a team of builders. In 2005 they got a job directly from an employer in north-west London. It was a three-month demolition project, and they were paid a daily wage of £40 with food and accommodation included: riches after Exeter. Ren sounded relieved when he said to me: 'Our livelihood is fixed for three months from now.' (Although Ren and his colleagues were content with the job, the rate of pay was in fact only acceptable for workers without papers. Today, the average wage for an undocumented Chinese builder in London is £50 a day, at least half the rate of pay for local builders.)

I asked him how Xiao Yun was. She'd completed her training, he told me, and was starting work as a massage therapist at the Chinese clinic. This made her an object of envy: you can't do much better than that if you don't have status. 'She told me she's looking for a Chinese man with status. Or, better still, a local man. She says she needs to get her status problem sorted.'

Six months later, Xiao Yun called Ren to say she was getting married to a fifty-year-old Singaporean Chinese man. In exchange for the man's help with her status, she was paying him a fee of £5,000, a sum she'd been saving up over two years.

There was no bitterness in Ren's voice as he told me about this over a pot of green tea in his flat in Turnpike Lane. 'I completely understand her thinking. The system is abusing us, daily. What else can we do but try to use the same system to protect and benefit ourselves? That's survival. Many women without legal status would do the same, I think.'

Ren's work as a builder lasted for two years. During this time, he saw and heard how other Chinese builders were mistreated by middlemen and private companies, who were able to delay wages as they wished, or ended workers' contracts towards the end of their work to avoid paying them. He saw how his fellow workers had to be responsible for their industrial injuries. 'There was one Chinese builder,' he told me, 'who fell off high scaffolding after being told to carry up heavy things. The man was admitted to A&E a day before Christmas, with his arm smashed to pieces. After endless requests for compensation, the company pushed the man away by giving him £100. The company called it "compensation". The man struggled through Christmas in hospital. He couldn't bring himself to tell his wife about the injury that had disabled his arm.'

One day early in 2007 when I came out of the tube at Mile End station I saw Ren there, selling the *Evening Standard* in the rain. '*Standard! Standard!*' he'd been instructed to shout. 'I'm paid £30 a day for this job,' he told me. 'At least we get paid at the end of each day.'

His years in Britain have changed him beyond measure. 'When I arrived, I was thirty-eight. Now I'm forty-four, properly middle-aged. I feel ancient and exhausted.' He has never recovered from the compromise he's had to make with his self-respect during his time in England. 'For every pound I'm making here, I always feel I'm sinking further to my knees.' His generosity and his enthusiasm for life have been crushed out of him. Now he's a reserved and untrusting man. He's learned to be emotionally thick-skinned. But, he told me, the hardship has never become easier to bear. His health has deteriorated: he's developed kidney problems. Having no GP, he recently had to resort to A&E in a hospital in north London. Although he was treated as an emergency case, he wasn't able to receive any follow-up check-up or treatment. 'The hospital kept telling me to go to my GP,' he told me. 'They knew I couldn't register with one, because of my lack of status.

'You work like a slave every day,' Ren said. 'You contribute your cheap labour to this country. But when you're ill, how does this country treat you? I've seen the true face of the old capitalist country that I'd imagined to be civilized.'

★

Gao Jun – our friend in Selsey who was so excited when he bought a camcorder at a car-boot sale – got a job as a kitchen porter at a popular Chinese restaurant chain, Aroma, in Stevenage, early in 2005.

The language spoken in Aroma was Cantonese. So Gao Jun not only couldn't speak the language of the country he was in, he couldn't speak the language of the Chinese restaurant he was in either. And (not to his surprise) the employer made use of the language barrier to exploit him. On top of the unbearably hard work, he suffered the torment of being shouted at by a bad-tempered chef in a language he couldn't understand. He put up with the job for a month, but could stand it no longer and decided to leave. He gave a week's notice. The manageress refused to pay the week's wages. Gao demanded them. The manageress put her wrists together in a gesture implying 'you're going to be in handcuffs if you don't leave'.

'I was really frightened of having my status exposed,' Gao said to me. 'But I was so infuriated with this treatment that I refused to go away. The manageress did eventually call the police, and told them I was making trouble at the restaurant. She didn't tell them I had no papers, because that would have incriminated the restaurant. The police handcuffed me, took me away and in the end drove me back to my flat. I had no idea what was said between them and my boss. All I knew was I'd never get my wages.'

Aroma's spokesman Colin Wong said: 'We confirm the allegations are not true. When an employee gives us the appropriate notice to terminate his/her employment, all wages and entitlements due are paid or given to him/her on or before the last day of the employment. We invite you to produce evidence to the contrary. We ask you to ask yourself: 1) Why would we refuse to pay wages due when the appropriate notice is given? 2) If we had refused to pay wages due, why would we call the police? The police would surely have taken the side of the employee as it would appear that we are in the wrong. 3) If we had refused to pay wages due, why didn't the employee take action then, for example seek legal advice? In fact, s/he can still seek legal advice now and take the appropriate action.'

Gao came to London and stayed with his older brother who'd found work as a builder. He called me to say he'd found a new job as an assistant cook at a bakery in Chinatown. 'I'm lucky to get the job. They're not easy to come by. My wages are £225 a week – not bad, though accommodation isn't included. I'm hopeful but not too optimistic, because we all know about the high turnover in Chinatown jobs. There must be a reason for it.'

The bakery was on Gerrard Street. In the evenings it reopened as a restaurant, so Gao worked from morning till late at night, first baking, then frying rice and noodles. He was exhausted at the end of each day's work. But by now he was used to being exhausted in Britain. He expected nothing less. What made life hard, again, was the language barrier. 'It's hard to pick up the Cantonese language quickly,' he told me. 'It has more tones than Mandarin and it's difficult to get the right pitch. Also, they seem to speak so fast here. You can't blame them – they're working in a busy kitchen. Who has time to teach me the language?'

But he had no intention of leaving. He knew how precious Chinatown jobs were, especially now that EU workers were arriving in large numbers to take the factory jobs. I visited him during one of his short breaks at the bakery, and noticed he'd lost weight. 'I'm terrified of losing this job. I haven't yet paid back the loans – the money I borrowed to leave China,' he confided to me with a self-mocking laugh. 'You've at least got to pay off your borrowings. It'll be ages before I can earn enough to return home.'

His fears for losing the job were realized one morning when he arrived for work, two months after starting. His employer told him he wasn't suited to the job. There was no notice period.

He went on the job hunt again. 'It doesn't upset me any more,' he told me. 'It's just part of working life in this country. Everything's up to the whim of whoever's in charge. I'm just an exchangeable tool.' Three weeks later, through his flatmates from Tienjin, he heard about a job in a Greek-owned garment factory in north London. He was offered a job there immediately, ironing clothes for £3.25 per hour. Local workers were paid the minimum wage: but this was no different from what he knew of the workplaces in England.

'I ask myself,' Gao said to me – and I saw the despair on his face, 'how long will I have to live with this "normality" that I've lived with for four years in this country? What have I gained? I'm cut off from home and cut off from England outside my little circle. I haven't picked up English, or Cantonese. Living and working in this environment has stagnated me. I've made no progress at all.'

I recalled the first time I'd met him in Selsey. I remembered him holding the camcorder in his hand and filming everyone. His expectations had been so high: he'd been a dreamer then. I looked at his anxious face now, and saw what four years in England had done to him.

'Work, work and work. But being a hard-worker isn't enough in England. You've got to be on the alert all the time. I'm no longer surprised when employers delay my wages or don't pay me at all. I no longer expect to have any control over what happens to me. Like we say, it's a jungle in England.'

But there must be one or two things he likes about England, I suggested. Gao then pondered on the rare moments of joy. There was a long pause. He looked embarrassed. Then he said, 'I knew about the red double-deckers before I came to England. They're such romantic-looking things, aren't they? And I suppose they're one of the things I like about England. I love to be on the Number 38 bus. It wasn't till I came here that I realized how indispensable buses are to us, not being able to afford to go on the tube. When people ask me where I live,

I can't tell them in English. But I remember where I live by the bus number I take, and I'll tell people which stop to get off at.'

Gao didn't last long at the Greek garment factory. He couldn't cope with the daily racial abuse from his employer or the two-tier system under which he was made permanently inferior to the locals. Having no work and no cash in early 2007, he stayed indoors for a while. The flat he was living in was becoming more and more overcrowded, as friends of his flatmates flocked to London after losing their jobs on the farms and factories of East Anglia.

Since the government tightened internal immigration controls in May 2004, large numbers of Chinese workers have gradually left the farm and food-processing factory work in East Anglia. The tightening of immigration rules quickly led to Chinese workers losing out in the competition with new EU workers. Steadily, these new workers – their number now reaching 50,000 – are replacing the Chinese as the main work-force in the region. 'This is affecting the Fujianese workers much more than us northern Chinese,' Gao told me. 'A lot of them used to work in East Anglia. Now they're all flooding back into catering jobs and the DVD trade in the city.'

I visited Gao in the cramped flat where he was living. He told me he felt helpless in the face of the decreasing amount of work on offer. 'What can we do?' he said to me. 'Our space in the labour market is getting smaller and smaller. The jobs open to people arriving in London from East Anglia are in the Chinese-run food manufacturers and wholesalers. They pay just over half the minimum wage, and the attitude of the employers is "take it or leave it". I'm in exactly the same boat as my flatmates who've been pushed out of East Anglia.'

One of his flatmates told me: 'As we've been forced even more underground, we have less and less bargaining power. Wages have declined and conditions have become harsher. The weekly wage for the lowest-level kitchen porter in London had actually gone down recently, from £170 a week to £140.'

Another of his flatmates was lying in his bunk bed with his arm in a bandage. He told me he'd been dismissed by his Chinese restaurant employer after his arm was badly burned in a kitchen fire. 'My employer's last words before sacking me,' he said, 'were, "Why didn't you get burned to death?"'

Two weeks passed, and there was no sign of any catering work for Gao. Like so many others, he had to resort to working in a Chinese-run food factory. He got a job at a bean-curd factory in Brettenham Road in north London: the New Kong Nam Food Production Co that has been in business for two decades and is one of the largest bean-curd factories in England, supplying restaurants and supermarkets in Chinatown. His job was processing and packing bean curds and delivering them to Chinatown. When I spoke to him in October 2007 he was working there for ten hours a day, six days a week, for just under £3.20 an hour.

Mr Zichun Chen, managing director of New Kong Nam Food Production Co, said: 'Our workers work eight hours a day and have two hours' unpaid break, making their working day 9.5–10 hours in total. Our workers are paid different wages according to their different jobs, and the lowest is £190–200 per week for a porter, who does a bit of everything. This wage isn't too low, because workers are provided with food and accommodation.'

'I'm determined to stay in this job,' Gao told me – just as he'd told me before. 'There's no other choice. I'm planning to pay off my debt by the end of the year. Then I want to start saving before I go back to China. There's nothing for me in this country. I'm so tired. I just want to go home.'

Xiao Li – the rebel we met at the factory in Hartlepool in 2001, who gave himself more breaks than were allowed – was quite a different man when I met him again in 2006. He'd come to London after his colleague Zhang died, and had worked in the kitchens of takeaways and restaurants. But because of his previous catering experience in China and his outstanding skills as a chef, he was able to set a high wage standard for himself, even without status, and – brazenly, in employers' eyes – had *turned down* jobs that would pay him less than he felt he deserved.

Over five years he'd established good contacts and working relationships in the Chinese catering trade. His name had spread among the customers at the takeaway where he'd been working: some customers asked him to do the catering for their lunches and dinner parties. Having worked as a Sheraton chef in China, he was good at cooking for large numbers in a short time. 'They loved my chilli seafood dish and Tienjin-style garlic mussels,' he told me, the day after one of those private parties. Such jobs could earn him £300 for half a day's work.

Encouraged by these experiences, he began to consider starting his own catering business. The opportunity arose when a contact of his from Tienjin was looking for someone temporarily to take over his Chinese takeaway in south London. Xiao Li got the job.

To save costs, Xiao Li decided not to hire any workers: there'd just be him and his partner Xiao Hong, a student who spoke better English than he did. She'd be the receptionist taking orders, and he'd be the chef.

He wanted to introduce northern Chinese flavours to the menu; he refused to continue providing predictable sweet-and-sour Cantonese meals. He developed a new collection of dishes from his hometown of Tienjin: a new range of meat and vegetable starters, and a northern stew. 'It's an experiment for their taste buds,' he told me. 'If they like it, we'll add more.' To his delight the local customers welcomed the new additions. Praise from customers poured in, and word spread. Occasionally Xiao Li put his head out from the kitchen, and customers would greet him and give him the thumbs-up sign. 'Sank you, sank you!' was all he could reply.

In spite of the success Xiao Li and his partner were only just breaking even. The takeaway was in a down-market area and the number of customers was limited. Also, as word was spreading about the excellence of the food, word was also spreading among local youths that there was a good takeaway to target. These local 'kids', as Xiao Li described them, were aged between fourteen and eighteen, and hung around the doorway. One day they got bored with staying outside. They came inside, shouting and throwing beer bottles. Xiao Hong told them to stop, but they took no notice. Xiao Li asked them to leave. They started shouting abuse at him. Reminded of the racist abuse he'd suffered in Germany and in the north of England, Xiao Li lost his temper. He chased the youths out of the shop, shouting 'Get out!' in Chinese.

The next day, they came back. They littered the place again, and stood in the doorway to obstruct customers. Xiao Hong called the police but they didn't arrive. The following day the harassment started again. This time Xiao Li came out of the kitchen holding a chopper in his hand. The youths fled at the sight of the knife. Xiao Li chased them along the street, determined to teach them a lesson. When they reached the end of the street they realized it was a dead end: there was nowhere else to run to. With Xiao Li standing in front of them wielding his chopper, they screamed 'like lambs before slaughter', as Xiao Li described. 'I wanted to show them the consequences of their racial harassment, so they wouldn't dare to do it to other people.'

The teenagers huddled together, shouting for help, and Xiao Li took aim. With all his concentration, he threw the knife in their direction. As they shrieked, the chopper landed on the trunk of the tree behind them.

'Having witnessed my flying-chopper technique,' Xiao Li told me, 'they ran for their lives. We haven't seen them since. I'm capable of dealing with racism now, after living in England for so long. Racism can't touch me without me touching it back.'

He continued to work ten hours a day, six days a week, all through 2006, and managed to earn enough to help with his father's medical treatment in China and to improve the living standard for his younger sister and her family.

Early in 2007 his temporary management of the takeaway ended when the owner returned to England. He asked Xiao Li to stay on, but Xiao Li wanted a change. 'My dream,' he told me, 'is to set up a café that serves both Chinese and English food, in a good location in the capital. I'd like to introduce all my hometown delicacies, and change the British taste for Chinese food. I know they'd love it.' But he understands that, without status, he'll never be able to realize his dream. He'll have to continue being employed for the time being. Now he's working as a chef in a Chinese restaurant in East Croydon. He works seven days a week and commutes from Brixton.

'I'm not planning to return to China,' he said to me in late 2007. 'I've become attached to this place, believe it or not. I don't feel as much of an outsider as I used to. I've grown to like the streets of London, the weekend markets, the pub-goers socializing round big pub tables. I like the diversity of people, the football and the rain. I love the space I've found for myself. I've built my home here.'

What of Ailing and Ah-Fang, the two women whose stories we've followed? For a long time after Ailing left the Midlands at the end of the spring-onion season in 2005, I wasn't able to get in touch with her. It seemed that talking to me would remind her of what had happened on that first domestic job in Birmingham. But in late summer 2007 when I called her she told me surprising news: she'd gone back into domestic work, which she'd said in 2005 she never would again. It seems to be the best option available for a female Chinese worker without status. The other favoured job choices for women are in the cleaning services and housekeeping in hotels.

'A friend of mine,' Ailing said, 'told me about possible work in a four-star hotel at Heathrow Airport, via a Fujianese agency that gets you in through the back door. I was tempted. But weighing up the odds about the risk of exposure, I decided to take on the domestic job in a private household.'

Her bosses are a Chinese couple. 'They aren't too bad to me, although I'm only earning £150 a week and I haven't been given a separate room but have to sleep in the same room as the young child I'm looking after.' She's planning to return home to China next summer, to be reunited with her son.

Ah-Fang has been calling me a lot. When she lost her massage-parlour job in Archway, she lost her accommodation too, and had to seek temporary shelter at Angel Family Hotel, a Chinese-run hostel in Raynes Park that charges £15 per day – a lot of money for her – for two daily meals and a bed in a room shared between four. The hostel's tenants are primarily workers like her, who are in between jobs and need a bed for a few nights.

In late 2007 she was in employment again, working as a receptionist at a massage parlour in Portsmouth. 'What other choices do I have?' she said to me. 'Many Chinese women want domestic jobs because they're seen as more secure and less prone to immigration raids. So I've been ousted by the competition! The only jobs left for women of my employment experience are the massage-parlour ones.'

She still clings to her Buddhist beliefs. After receiving her wages from the parlour manageress, she sent some of the money to the monks at the True Buddha Temple in Willesden Green. 'Those monks have helped me so much during my bad times in this country.'

9. The Status-less and the Status Quo

Nagging at you, making you uncomfortable, perhaps, as you've come face to face with undocumented workers like Zhang Guo-Hua, Ren Xiang and Gao Jun in this book, is another image in your head: a much more detached, impersonal image, of faceless 'illegal immigrants' crowding into the country and being a 'problem' at the heart of the national agenda. Every day on the news, we hear that Britain is overcrowded (although the arrival of a million new migrants in the past decade represents only a 1.7 per cent rise in the population). Government ministers hammer home the message to us: space in schools and hospitals is limited; locals need primary access to jobs and housing ('British jobs for British people'); Britain should not be a 'soft touch'; despite its ageing population and thus its need for new labour in the coming years, Britain cannot take on another million migrants.

While you carefully weigh up both sides of the immigration debate, the crackdown is proceeding with no care at all. Britain's Immigration Minister Liam Byrne tells us proudly that an 'illegal' is removed from the country every eight minutes. The Border and Immigration Agency is making its presence increasingly felt, with arrests all over the country. As you queue to show your passports on arrival at Heathrow Airport, you're now shown a warning film in which policemen with sniffer dogs search lorries arriving at Dover, and conduct on-the-spot immigration raids. The message is clear: do not enter the country illegally, do not outstay your visa, or you will be removed by force. The 'points-based system', whereby migrants will have to fulfil strict criteria in order to reach the appropriate 'tier' to be allowed to work in Britain, has come into force in 2008, aiming to clean up any irregularities.

The preceding chapters show how closely connected our daily lives are to these irregularities, and how every British person benefits from the existence of these nameless people living and working around us. Undocumented migrant workers are not an anomaly in the system in which we live, but very much part of it. The British economy thrives on this army of workers, who number between 700,000 and a million. Businesses survive on and make profits from their cheap, flexible labour. Every time we pick up a pack of skinless chicken breasts or a bag of washed lettuce, we may be unknowingly colluding with the system that exploits them. Doing jobs no locals want to do, for wages and working hours no locals would accept, they are producing social wealth for a country that permanently excludes them.

Having demonstrated to you the silent contribution of these undocumented workers, and their exploited existence in this country, I'd like to suggest that we move beyond the debate about numbers ('How many of them are coming in?') and their effects ('What can they do for Britain?'). Is it not time to ask, what is Britain doing for the undocumented, as workers and as human beings? What should a First World country like Britain do in order to protect and uphold the rights of workers, regardless of their immigration status?

The phenomenon of migration is a global one, and is not going away. The stories we've heard of the Chinese workers are a mere microcosm of the story of the system in which the whole world lives. The fluctuations of capitalism, which have been going on since the nineteenth century, cause an endless global movement of labour that never ceases to grow. The number of people living outside their countries of origin more than doubled between 1975 and 2000, from 75 million to 175 million, and is likely to double again in the next twenty-five years, according to the International Labour Organization

(ILO). Among the 175 million away from home, migrant workers and their families now account for 120 million people globally. It's estimated that undocumented migrant workers constitute about twenty per cent of global migration: which means that there are around 24 million 'illegal workers' world-wide.

The 5.5 million undocumented workers in Europe are the backbone of industries, yet they are not entitled to basic rights. The Council of Europe's report 'Regularizing Irregular Migrants', issued in autumn 2007, points out that a large proportion of undocumented migrants in the EU will not or cannot be returned to their countries of origin, because they were asylum seekers who may face imprisonment or the death penalty if they return – or because they were smuggled to Europe, which means they have no documents for their countries of origin to accept them as citizens. They are here to stay: truly the 'ghost citizens' upon whose labour Europe's wealth is built.

Zhang Guo-Hua, Ren Xiang, Gao Jun, Ah-Hua and many others you've met in this book are all part of this global working class, whose livelihoods in their home countries continue to be destroyed by global capitalism and its agents. Today, millions of people in China are living through the economic upheavals that have changed the face of China in the past two decades since China's rulers initiated the Reform and Opening to world capital. The dismantling of state-owned enterprises, the mass lay-offs and unemployment, and the privatization of public services and education have all led to the impoverishment and desperation of the urban working class and the rural population, pushing the latter to sell their cheapest labour in the cities and the former to migrate to advanced capitalist countries to work. While China is trying to project a liberalized image to the world as it prepares to host the Olympics in Beijing, the millions without a voice continue to be on the move, struggling to make ends meet.

Behind the picture of the permanently packed shopping malls, posh yuppie flats, the shiny Pearl Tower above a prosperous city with buildings ascending every day and the three-generation family sipping coffee at Starbucks on a Sunday afternoon, is the bitter reality of low pay, long working hours, no health and safety, no job security and all the hardship that working-class people have to live with.

Campaigners depict a reality contrary to the happy-consumer society that China's rulers and the Western media would love to portray. Geoff Crothall from China Labour Bulletin observed first-hand how things have changed from bad to worse: 'Long hours and low pay in China are as nothing compared to the problem of the non-payment of wages [which is prevalent in the private enterprises]. Between January and September 2005, for example, the Guangzhou Labour Bureau handled 36,408 complaints about the non-payment of wages. In April 2006, more than 300 workers at Jinbao factory in the southern industrial city of Shenzhen staged street protests demanding the payment of over two million RMB [£133,000] in back wages.'

'Companies can get away with not paying wages, because the local labour bureaux don't have the power to force them to pay, and in the vast majority of cases there's no trade union to represent the workers' interests. The official All-China Federation of Trade Unions has made a high-profile bid to bolster its presence in the private sector, but most of the unions it has set up are adjuncts of management rather than genuine representatives of the workers.'

In the ruthless world of China's market economy, profits come before workers' health and safety. 'Dangerous Levels of Lead in Made-in-China Toys.' The news burst on to the British front pages in summer 2007, when Mattel, the largest toy factory in the world, did a product recall of millions of its China-made toys. This was as much a health hazard for Chinese workers as it was for Western consumers. As with the Dover tragedy and the Morecambe Bay cockling tragedy, the curtain was lifted, just for a few days, on the dark world beneath the shiny one most of us live in. The horrific working conditions in China came briefly into the news, then vanished again.

I talked to the campaigner Li Qiang from China Labour Watch, who's been investigating Chinese toy factories since 1997. He returned to Shenzhen in July 2007, and found that little has changed. 'Today,' he told me, 'in Sunyick Plastic Products (Shenzhen) Co Ltd, who produce for Mattel, Wal-Mart and many other multinationals, the electronics department workers are working fourteen hours a day at peak season, and have only one day off every month. Their monthly wage is about 1,000 RMB [£67]. The 5,000 workers at Sunyick have never received health-and-safety training and are exposed daily to dangerous chemicals they know nothing about. The oil-paint department has the worst working conditions of all. The chemicals spread many metres from the building, and workers aren't provided with the necessary equipment to avoid chemical poisoning. In August a female worker at Sunyick fainted and died. She'd been working twelve hours a day, seven days a week.'

Regarding the above, Simon Wong, admin manager of Sunyick Plastic Products (Shenzhen) Co Ltd, said: 'There are [sic] standard Code of Conduct (COC) detailed by buyers within the manufacturing industry. ICTI [International Council of Toy Industries] has a comprehensive way to measure the factories and issue acceptance when it sees fit. Our company has been approved since 2005 and maintained certified [sic] without interruption until now. Auditors from Walmart, Mattel, Disney and ITS all confirmed the same ... In other words, we have been operating within the limits of all COC rules from time to time. It was untrue that the electronic department worked fourteen hours a day and one day off every month at peak season. We worked on the limit of twelve hours a day and six days per week and that is acceptable by the COC for peak season. Of course, we plan work based on eleven hours per day and 5.5 days a week. The female worker who died had been working twelve hours a day but six days a week at our peak season. Although we are very sorry that it happened, we were operating within the COC requirement. Death diagnosis certified that she died of normal illness.'

Regarding the wage level, Simon Wong of Sunyick said: 'It was true that the monthly wage was about 1,000 RMB back in 2007.' But the company denied that there was no health-and-safety training. 'Without exception, all workers need to go through a three-day training programme in the training room before they are released to work in the plant. They have to pass a test on the taught materials before release. Among other things, the training included industrial safety, first aid, fire prevention and GMP, etc. We comply completely the ICTI requirement that all chemicals must be labelled, and Material Safety Data Sheets [MSDS] must be available in local language at the spot. Our workers are well informed of dangerous chemicals if they are required to handle them and we have no substantial injury in this regard.'

The company also said: 'It may be true that the oil paint department is least preferred environmentally because of its nature. However, our people and the Environmental Auditors from the government did check our air composition regularly. Our air has always been within the limit. It was true that the exhaust to outside of the factory has not been properly monitored, but it has been rectified now.

'All in all, we operate under the COC requirement to a very high standard. I could not impose your belief, but I hope truth will speak for itself. It's true that some local companies do not comply to [sic] the labour law, but most foreign-owned companies do comply, especially companies of our size.'

'The health-and-safety record of many factories in the southern coastal region of China is particularly appalling,' Geoff Crothall told me. 'When employees suffer injury or contract a work-related disease, it can be very difficult to get proper medical care. In 2004, when gemstone workers in Guangdong contracted the potentially fatal lung disease silicosis through breathing in silica dust, the managements of the various factories either refused to provide workers with medical check-ups or forged the results of those check-ups in an attempt to avoid liability.

'It's common for factory workers to live and sleep in the same building as the workshop. In October 2007, thirty-seven people were killed and nineteen critically injured when fire swept through an unlicensed shoe factory in Putian, Fujian. The workshop had been illegally set up in a residential area. The ground floor was used as a warehouse, the workshops were on the first and second floors, and the dormitories were above. The workers were asleep when the fire broke out.'

For workers in China's construction industry, the situation is also dire. The economic boom in the south-east has led to a huge upsurge in construction – as well as being the world's factory, China is also the world's building site. With this rise there's been a corresponding increase in the number of industrial accidents and deaths. According to the State Administration of Work Safety, there were 419,000 recorded industrial accidents and 79,000 recorded industrial deaths between January and October 2007. Construction workers are almost exclusively from the countryside, they work long hours for low pay and rarely have any form of medical insurance.

'If they're ill or injured,' as Crothall explained, 'they have to pay for their own treatment, and the only way to get compensation is to sue the employer. Even if they – or their surviving family members – do successfully sue the employer, workers from the countryside get less compensation than urban workers, because of their "temporary status" as urban residents.'

Mass protests and spontaneous strikes are illegal in China, but they've been happening nonetheless, as working conditions have become increasingly intolerable. The number of protests and strikes grew from 10,000 in 1994 to 87,000 in 2005 – and the social unrest has worried China's rulers. They've been compelled to pass the Labour Contract Law, which comes into effect in 2008. It's full of 'pro-worker' initiatives: reading it, you feel there's hope for workers at last. But strong objections to the new law have been voiced by US corporations and investors, led by the US Chamber of Commerce in China (and endorsed by the Bush administration). It said: 'We believe it [the new Labour Law] might have negative effects on China's investment environment.' Li Qiang and many campaigners are worried that the US companies' objection, along with the reluctance of local governments to challenge these companies, will be a huge barrier to the implementation of the new law.

From the hell that is China, workers like Zhang, Ren and Gao travel to the hell that is the undocumented person's Britain. Pushed off the train of 'economic progress of the Chinese nation', they have few alternatives. The precise number of undocumented Chinese workers in Britain is intrinsically hard to gauge, but it's estimated to be between 170,000 and 200,000. The money sent home from Britain by undocumented workers helps to rebuild communities across the world: according to the ILO, undocumented workers (of all nationalities) send home total earnings of around US$100 billion a year, a larger sum than all overseas development aid.

The British government's chosen role in all this has been to install ever-more draconian immigration policies, as immigration controls have become tougher across Europe. No First World country wants to allow in the world's poor. Let the problems caused by the world's economic greed be dumped on someone else's doorstep, not ours. Over the last decade there has been a long, steady process of illegalization of status-less migrant workers.

First, in 1998, came the 'Fairer, Faster and Firmer' approach, which provided the substance for the 1999 Immigration and

Asylum Act – the greatest tightening of controls since the 1905 Aliens Act. This act installed a forced dispersal scheme, kept asylum seekers outside the welfare system, speeded up deportations and introduced the 'voucher' system, which branded asylum seekers as second-class citizens. Under this Act, many asylum seekers were turned overnight into 'illegals'. The social environment became more hostile. In the six months leading up to the Dover tragedy in June 2000, Britain saw the largest wave of racist attacks since the 1960s against 'outsiders': asylum seekers, refugees and migrant workers.

The deaths of the fifty-eight smuggled Chinese people in Dover opened the murky underworld to the media's blinding spotlight for a brief time. But the mainstream British media acted as the 'watchdog that never bites'. The papers commented on the tragedy, horrified at the deaths – but instead of protesting about the human rights of migrants, they tended to whip up panic about the country's over-population and the burden on public services. The government was able to introduce its Secure Border and Safe Haven approach in 2002 without much opposition. It focused on controlling and removing unsuccessful asylum applicants, and 'creating a seamless process of managing asylum seekers' in their own cut-off asylum processing system. Since July 2002, asylum applicants are no longer allowed to work until they are given a positive decision on their application by the Home Office, no matter how long they wait for such a decision. The government said this was because employment was a 'pull factor'. (Section 55 of the Immigration and Asylum Act of 2002 even took away asylum seekers' rights to state-funded food and shelter if they failed to apply for asylum immediately on arrival. This was so inhumane that the High Court ruled against it in 2003.)

The result of these policies was to push many more people into becoming hidden 'illegal' workers.

In the aftermath of the US-led attack on Iraq, the government has intensified its war on 'illegal immigrants'. The status-less are seen not only as an unwelcome cause of over-crowding, but also as a national security risk. As a crowd-pleaser for the electorate, Tony Blair claimed in 2003 that Britain would halve the number of asylum seekers by that September. He said that Britain would withdraw from Article 3 of the European Convention on Human Rights if Britain failed to reach the target. (Article 3 of the Convention prohibits the extradition of a person to a foreign state if they are likely to be subjected to torture or the death penalty.) Three months after the Morecambe Bay tragedy (which involved the highest number of industrial deaths in Britain since the Piper Alpha disaster of 1988, when 167 workers were killed in a fire on the Piper Alpha North Sea oil rig due to poor safety procedures), the government triumphantly announced in May 2004 that it had successfully cut down asylum applications by twenty per cent in nine months.

The asylum figures have declined steadily since. Chinese asylum seekers formed the third-largest nationality for asylum applications in the first quarter of 2007 – and that was only 480. In 2006 there were 1,960 Chinese applicants. Of these only two per cent were granted refugee status in Britain. But if you look at the records of asylum seekers *removed* from the UK, you'll find that China is not even one of the top ten countries. This is partly because there are tens of thousands of Chinese asylum seekers who are still waiting for their cases to be dealt with by the Home Office, and thousands who cannot be returned after their applications have been refused or even after their asylum appeal, because their country won't take them back. These people have no support from the government, and are not allowed to work. It's a situation that pushes them into destitution, driving many of them into high-risk illegal work such as selling DVDs on the streets. (The thirty-three-year-old DVD seller Xiong Zhang, who died from head injuries after being assaulted and robbed on a towpath in Barking in 2007, and another DVD seller, twenty-nine-year-old Xiao Mei Guo, who was murdered and mutilated in Whitechapel where she worked, were both failed asylum seekers.)

The Gangmasters Licensing Act was passed in June 2004, while gangmaster exploitation continued along Morecambe Bay and in hidden pockets all over Britain – as we've seen in these chapters. After a seven-month-long trial ending in March 2006, the Chinese gangmaster Lin Liang Ren was given a fourteen-year prison sentence for twenty-one counts of manslaughter. And the case closed. Britain put the tragedy behind it. The deeper cause of the deaths – unreasonable production targets imposed by companies via gangmasters under unsafe conditions in a country where migrant labour enjoys little protection – was conveniently forgotten.

I spoke to Xu Li Ying, whose brother and his wife both drowned at Morecambe Bay, and heard about the tragedy's appalling after-effects. Victims' families have fallen apart, unable to cope with debts ranging from £10,000 to £20,000. 'The British government refused to compensate us for the deaths of our loved ones because they were illegal,' Xu Li Ying told me. 'The British government didn't mind about their illegality when they were working like hell on their soil.'

The Chinese government, she said, cared only about covering up. 'The local officials tried to stop journalists from talking to us. Our lives have been torn apart. The children of the victims have had to discontinue their schooling and go out to work. Where's the justice in this? The workers who died were selling their cheap labour to feed their families. Did their lack of status make their lives cheaper?'

The British government has turned a deaf ear to such clamourings for fair treatment. It has refused to build up legislation to protect migrant workers, who continue to be subjected to an unregulated world of labour intermediaries and corporate interests. We've seen, time and again here, how employment agencies exploit workers, illegally charging them registration fees, charging them again to find a replacement job if they're dismissed, housing them in overcrowded flats and making random deductions from their wages. In 2007, the government, yielding to pressure from the Confederation of British Industry (CBI, the UK's leading employers' organization), decided not to pass the Agency Workers Act, which would have provided protection for migrant workers who have to go through agencies. At the EU summit in December 2007, Business Minister John Hutton delayed the implementation of the Agency Workers Directive, which would have given full employment rights to agency workers after six weeks of starting a job. There are only four EU countries that do not require temporary work agencies to be licensed: they are Denmark, Finland, Sweden – and Britain. The TUC's 2007 report, 'Agency Workers: Counting the Cost of Flexibility', points out that an agency worker receives, on average, 80p for every pound paid to a permanent worker. However, even these statistics are optimistic. In many cases – as we've seen in this book – migrant agency workers are not receiving the minimum wage and are sometimes not paid at all.

The Gangmasters Licensing Act, which came into force in October 2006, has been far from effective. Apart from its limited scope (the Act only covers labour providers in the fresh food produce and packing industry, shellfish gathering, agriculture and horticulture), many of those who should fall under the Act aren't licensed. The current number of licensed gangmasters is 1,113. The overall number of gangmasters who should fall under the Act is more than 3,000. And for those who are licensed it's not hard to find loopholes to avoid meeting the standards of the licence. According to industry estimates, only twenty per cent of GLA-licensed labour providers are genuinely abiding by the standards.

'Controlling Our Borders: Making Migration Work for Britain.' This was announced in 2005, and its culmination is the bringing into force of the points-based system in 2008. Under this system, sponsors (primarily employers) will be the focus point of immigration control. Only highly skilled migrants such as scientists and entrepreneurs, placed under Tier One – considered most useful for Britain – will be exempt from the need to seek sponsorship from employers. In the case of the other categories – Tier Two for skilled workers, Tier Three for low-skilled workers and Tier Five for temporary workers – employers will have more power than ever over workers, as workers' immigration status will be tied to their employment. They won't be able to change jobs without making a fresh visa application. (Tier Four, for international students, will be launched in 2009, and these students will have to find sponsorship from educational institutions recognized by the government.)

Under this regime, migrant workers become mere commodities, classified only according to what they're thought to be able to bring to the British economy. Their rights and entitlements are only work-given and are defined by the category of their economic use. Many trade-union activists are aware of the racial and class implications of the new migration regime. Javier Ruiz, a TGWU (now part of UNITE) organizer, told me: 'It's hard not to see the racist element of the new system. Its aim is to phase out labour migration from outside of the EU. It tends to keep out the semi- and low-skilled workers from Asia, Africa and Latin America, by replacing it with the use of Bulgarian and Romanian labour.'

As to the subject of undocumented workers and their hidden contribution to the economy, the government will leave those issues to the Border and Immigration Agency. The Home Office document explaining the points-based system portrays a squeaky-clean future, in which everyone is accounted for. This rigid new system is in line with the European approach to labour migration, recently made clear in a speech given in summer 2007 by Franco Frattini, the European Commissioner for Justice, Freedom and Security. His speech was entitled

'Enhanced Mobility, Vigorous Integration Strategy and Zero Tolerance on Illegal Immigration', and in it he argued that migrant workers coming to the EU should have work-related rights rather than universal human rights. This trend in European policy will no doubt encourage smuggling, trafficking and enslavement in the informal economy. The existing 170,000 to 200,000 undocumented Chinese workers in Britain will continue to be maltreated and trapped.

By tightening controls and refusing to protect rights, the government maintains the workers' illegality and their exploitation.

The beneficiaries in all this are the government's close allies: businesses. As First World countries like Britain keep their doors firmly shut, a world dominated by wealth and power is kept intact. Global workers, like the people you've met here, will continue to become illegalized on their journeys to lift themselves out of poverty.

'Is it not time for the trade unions to act?' This is a question many are asking. Do the trade unions, as workers' organizations, not have the responsibility of formulating a principled opposition to these policies and controls that continue to divide the workforce and weaken the labour movement? Is it not time for the unions to advocate an internationalist approach, one that argues for unionization and protection regardless of workers' status?

Some union organizers, like TGWU's Javier Ruiz, are frustrated. 'The unions have a long way to go to understand and address issues of migration. But we have no time to wait for the unions. We are in urgent need of a mass movement to challenge government policies.'

The status-less continue to hope for change. I'll give Xiao Fan, the kitchen worker in Chinatown, the last word. He said simply this: 'As breadwinners for our families, we want to maintain our dignity. While having to sell our labour, we don't want to sell our basic self-respect. With or without papers, we're all workers doing a job, trying to improve our lives. We want to be given the chance to live and work in the open, with our heads up.'

Acknowledgements

This book is dedicated to all the status-less workers who are selling their labour without a name to be remembered by.

I'd like to express my gratitude to the people who made my research possible: to Lao Zheng and Li Fulin who helped me get into a number of workplaces, at times putting themselves at risk; to Xiao Guo, Gao, Xiao Liu, Lao Liu, Lao Yang, Ah-Ying and Ray, whose precious advice and kind help I couldn't do without. I'd like to thank Biser Ivanov for his comradely support, not least in offering to drive me around workplaces and even following minibuses in pouring rain!

Special thanks to the *Guardian* for bringing this subject to the mainstream. Without their commitment and help, an ethnic minority journalist like myself would never be able to have a voice. I'd like to thank Ed Pilkington for commissioning the news stories that are now part of Chapters 1 and 2. Many thanks to David Leigh, investigations editor, for his reassuring visit during my first undercover job and for all his kind help and advice in subsequent years.

I'd like to express my sincere thanks to William Ong, publisher of *Chinatown Magazine* (now *Pearl Magazine*) and the editor Davidine Sim, who appreciated my Chinese-language work on this subject and put me in touch with Karolina Sutton, my very helpful agent, who patiently saw me through the writing with her most valuable advice. I'd like to thank my editor, Ysenda Maxtone Graham, for her skilful work and brilliant advice on the language of the book, and her encouraging enthusiasm about the subject. Many thanks to Juliet Annan and Jenny Lord of Penguin, for their insightful reading and advice on the book. And thanks to Samantha Mackintosh and Sarah Hulbert for the final copy-editing.

I'd also like to thank activists Jabez Lam, Lisa Mok, Don Flynn and Javier Ruiz, for their thoughts on the bigger picture: the socio-political context of the issues dealt with in this book. Many thanks to Richard Adamson, lecturer of investigative journalism, and Professor Colin Sparks, for helping and encouraging me to pursue my interests. Thanks to *UK-Chinese Times* for supporting me over the years and serializing my work.

Warmest thanks to my partner John Davies, for his understanding (especially of my endless 'nights-out' during the undercover work) and his lasting emotional support. His activism has been a constant source of inspiration for me. I'd like to thank my parents, for their love to such an 'unfilial' daughter who always delays our reunion. Thanks to Yuren, for giving me courage before my first undercover job, and to Hsiao-Lan, for listening! Many thanks to Valerie and James, for their caring words; and finally to Paul O'Kane, for his socialist spirit, which encourages me.